VEDANTIC APPROACHES TO GOD

LIBRARY OF PHILOSOPHY AND RELIGION

General Editor: John Hick, H. G. Wood
Professor of Theology, University of Birmingham

This new series of books will explore contemporary religious understandings of man and the universe. The books will be contributions to various aspects of the continuing dialogues between religion and philosophy, between scepticism and faith, and between the different religions and ideologies. The authors will represent a correspondingly wide range of viewpoints. Some of the books in the series will be written for the general educated public and others for a more specialised philosophical or theological readership.

Already published

William H. Austin	THE RELEVANCE OF NATURAL SCIENCE TO THEOLOGY
Paul Badham	CHRISTIAN BELIEFS ABOUT LIFE AFTER DEATH
Patrick Burke	THE FRAGILE UNIVERSE
William Lane Craig	THE *KALĀM* COSMOLOGICAL ARGUMENT
	THE COSMOLOGICAL ARGUMENT FROM PLATO TO LEIBNIZ
Lynn A. de Silva	THE PROBLEM OF THE SELF IN BUDDHISM AND CHRISTIANITY
Padmasiri de Silva	AN INTRODUCTION TO BUDDHIST PSYCHOLOGY
Ramchandra Gandhi	THE AVAILABILITY OF RELIGIOUS IDEAS
J. C. A. Gaskin	HUME'S PHILOSOPHY OF RELIGION
H. A. Hodges	GOD BEYOND KNOWLEDGE
Hywel D. Lewis	PERSONS AND LIFE AFTER DEATH
Eric Lott	VEDANTIC APPROACHES TO GOD
Hugo A. Meynell	AN INTRODUCTION TO THE PHILOSOPHY OF BERNARD LONERGAN
F. C. T. Moore	THE PSYCHOLOGICAL BASIS OF MORALITY
Dennis Nineham	THE USE AND ABUSE OF THE BIBLE
Bernard M. G. Reardon	HEGEL'S PHILOSOPHY OF RELIGION
John J. Shepherd	EXPERIENCE, INFERENCE AND GOD
Patrick Sherry	RELIGION, TRUTH AND LANGUAGE-GAMES
Wilfrid Cantwell Smith	TOWARDS A WORLD THEOLOGY
Robert Young	FREEDOM, RESPONSIBILITY AND GOD

Further titles in preparation

VEDANTIC APPROACHES TO GOD

Eric Lott

Foreword by
John Hick

BARNES & NOBLE
BOOKS
10 East 53d St., New York 10022
(a division of Harper & Row Publishers, Inc.)

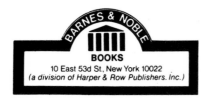

First published 1980 in the U.K. and all other parts of the world excluding the U.S.A. by
THE MACMILLAN PRESS LTD
London and Basingstoke

First published in the U.S.A. 1980 by
HARPER & ROW PUBLISHERS INC.
BARNES & NOBLE IMPORT DIVISION

Filmset in Great Britain by
VANTAGE PHOTOSETTING CO. LTD
London and Southampton
Printed in Hong Kong

British Library Cataloguing in Publication Data

Lott, Eric J.
Vedantic approaches to God – Library of philosophy and religion)
1. Vedanta
I. Title   II. Series
181′.48   B132.V3

MACMILLAN ISBN 0-333-27109-2

BARNES & NOBLE ISBN 0-06-494365-8
LCN 78-17886

To
Chris

Contents

Foreword

Vedanta is known in the west as a school of Hindu philosophy. It is in fact a family of schools of Indian religious philosophy; and Dr Lott is concerned to bring out its diversity, and in particular to remind us that to a great extent Vedanta is theistic. The different members of the Vedanta family are all attempts to speak about Brahman, the Ultimate Reality, described by Dr Lott as the 'trans-empirical, immortal Being, the supreme Ground of all beings'. But western interest has tended to concentrate upon one member of this family to the exclusion of the others —advaita Vedanta, centring upon the idea of Brahman as the non-personal Absolute. The most considerable thinker of this school was Shankara, in the ninth century A.D., who has been aptly compared with Thomas Aquinas as a great constructive systematiser who was also a saint. It is this advaitic form of Vedanta that has been likened in a number of comparative studies to nineteenth century German Idealism and to the thought of such twentieth century writers as F. H. Bradley and Paul Tillich. According to advaita Vedanta the personal God of religious devotion represents the way in which the trans-personal Brahman is experienced by finite persons in their state of illusion, so that the worship of a personal God belongs to a preliminary stage of men's advance toward full enlightenment. This type of Vedanta has often been equated by western writers with Vedanta as a whole; and in this book Dr Lott redresses the balance by giving proper attention also to the leading theistic Vedantists, Ramanuja (in the twelfth century A.D.) and Madhva (in the thirteenth century).

Ramanuja was a great theologian and saint of *bhakti*, the loving adoration of the personal God, who was for him the ultimate Brahman. Instead of seeing the human self as identical, in the depths of its being, with Brahman, he saw finite selves as dependent upon God, and the whole universe as related to God in a way analogous to the body's relationship to its controlling conscious self. Madhva went yet further and taught a total distinction between the divine Self and human selves. If Ramanuja's thought might be described as a form of panentheism,

Madhva's is a form of strict monotheism. God, for him, is the sole creator of the universe, and all creaturely being exists in absolute dependence upon its divine source. And yet the divine Lord also indwells his creation, giving life and guiding souls.

It is clear that the Hindu tradition has become increasingly theistic and has for approximately the last thousand years taken centrally the theistic-devotional form of *bhakti*. Indeed the *Bhagavad Gita*, which is dominated by the idea of the personal Lord, and which has long been India's most influential scripture, was written before the time of Christ. Dr Lott's book, with its restored emphasis upon this theistic movement, will help many western readers to a better proportioned understanding of Vedantic Hinduism than has been common since the nineteenth century. He enables us to see Vedanta again, not as an abstract philosophy of the impersonal Absolute, but as a living approach to God.

JOHN HICK

Preface

Any attempt in one book to introduce Western students of religious thought to the full range of Vedantic ideas is more than a little ambitious. It has, for one thing, been necessary to balance on a formidable hermeneutical tightrope. Without some kind of selection, systematising, and interpreting of the material, Vedantic thought would be likely to remain obscure by reason of its unfamiliar form of expression, even in translation. And yet, unless there is sufficient loyalty to what Vedantins actually wrote, the result is likely to be the usual 'Vedanta-for-Western-man', bearing little resemblance to actual Vedantic systems. I can only hope that my interpretation has not distorted any of the systems, and that my loyalty to the texts does not look like obscurantism. Unfortunately, studies in this field have tended to overbalance on one side or the other.

I cannot claim to be without any personal bias in my approach to these three great Vedantins, though I have made every effort to get inside the mind of each of them and represent their position fairly. My defence for tending to favour theistic Vedanta is that few writers in the past have given the theists a fair deal. Virtually no Vedantic scholar has attempted the kind of parallel description, giving equal weight to each, that has been done here. And I trust that my concern to make Vedanta in general more widely understood will come through more clearly than my particular preference for the theists.

The title speaks of 'approaches to *God*', though almost invariably one or other of the Vedantic terms—Brahman, supreme Person, highest Lord, etc—has been used in the book. For the Western reader, however, the term 'God' seems to be the most immediately meaningful, and the study itself will show to what extent this is a valid appellation for Vedanta's Object of enquiry. Personally I find Vedanta to be essentially a *theological* discipline, and many of the basic questions it raises are those raised in Western theological discussion. The nature of divine transcendence and its relation to cosmic immanence, ways of knowing that transcendent Being, description by way of analogy, the relation of the transcendent Being to human action and the question of divine grace, divine purpose and spontaneity of being, the relation of supreme Cause to other causal factors, the nature of the divine-human relationship, the soul's destiny—these are but some of the topics as central to Vedanta as to any theological system. Other aspects of Vedantic thought will appear very new, probably even alien, to Western ways of theological thinking. I trust that I have brought out this distinctive stance of Vedanta clearly enough also.

Many of the primary sources are available in English translation, and where I have thought these to be both accurate and intelligible I have made some use of them, usually with changes of my own. Extensive use of Sanskrit has been avoided for obvious reasons. In transliterating Sanskrit terms it has not been possible to be absolutely consistent. In some cases it has seemed most natural to keep the spelling that readers have become accustomed to —Vedanta, Upanishad, Krishna, for example. Mostly, though, I have used standard transliterative forms. A few very frequently used terms are written without diacritical marks. The 'correct' forms are: Śaṅkara, Rāmānuja, Gītā, Sūtra, Sāṅkhya, Vedānta.

This work is based largely on research carried out in 1976–7 at the University of Lancaster. I am happy to record my gratitude to Professor Ninian Smart for guiding my study then, as he has on previous occasions also. I am also indebted to a number of Indian scholars of each Vedantic school for suggestions made in conversations with them at various times since my coming to India in 1959.

Bangalore 1979 ERIC LOTT

List of Abbreviations

Anu-Vyākhyāna of Madhva	AV
Bṛhadāraṇyaka-Upaniṣad	BU
Bṛhadāraṇyaka-Upaniṣad-Bhāṣya of Śaṅkara	BUB
Bṛhadāraṇyaka-Upaniṣad-Bhāṣya of Madhva	BUB(M)
Bhagavad-Gītā	BG
Bhagavad-Gītā-Bhāṣya of Śaṅkara	BGB
Bhagavad-Gītā-Bhāṣya of Madhva	BGB(M)
Brahma-Sūtras	BS
Brahma-Sūtra-Bhāṣya of Śaṅkara	BSB
Brahma-Sūtra-Bhāṣya of Madhva	BSB(M)
Chāndogya-Upaniṣad	CU
Chāndogya-Upaniṣad-Bhāṣya of Śaṅkara	CUB
Gītā-Bhāṣya of Rāmānuja	GB
Kaṭha-Upaniṣad	KaU
Kena-Upaniṣad	KeU
Kena-Upaniṣad-Bhāṣya of Śaṅkara	KeUB
Māṇḍukya-Upaniṣad	MaU
Muṇḍaka-Upaniṣad	MuU
Śrī-Bhāṣya (on Brahma-Sūtras) of Rāmānuja	SB
Śrī-Bhāṣya, Thibaut's translation (of first Sūtra)	Thib.
Śvetāśvatara-Upaniṣad	SU
Taittirīya-Upaniṣad	TU
Taittirīya-Upaniṣad-Bhāṣya of Śaṅkara	TUB
Upadeśa-Sāhasrī of Śaṅkara	US
Vedārtha-Saṅgraha of Rāmānuja	VS
Viṣṇu-Tattva-Nirṇaya of Madhva	VTN

1 Orientation to Vedanta

Indian religious thought has in recent years attracted considerable interest in the West. Indologists of all kinds must find it encouraging to hear terms like *karma*, *bhakti*, *dhyāna*, *yoga*, *brahman* and so on being used quite frequently in religious discussion today. Yet the deplorable fact is that Western thought generally, and Western theology in particular, still has a very inadequate idea of what Vedanta, the most important of India's living conceptual systems, is all about. Indeed so prevalent are positively mistaken ideas about this religious system, that anyone studying Vedanta with serious intent for the first time will quite likely begin with a number of false assumptions.

One of the most common misconceptions is to think of Vedanta as a single system within which there is no significant divergence either in method or in conceptual content. There may well be the further mistaken idea that its one definitive concern is for the realisation of pure Selfhood, wholly transcendent to all empirical existence. In other words Vedanta has tended to be identified with the non-dualism (*advaita*) most effectively expounded by Sankara in the early ninth century. Another notion consequent to this is that Vedanta is in no sense a theological system; any such method of self-realisation will inevitably be thought of as transcending all the usual apparatus of theology—revelatory scripture, doctrinal affirmations, belief in a cognisable supreme being, and so on.

The partial truth in these notions does not make them any more acceptable. There *is* a body of thought recognisable as Vedantic; Vedanta *does* look for a level of being that transcends the empirical, and *some* continuity of being is affirmed of all beings; Vedantic method does *not* fit exactly into Western theological categories. But half-baked Vedanta is as inedible as any other half-baked fare. In any case it will be useful to look a little more closely at these ideas. At least we should be able to recognise that they leave some rather important Vedantic facts out of the picture, and are really no more than current value-judgements.

Firstly there is the claim for Vedanta's *homogeneity*. We shall see in the next chapter that there are good reasons for speaking of Vedanta as a single discipline, both methods and concepts being shared in common by all types of Vedanta. To speak of a single system of Christian theology would be somewhat analogous, though Vedantic divergence is undoubtedly greater. In Vedanta as well as in Christian theology what is often ignored is that the distinctive features of the various schools are just as significant as those found to be in common. By recognising and even drawing attention to such distinctive positions we do not devalue or relativise Vedanta, even if it does mean taking historical facts more seriously. But to ignore the variety not only means a diminishing of the doctrinal richness of Vedanta; it also means that each school is not treated with the conceptual seriousness it deserves. From the point of view of the neo-Vedantic apologist, of course, the claim that each school complements the other has its obvious attractions. An excess of richness in the form of divergent schools is usually something of an embarrassment to the exponents of the tradition as a whole.

No definitive viewpoint, however, can be found in the earliest Vedantic sources, the Upanishads, written probably between the eighth and third centuries BC. Everything expounded later can perhaps be found there in seminal but certainly not in systematic form. It may be that around the first century AD the Vedantic discipline did reach something like an orthodox consensus, as represented by its basic principles (*Sūtras*, literally a thread) said to have been compiled by Bādarāyaṇa. Even prior to this there was the Bhagavad-Gīta, which included some basic ideas of Vedanta as a determining viewpoint in its remarkable synthesis of ideas from various sources. Certainly it became axiomatic for any would-be Vedantic teacher, as evidence of his orthodoxy, to write commentaries on the five hundred or so Sutras and on the Gita. Unfortunately the Sutras are so aphoristic and enigmatic in style that they make little sense apart from their commentaries. They were intended presumably as a summary of a clearly defined oral tradition. But when the commentators differ so radically in their interpretations at crucial points it is very difficult to say conclusively which are more loyal to the original meaning. The Gita's meaning is not so obscure. It is inclusive enough to afford seeming legitimacy to various versions of the Gita's themes, especially of the order of priorities in making them into a system. In the case of the Gita, however, there seems sufficient reason to think that a theistic perspective determines the author's intention in bringing together such a variety of themes including what look like monistic passages. But more of the Gita's perspective later.

We can assume then that some kind of inclusiveness is necessary to any proper Vedanta in which both the oneness and the distinct nature of things, both a self-oriented and a God-oriented outlook, must find some role. Such an inclusive viewpoint, however, cannot escape the matter of priorities. Each Vedantic school will necessarily set out from some determining perspective, differing one from the other. It is this perspective which decides the conceptual structure of each system—which are to be first-order and which second-order doctrines, and how these are to be fitted together into the one system. Once the primary perspective is discovered it becomes possible to see how the same doctrine can play a very different role in different schools, for all doctrines will be subordinate to this determining viewpoint. The fact, therefore, that Vedanta is synthetic in style does not preclude analysis as a way of understanding Vedantic self-articulation, even if something more than analysis is called for when it comes to entering into the experience aimed for by each system. But this is equally true of any religious system, even those with less elaborate conceptual structures.

Two questions then arise: Is it possible to work out within Vedantic terms criteria by which to test the validity of each school? More often than not Vedantic scholars today merely take it for granted that the absolutism of Sankara and his followers is both the more valid Vedanta and the more valuable system ontologically and epistemologically. Yet neither conclusion follows except as a value-judgement made on the largely subjective assumption that one should be aiming for pure Consciousness, an absolute identity of Being. On Vedantic grounds this is at least debatable as an ultimate goal. And in terms of a more general evaluation we see that the 'superiority' of one system over another is entirely a matter of what one is looking for. Perhaps it is possible to establish that one goal is ultimately more desirable than another, though it is doubtful if this can be done without bringing in criteria probably not part of the system being examined. Certainly disparate goals will require disparate systems and methods for realising those goals.

An important evaluative canon, therefore, is—which system provides, along with its inclusiveness, the most convincing inner coherence in its attempt to 'enquire into' the supreme Being and to express the transcendent character of that Being? As we shall further see, it is the question (perhaps we should say the *mystery*) of transcendence that is at the centre of the Vedantic debate. And if an adequate concept of such divine transcendence must at least be attempted by each Vedantin, then it becomes equally important to integrate convincingly all related, secondary concepts with this primary Vedantic truth. It is not so much the rigorous logic with which each idea is presented that is more important, but rather the structure of the system as a whole. Such inner coherence is certainly a quality that Vedanta itself requires of its exponents. However, it must be confessed that this too can never be a matter of purely objective assessment when faced by such a variety of systems, each with a distinct principle of coherence.

Secondly, there is the frequent assumption that the Vedantic system *par excellence* is the non-dualism so ably expounded by Sankara. The idea of the one Vedanta is rather closely connected with this monistic monopoly. Recent attempts to up-date Vedanta and to expound it as one unbroken system invariably assume that whatever provisional concerns might be permissible at the lower stages of the spiritual life, the ultimate concern must be for an immediate experience of transcendent selfhood. This means that all non-monistic concepts are to be taken as only relatively valid. Such theistic systems are cases of 'arrested development',[1] remaining incomplete until they have been transcended by the larger vision of an absolutist like Sankara. Neo-Vedanta apart, even a usually reliable historical guide like Surendranath Dasgupta was so impressed by monistic dominance in the Vedantic system that he could write: 'Whenever we speak of the Vedanta philosophy we mean the philosophy that was propounded by Sankara.'[2]

One reason for such partiality is Sankara's detachment from sectarianism. It is in the very nature of a theistic interpretation of Vedanta to remain closely associated with a particular religious community. Not that the theist would intend his Vedantic writings solely for his own sect. Ramanuja, for example, writing in the eleventh century, clearly had a much broader readership in mind; hence the striking difference in style between his Vedantic and his devotional writings. There is a remarkable avoidance of strictly sectarian material when he writes as a Vedantin, even though his Vedantic formulation remains based scrupulously on the theology of his Vaiṣṇava tradition. He cannot, like Sankara, point to an esoteric knowledge that utterly transcends all empirical religious categories. His was a serious theistic religious commitment.

A related question concerns the rationale for choosing Madhva (thirteenth century) as the third representative in making this kind of comparative Vedantic study. He has received rather cursory treatment from most recent historians of Indian religious philosophy, again largely because of the somewhat esoteric sectarian style of his writing. In his comparative study of the major Vedantic commentaries V. S. Ghate at least gave some consideration of Madhva. Unfortunately, Ghate's evaluation is often based on the notion that the majority must be right. Another rather subjective judgement is that 'the more advanced [in] systematisation the further removed from . . . the Sūtras',[3] a canon of evaluation suggesting that Vedanta essentially lacks a coherent system. When Ghate goes on to say that 'in a majority of cases [Madhva's] explanations are far-fetched, fantastic and too sectarian in character', 'quite irrelevant', 'most unnatural', and so on, it must be admitted that Madhva's style does sometimes lend itself to such a criticism. His commentaries certainly lack the sophistication of Sankara's. But sophistication is not all that matters, and Ghate greatly exaggerates their non-Vedantic character. Unfortunately, a generation or two of students in India have tended to accept this judgement without question and Vedantic studies, indeed the religious debate in general, have been the poorer. However much Madhva may have deviated from accepted Vedantic tradition on particular issues—for example his refusal to accept Brahman as substantial cause in any sense—there is no denying the remarkable vigour and consistency with which he expounded his form of theistic Vedanta, a theism which rightly makes the transcendent perfection of the supreme Being a key issue. And Madhva's stance is especially significant in showing that on the question of how Brahman can be transcendently immanent there is no simple division between monists and theists. Madhva's more radically transcendent theism leads him at times to take a position in some ways closer to Sankara's monism than to Ramanuja's style of theism. Often, of course, Madhva's affinity will be with his fellow-theists, but at other times he differs from both the others. This distinctive stance of Madhva's not only helps us to understand the full range of the Vedantic debate, it also gives us a clearer view of the implications of the monistically inclined systems. In any case the superiority of Sankara's style of Vedanta cannot be merely presupposed.

The third questionable assertion frequently made of Vedanta is that it follows a philosophical method, free from all the dogmatic inhibitions of theological systems. In fact it does not correspond exactly to either philosophy or theology as they are generally known at present in the West, though here one has to recognise that logical analysis and empirical positivism have not wholly destroyed metaphysical enquiry in matters philosophical, nor has neo-orthodox dogmatism done so in Christian theology. In other words, it is not entirely clear what methodology is assumed when we speak either of philosophy or theology.

To some extent this is equally true of Vedanta, despite its common 'enquiry into Brahman', and the commonly accepted means by which valid knowledge is said to be acquired—perception, inference and testimony. These two aspects of Vedanta do, of course, involve a great deal of ontological and epistemological discussion that could lend weight to the assertion that Vedanta is primarily philosophical in style. It was the nineteenth-century pioneer Indologists who set the trend here by comparing this discussion, especially the conclusions reached by the monist school, to the Idealist metaphysical outlook then in vogue in the West. The fact is, however, that the consistent classification of Vedanta as 'philosophy' has seriously weakened essential aspects of the tradition. This is especially true when theistic Vedanta also is treated as non-theological. One prominent exponent of theistic Vedanta refers disparagingly to theology as the 'dogmatic formulation of a system of thought on the authority of Scripture. It means a creed fashioned out of dogmas, not pursuing truth for its own sake and not employing methods of free rational and philosophical investigation. It is reason fettered by faith.'[4] Vedanta, it is claimed, is not of this kind.

Whatever the reasonableness required of the Vedantin and however objectionable dogmatic theology might seem to him, it is a distortion of the method necessary to his discipline to think of it as reason in no way fettered by faith, or to think that he will be 'pursuing truth for its own sake'. We may note five ways in which Vedanta's essential character contradicts this notion of free philosophical investigation.

1. As *Veda-anta,* meaning the 'end of the Vedas', the historical roots of the system are unquestionably religious. Vedanta emerged in the context of the theistic ritualism of the Vedas, even though it sought in some sense to transcend the ritualist perspective of the Vedic age. Even the theism of the earlier period, with its henotheistic tendency, was found to be inadequate to provide either an inclusive enough account of the origins of the universe—despite various cosmogonic myths attempting just this—or a way of release from the sense of bondage which appears at the end of the Vedic age, i.e. in the Upanishads.

There was a significant transition from being content with offering sacrifices to seeking deep within the inner self for the solution to the mystery of the universe. Yet it does seem to have been ritual that provided the continuity between what might appear to be two very different ways of looking at things. To Vedic man the sacrifice was a microcosmic representation of his whole universe, his whole being. Then by reflection on this ritual microcosm, gradually he came to see his inner being also as microcosmic in nature. The underlying, integrating ground of the universe was seen as reflected in that ground of his own being, his vital selfhood. Such a probing into the deepest levels of the self as a means of attaining liberating, transcendent knowledge was bound to diminish the importance of the various deities of the Vedas. They were in fact threatened on at least three counts: as subject to karmic law and the cyclic process of re-embodiment they were felt to be soteriologically impotent; in that they were many, they did not seem to provide a fully convincing cosmological solution; being distinct from the inner self they could not contribute directly in the attempt to probe the transcendent mysteries of the self, though they were taken to be controllers of various aspects of the inner life. A supreme Being transcendent to and yet immanent within this whole universal process mirrored in the inner life of man had become essential. Yet meditation on this supreme Being would still be done within the context of the Vedic ritual. For Brahman-knowledge arises out of and in conjunction with, even though transcending, that microcosmic action. Indeed, the precise nature of the relationship between the two—action and liberating knowledge—was one of the issues on which Vedantins, and Vedantins and Ritualists, were later to join battle vigorously.

2. Vedanta, like almost all other religious systems in India, was motivated by a very practical soteriological aim, which is hardly a characteristic of philosophers pursuing truth for truth's sake. The goal was determined by a belief that the soul is bound to ever-recurring embodiments because of the necessary outworking of the consequences of actions associated with that soul in its previous embodiments. The fruit of action must ripen and work itself out in the experience of the soul which has done that action. Despite the positive side of this theory—that a person's action is creative, and able to determine his future destiny, that virtuous action is equally potent in producing favourable consequences, and that human history is assumed to be part of an essentially moral process, controlled by an essentially merciful God according to Vedanta and some other schools—in general *karma-samsāra*, or the action-cycle, was taken to be a mortally inhibiting state of suffering and mutability, a state to be escaped from by those suitably enlightened. The dilemma is that a person must somehow transcend the results of his own actions. Release (*mukti*, *mokṣa*), then, was the principal concern motivating the Vedantic enquiry. It is not a matter of sheer intellectual enquiry. So there is no question of doing justice to its logical structure, both ontic and epistemic, without first taking seriously the dynamics of its underlying doctrine.

3. The Vedantic enquiry has also its esoteric dimension; it goes far beyond a merely intellectual exercise, for its content is a matter of wonder and mystery. The 'Upanishads' that formed the basis for later Vedanta came to mean 'secret formulae', though the literal meaning seems to be 'near-down-sit', indicating the posture of the initiate as he sat at the feet of his teacher to receive secret instruction. In order to begin

such an esoteric enquiry various spiritual qualifications were first required. It was not open to anyone. Vedanta, then, is no merely formal intellectual pursuit. It concerns an Object of enquiry that is 'wonderfully beheld, wonderfully spoken, wonderfully heard'.[5]

4. To be more precise, Vedanta claimed to have acquired the knowledge of a trans-empirical, immortal Being, the supreme Ground of all beings, as the means of overcoming the problems posed by existing and acting in a world of mortality and suffering. If this supreme Being is thought of as ultimately personal, then there is no doubt that the enquiry into his being has a theological character. Even if an impersonal, unqualifiable Absolute is taken as the higher form of Brahman, as long as the 'enquiry' continues it will be a qualifiable Brahman that is the Object of the cognitive and conceptual process necessary to such an investigation. At the point of ultimate enlightenment, of course, the absolutist would claim that Brahman is the Subject, no longer limited by determinable, conceptual, objective forms of knowledge. Perhaps even with this unqualifiable Subject as the seeker's ultimate goal, it is still fitting to speak of such a process of enquiry as theological in nature, rather than as 'pure philosophy'. Brahman is the 'great Being', the saving end of man's existence.

5. Just as important as Vedanta's religious roots, its soteriological aim, and its ontological subject-matter, is its method of basing itself on an authoritative source, viz. the revelation of scripture. Knowledge of the transcendent Brahman is said to be dependent upon this revelation. Even the least theological Vedantin, Sankara, acknowledged that 'reason is only recognised by us in so far as it is ancillary to revelation' (*śruti*, literally 'that which is heard').[6] This avowed dependence upon scriptural authority has been something of an embarrassment to those who espouse the pure philosophy idea. Even while recognising the theological aspect of Sankara's system, they may well feel such a scriptural basis to be more an obstacle than an aid to the development of his system.

Many pro-Sankara exponents argue that Vedanta is based essentially on transcendent Experience rather than on any external authority, even that of rational argument. This, they claim, indicates its non-theological character. Scripture is merely a witness to such transcendent realisation of the Absolute, and the experience would stand even without scriptural witness. But again it has to be said that the acceptance of certain given insights into the nature of reality, whether such insights are given in intuitive experience or in scriptural texts, can hardly be called a philosophical attitude as this is generally understood today, at least in the West. And theology is certainly not merely a matter of scriptural exegesis; the interplay of experience, scriptural revelation and reason has always been essential to theological method, even when such an interplay is not recognised.

2 Common Features in Vedanta

The first chapter tried to make clear that different Vedantic schools have very different assertions to make about the nature of reality, and often use very different methods to reach such conclusions. It is now necessary to note that they also cover a great deal of common ground, though we can here do no more than outline ten of the more important of these shared features, remembering that each of them can take a distinct role in each system.

1. All Vedanta is expected to be based on the three foundations (*prasthāna-traya*)—Upanishads, Bhagavad-Gita, and Brahma-Sutras. Eighteen Upanishads are usually accepted as being ancient enough (*c.* 800–300 BC) to carry Vedantic authority, though some Vedantins also ascribe Vedantic weight to some of the hundred-odd secondary Upanishads. It has already been noted that the term Vedanta means 'the end of the Vedas', the idea being that the intention of the Vedas (to one or other of which each of the Upanishads is attached) has been realised in the Upanishadic insights, some of which arise out of meditation on the inner significance of Vedic sacrificial ritual. The whole body of Vedic literature is the *śruti*, that which is 'heard'; it is the primary revelation for the knowledge of Brahman, having been heard by the ancient seers. That there are significant differences between the earlier Vedic attitude and that of the Upanishads regarding the world and man's role in it can hardly be denied, in spite of the few Vedic texts that anticipate the Vedantic concerns of the Upanishads. The action-knowledge tension seen in the Vedantic debate reflects something of this Veda-Upanishad difference.

All subsequent scripture is regarded as secondary tradition; it is what is 'remembered' (*smṛti*). This includes both the Bhagavad-Gita (late pre-Christian era) and Brahma-Sutras (*c.* AD 100), as well as the great

Epics, Puranic and sectarian traditions, the lawbooks, and the authoritative summary statements of other schools. Vedanta generally held that such secondary scriptures were to be used only to corroborate what had been established by primary revelation. Yet the acceptance by all Vedantins of this common revelatory basis in no way guaranteed a single Vedantic system, for each one used a distinct hermeneutical procedure. Each of the sources was inclusive enough for each system to be able to draw on material that best fitted its distinctive presuppositions; even texts commonly accepted as very important could be interpreted in a similarly distinctive way. And in the case of Madhva, he did not feel it necessary to limit even his primary proof-texts to the principal Upanishads, but ranged much wider afield, freely using both Vedic and Puranic passages in the exposition of his system. Sankara, on the other hand, gave ultimately determining hermeneutical significance to the relatively small number of 'identity texts'.

2. Then there are the commonly accepted means of valid knowledge (*pramāṇa*, meaning that which measures, a canon). On this issue Vedanta was obviously much indebted to the Nyāya logicians, who had given sustained thought to this *pramāṇa-śāstra*, or the science of proper knowledge, and to epistemological questions. All Vedantins accept at least three such ways of knowing—perception (*pratyakṣa*), inference (*anumāna*), and testimony (*śabda*). It is denied that inferential argument can lead to reliable knowledge of Brahman, though Sankara uses a variety of arguments at least as pointers to the existence and character of Brahman.

Both perception and testimony, however, are taken as operating at two levels—at the empirical, secular level, and at the transcendent, spiritual level. In the case of testimony obviously it is scriptural testimony that carries most weight. Indeed, all Vedantins asserted that scriptural revelation is the only fully reliable authority for our knowledge of the supreme Being. Perception normally means empirical experience mediated through the senses. But there is also perception of an immediate kind, by-passing the usual sensory and mental process of experiencing things. Sankara claimed that all perception in reality is of this direct kind. Only then is it fully authentic perception.

Madhva, on the other hand, while agreeing with Ramanuja that all proper perception must be of some determinable entity, in accordance with his greater individualism, introduced the idea of an inner 'witness' or arbiter of all experience, whether received by way of perception, inference, or even scriptural testimony. In the last analysis, argues Madhva, the validity of all experience will depend on this inner judgement. So here again we see that general agreement on acceptable ways of knowing did not prevent each Vedantin from working these into his system in a distinctive way.

3. The most inclusive common Vedantic feature is the 'enquiry into Brahman' (*Brahma-jijñāsa*), or 'the desire to know Brahman', as the first of the Brahma-Sutras puts it. To quote Sankara on this Sutra: 'Knowledge thus constitutes the means by which the complete understanding of Brahman is desired, this being the highest end of man. . . . Brahman exists as the all-knowing, all-powerful one, whose essential nature is eternal purity, intelligence, and freedom. For when we realise the derivation of the word "Brahman" from the root *bṛh*, "to be great", we immediately understand that eternal purity, and suchlike [super-eminence] belongs to Brahman.'[1] And yet all agree also that further investigation is required in order to ascertain exactly of what nature is this super-eminent perfection. At this point there was a crucial divergence, depending on whether such perfection was thought to be essentially personal or not. The existence of personal or qualifiable Brahman (*Saguṇa-Brahman*) or at least a personalised conception of Brahman, had to be allowed at some level, for Vedanta's sources clearly testify at various places to such a Being. This theistic dimension had to be incorporated in some way into any authentic Vedanta. However, it is not so much theistic doctrine as such, but the Vedantic conviction that Brahman is the one, supremely perfect universal Cause, the transcendent Goal of all existence, that marks this system off from all others.

4. In the Vedantic discussion one of the most important concerns is how Brahman-*knowledge* (*jñāna*) relates to the ritual *action* (*karma*) preceding it. Another way of putting this is to ask how doing relates to being (*Sat*, 'being', is one of the earliest synonyms for Brahman). We can also see this as the question of the relationship between Early Exegesis (Pūrva-mīmāmsā, i.e. the Ritualists) and the Later Exegesis (Uttara-mīmāmsā, i.e. the Vedantins), the former taking injunction to action, ritual action in particular, as the essential subject-matter of the Vedas. This ritualist school also had its transcendent dimension, even though it was thought of as some unseen power inherent in the ritual action. The issue is not merely one of how transcendent Brahman relates to empirical world. Perhaps the ritualist concept of the 'unprecedented power' was merely a conservative exposition of an earlier Brahman-concept, in which 'Brahman' was the ultimate sacred power accompanying the word and action of the priestly ritual.

Vedanta, however, contended that the supreme Brahman transcends all action, even though in some sense initiating and including it. In any case this transcendent Being can never be attained by means of action, for his essential being is beyond the realm of doing. Even though all agree in this, however, there is sufficient difference in their interpretations of the nature of Brahman, and the knowledge by which his nature is properly understood, to give a different place to action also.

5. Vedanta assumes, along with virtually every Indian religious system, that action is binding. We have already noted something of how this basic Indian idea was worked out. One Upanishadic text puts it thus: 'As a person desires, so he acts . . . as he acts, so he becomes'[2]—an endless series of lives or cycle of rebirths (*samsāra*) being the way in which his actions eventually bear fruit and bring about this 'becoming'. There is no escape for the soul from these action-consequences, for cannot the cow find its own calf among a thousand other calves? However, this determining potency of action is not an externally mechanical process. It also depends upon the inner desire, the intention with which the action is done. And this made possible the Gita's solution to the problem—duties are to be done, but without any desire for the benefits that normally could be expected from such action. Thus the soul will remain detached from action-consequences and can hope for release from its bondage to the mortal realm in which such consequences have to be experienced. Possibly we can detect some Buddhist influence here, in this idea of the creative misery-causing role of desire. In any case, the universal sense of bondage felt by the Indian mind made it necessary to find some way by which a person could transcend the consequences of his own actions and thus become a liberated *mukta*.

Hence, in traditional Hinduism there is thought to be a transition required from the proper fulfilment of social duties (*dharma*)—which also assumes the fulfilment of natural desire (*kāma*) and economic need (*artha*), the two other mundane goals of life (*puruṣārtha*)—to the ultimate liberation from all such attachments. Inevitably there is some tension here between the more proximate goals and the ultimate goal that transcends all the lesser aims of life. It is the nature of this tension about which the Vedantic schools differ so remarkably. But none can ignore the need for the proper functioning of society. Indeed, the *dharma*-concept plays a much more important role, even if as an unspoken presupposition, in all the religious traditions of India, than is usually recognised. The Gita's main concern is precisely this—to resolve the tension between the need for action in society and the goal of trans-social liberation. Its solution was that *karma* should be without *kāma*, or there should be continued involvement in the functioning of society without any personal desire for benefit from such involvement. It is first suggested that yogic detachment of mind from sensory enjoyment is the way to such desireless action. Then gradually this is supplemented by the idea of centering the mind on God and handing over to him both action and the consequences of action, with the recognition in any case that it is all under his cosmic control. Naturally no Vedantic system could ignore this development in the Vedantic tradition.

6. Then Vedanta's insistence that the knowledge of Brahman alone leads the soul into the transcendent realm implies that Brahman ultimately is both the goal (*upeya, sādhya*) of existence and the means (*upāya, sādhana*) by which to attain it. Various lesser 'means' are certainly necessary to the Vedantic discipline, but there is no question of any such spiritual method functioning as a direct means of realising what the soul seeks—its ultimate liberation. In fact this liberation is none other than the 'knowledge' of Brahman; it is not some state of the soul transcendent to Brahman. What is debated among the various schools is the exact meaning of 'knowing' Brahman. But all Vedantins would disagree with systems such as Jainism, or Samkhya-Yoga, in which the ultimate goal itself is the perfect liberation, or isolation (*kaivalya*) of the soul. Samkhya-Yoga may well find God a useful means for attaining this pure soul-state, being a suitable object of meditation. But this is not how Vedanta sees the supreme Being, the only ultimate End of all existence.

Some find the Gita's synthesis ambiguous, and many interpreters contradict each other on this issue, so it may be useful briefly to look at what this basic Vedantic document has to say about life's ultimate End. Early in the Gita the author makes it clear that he takes seriously the Samkhya dualistic analysis, the dichotomy of Self and Nature (*puruṣa* and *prakṛti*). Yogic discipline is taken to be the means by which the Self, or the many selves, can be detached from the complex psycho-physical world deriving from primal Nature. In particular the mind (*manas*) must be brought under control; the seeker must become what the Gita calls *buddhi-yukta*, yoked by his intelligent will, by that part of a person which can integrate his psychic powers, control his senses, and keep him free from attachment to objects outside himself. This is said to be true *yoga*, both this word and *yukta* deriving from *yuj*, which has the same root as the English 'yoke'. A preliminary goal of the Gita, therefore, is this mental-control, or integration of the will, which allows the Self within to realise its true nature, free from any confusing distractions by the objective world.

This dualism then merges into an apparently monistic analysis. It is said, for example, that the mind-yoked person becomes 'himself contented in the Self alone'. He is 'bound to Brahman', and even 'becomes

Brahman'. He 'sees the Self standing in all beings, and all beings in the Self; he sees the same in everything'.[3] It is not, however, difficult to see how the enstatic experience of the yogic discipline leads to this 'pan-en-henic vision',[4] in which everything is experienced as one.

The more crucial question is how to fit the Gita's theistic commitment into such a vision. For we are led directly into an intensely theistic passage just after this statement of universal oneness. And it seems reasonable to argue that the climax of the Lord's didactic revelation in the Gita is the glorious manifestation of himself, usually called the vision of his universal form (*viśva-rūpa-darśana*), described in Chapter 11. It is surely the recognition of this divine supremacy that is the ultimate goal of man according to the Gita. By seeing the universe in pan-en-theistic terms the earlier monism is transposed to a call to personal devotion: 'See me everywhere and see all in me.'[5] Such all-absorbing devotion to the Lord is the mark of the true yogi. While at first only isolated references anticipate this later theistic revelation, from the moment of seeing all things 'in the Self' the need for a loving relationship with the supreme Lord becomes increasingly explicit.

To be 'yoked' to the *Lord*, therefore, seems to be the ultimate goal of all the Gita's yogic self-discipline. Concentrating on him, doing all actions with the mind centred on him, making life a sacrifice to him, is said in the last analysis to be *the way* of liberation. This interpretation seems to be confirmed by what is usually called the 'final utterance': 'Give up all your duties (*dharmas*), and turn to me as your sole refuge. I will set you free from your sin.'[6] It is clearly not intended that all action should literally be renounced, for the whole previous scheme is based on the contention that action is necessary, despite the threat of bondage resulting thereby. The meaning then must be that action can be continued only in so far as it is offered up to the Lord in whom all universal action is contained. It is to be done for his sake. Not only is he the means for the soul to realise its ultimate destiny, he is also its ultimate Goal, transcending all other goals. In the Gita too, therefore, God's supremacy is such that the means and end of human existence become identical. Clearly this means-end identity implies a significant extension of the original aim to be released from karmic bondage.

7. As against most other Indian religious systems, Vedanta contends that '[Brahman is the one] cause of the world's origin, and so on', as the second of the Brahma-Sutras puts it. The Upanishads had used a variety of myths and metaphors to express this idea that Brahman is the one source of all. He is the one lump of clay from which a variety of vessels are made; the metal from which various instruments are made; the fire from

which sparks fly off; the spider emitting and withdrawing its web; the waves of the sea from which foam is stirred up; the One who, desiring a second, made himself into an embracing man and woman, from whom all beings derived; the one egg, by the splitting of which heaven and earth emerged; the one Self whose body this universe is. In all these pictures of creation the general intention is to show how Brahman 'in the beginning was one only, one without a second',[7] and from this one Being all finite beings have derived.

This is not all that Vedanta teaches concerning creation. It is accepted, for example, that creation is periodic, in which there is evolution from the single source, then a period in which the world is preserved in a more or less steady state, then a time of involution, when all is reabsorbed back into Brahman. Most Vedantins also accepted the Puranic elaboration of this into a more complex scheme of four ages (*yugas*), each of which shows moral deterioration, and which altogether make a great age (*kalpa*). And this vast period is but a day in the being of the creator God.

Perhaps it should be noted here that Vedanta did not reject outright the polytheism of the Vedas and Purāṇas. Thus it is often the masculine deity Brahmā who is described as taking a creative role, Śiva who is often associated with the act of dissolution, and Viṣṇu who takes the lead in maintaining the created state. But in any case Vedanta assumes that such divine activities will ultimately be dependent upon the supreme Cause, Brahman, though this supreme Lord of all will be taken as Viṣṇu in the case of the Vaiṣṇava Vedantins.

Brahman, then, is the one who wills this process of periodic creation, as well as the one from whose subtle, unmanifest being creation is achieved. He is, in other words, both effective cause (*nimitta-kāraṇa*) and substantial or material cause (*upādāna*). Only by some mysterious (*māyā*) process of self-transformation (*brahma-pariṇāma*) is it possible for Brahman to be the one great cause of this universe with its striking differentiations.

The precise nature of this self-manifesting act is the subject of very fierce debate among the Vedantins. Madhva, in fact, was unable to accept any form of the doctrine that Brahman is substantial cause, though he was perhaps more adamant than any other Vedantin that supreme causality belongs to Brahman. Sankara, on the other hand, found the whole notion of real causal relationships problematic. He seems to have accepted the Buddhist idea that what is caused is dependent and so cannot be real in the sense that uncaused existence is real. It is by way of manifestation, therefore, though in a veiled form, that

Sankara tends to describe the earlier Vedantic doctrine of Brahman's causal role. To some extent this interpretation would seem to be supported by two other creation-doctrines commonly accepted among the Vedantins. There is the idea that it is all the spontaneous, free 'play' (*līlā*) of Brahman, having no determining or benefit-oriented objective, and therefore neither having necessity, nor involving the creator in karmic bondage. Then there is the mysterious *māyā*-power by which the world is said to have been brought into being. But just what this means for the ontological status of created beings is the question at issue.

8. All beings, then, derive from the one being of Brahman, the one Self (*ātmā, puruṣa*), which means that there is but one Ground of all beings according to Vedanta generally. In some sense there must be a continuity of being and reality throughout the whole range of existents. But what exactly does this general monistic perspective mean in ontological terms? How does the one Being relate to the many beings? Or the one Self to the many selves? How are such 'identity-texts' as 'That [Self] thou art' (*tat-twam-asi*), or 'I am Brahman' (*aham Brahma-asmi*), to be interpreted? It is interesting to find that even Madhva's system has been called a 'non-dualism of the one, independent Brahman' by one or two recent exponents.[8] Certainly it has its monergistic side, even if it is not an ontological monism. Obviously much of the debate between theistic monism and absolute monism in Vedanta centres on this problem: What is the oneness of the universe, and how does the One relate to the many?

Returning to the cosmological side of this identity issue, we should note the general acceptance of the Samkhya theory that in creation's evolutionary process effect-states (*kārya*) always exist (*sat*) in their causal-states (*kāraṇa*); thus nothing ontologically new emerges. Later we shall have to examine in more detail the various modified forms of this *sat-kārya* notion. For the time being we can merely note how easily such a doctrine could be used to substantiate the Vedantic assumption that it is the one Brahman who is the cause of all subsequent effects, and that there is continuity of being despite changes in manifest form.

9. There was another basic tenet of the Samkhya school that became standard Vedantic doctrine, again in a modified way. We have already seen that Samkhya made a fundamental distinction between Self and Nature. Both are eternal entities and quite real, but while the Self is essentially unchanging and inactive—the detached though sometimes confused witness of all change—Nature is ever restless and active, mutable of form, essentially unconscious in its functioning, and hence existing for the sake of the Self. Nature exists to be experienced; the Self is the experiencer. It is just because of the Self's role as a passive witness

and potential enjoyer that Nature is somehow unconsciously compelled to exhibit herself, to manifest herself in ever more complex forms, like a dancer on a stage attempting the Self's seduction. In other words, it is the nearness of the Self that urges Nature into creative action, the two together bringing about creation 'like a blind [insentient] man carrying a lame [inactive] man'.

After the display of Nature's charms in the creative process, the Self becomes confused and no longer realises its true qualities. Using Nature, in the form of mind and senses, as a kind of mirror, the Self attributes to itself characteristics that in reality belong only to Nature. Nature is also distinguished by three constituent qualities—heavy darkness, vigorous energy, and pure goodness (*tamas, rajas, sattva*)—which further confuse the Self with their obvious moral connotation. To correct this confusion what is first needed is a 'discrimination' of the two essentially different principles. Then through yogic discipline the mind and senses can be controlled so that the Self, or rather each individual self, is able to realise its eternally immutable character.

Some aspects of this Samkhya-Yoga scheme clearly needed considerable reworking if they were to fit into Vedanta's Brahman-oriented thinking. The essential dualism of Samkhya had to be transposed to the ontological continuity required of the Brahman-system. The exact extent to which each Vedantin allows his doctrine to be influenced by Samkhyan categories makes an interesting study. But all agree that at some level a distinction is required between Self and Nature. In many theistic schemes a triadic distinction (*tattva-traya*) is introduced—God, nature, souls. Even Sankara begins his Brahma-Sutra commentary with the assertion that 'it is a matter not requiring any proof that the object and the subject [literally 'thou-ness' and 'I-ness'] . . . are opposed to each other just like darkness and light'.[9] Whether this difference has an ontological basis or not, and whether each self is ultimately distinct from other selves, is the question so sharply debated among the Vedantins.

10. Vedanta took much further than did Samkhya this need to discriminate the true nature of immutable Selfhood from the mutabilities of Nature. That the soul is ignorant (*ajñāna, avidyā*) of the real nature of things is a basic assumption. Hence the need for the Knowledge of Brahman. But this is also regarded as a positive confusion. For one thing there is the confusion of body and soul, when empirical life is taken as all there is. The monist may say in general that the removal of the veil of ignorance distorting the soul's vision is all that is required; it will then be seen that all things are in reality the one Brahman, pure Selfhood. But the epistemological distortion resulting from this ignor-

ance often seems to take on a creative role—the world of difference exists by reason of unenlightened differentiating vision, though this epistemic creativity has also to be squared with the monists' similar claim for the Lord's cosmic activity, by means of his deluding *māyā*-power.

The theist too accepts that the soul is confused in its understanding. But here the emphasis is primarily on the soul's ignorance of the supreme character of Brahman, and of its own utter dependence upon that supreme Being. It vainly imagines itself to be so independent that of itself it has the power to act and work out its own destiny. But whether monist or theist, in Vedanta some deluding ignorance is presumed, and liberating enlightenment, or the knowledge of Brahman, is sought.

3 The Transcendence of Brahman

The previous chapter should have made it clear that Vedanta deals with a variety of common themes, as well as in a variety of ways. If, however, Vedanta were to be reduced to one key concept, it would need to be the concern for Brahman's transcendent nature. When 'the enquiry into Brahman' is spoken of, as the principal subject of the Vedantic discipline, it is assumed that his nature is not known openly,with unquestionable certitude. In some sense his being is veiled and not accessible to empirical enquiry. It is just this otherness of Brahman that makes enquiry necessary. Vedanta is that 'by which the unknown becomes known'.[1] Initially it will mean simply attempting to arrive at a proper understanding of who and what Brahman is, for there are contradictory ideas about this, as even Sankara acknowledges. To declare and interpret Brahman's being, therefore, is Vedanta's principal task, though the principal goal of life goes beyond this. It is to 'attain Brahman' and his transcendent status.

Various reasons can be suggested for this over-riding concern with the transcendence of Brahman, though it would be quite improper to try to *explain* Vedantic commitment by reference to any such contributory concerns. To some extent such 'reasons' overlap with the proximate goals and common features outlined in the previous chapter. By exploring a little further those concerns which lead to the ultimate affirmation of Brahman's transcendent perfection we should be able to reach a clearer idea of *why* Vedanta functions as it does.

We shall also find that there is an immanental dimension intrinsic to Vedanta's exposition of Brahman's transcendence. Transcendence and immanence are certainly not taken as necessary polarities, each needing to counterbalance the other. It is true that some interpretations of the immanental dimension were felt by other Vedantins to jeopardise his transcendent perfection, so that it was in defining just how Brahman is immanently transcendent that Vedantins took their divergent paths.

The most dominant of their common themes proved to be the cause of their most fundamental disagreements.

Vedanta's initial *soteriological aim*—to escape the bondage of the karmic process—was an important factor making Brahman's transcendent nature 'necessary' to the system. To attain liberation from karmic bondage was the one common motivation lying behind all the major religious systems of India. Even though the Buddhists and Jainas had eliminated sacrificial ritual, each was still conscious of the imperative need for liberation from the binding effects of past actions. Jainism offered the way of the soul's purification and its attainment of omniscient isolation by means of ascetic practices. Buddhism offered the 'middle way' between such rigorous asceticism and the indulgence of desire (whether in Vedic sacrifice or materialist licence), and the eight-fold path leading from the proper awareness of the transitory nature of all things, including the soul, through the discipline of self-effacing deeds, to an eventual extinction of desire, the root of all misery. Vedanta offered the knowledge of the mysterious being of Brahman, the supreme Self who can elevate the suffering soul to partake in the bliss, the immortality, the infinitude of his own transcendent Being.

In each case what is offered is a level of existence which, unlike that of the benefit-giving gods, transcends the limitations of the sphere of action. Even the ultra-conservative Ritualists realised the need for some principle that transcended the level of action they held to be of ultimate importance. To meet this need they introduced the idea of the 'unprecedented power' that was both concurrent with and transcendent to every particular act of ritual. Only Vedanta, however, offers that which as the means to liberation is the perfect Object of meditation, and because of this transcendent perfection is also the ultimate Goal of all such meditation. Brahman, it is claimed, sets free from the oppressive chain of action and reaction, birth and rebirth, mortality and misery, precisely because he is the perfect Being, the immortal Self who transcends all such misery and the bondage in which the soul has become entangled. In inter-Vedantic debate the final thrust that was felt to clinch any polemic was to accuse the opponent of preaching a Brahman who is incapable of liberating the soul from its bondage. If it could be shown that the said Brahman was himself subject to bondage, then the argument was felt to be even more conclusive.

Yet it was clearly presupposed that the individual shares some kind of common being, certain common qualities, with Brahman, or there would be no possibility of his 'attaining Brahman'. Sheer transcendence with no immanental dimension would be soteriologically meaningless.

Concern for a single and sufficient *cosmic Cause* was another reason for Vedanta to teach the transcendent being of Brahman. The earliest Vedic search for the one source to explain the existence of the many beings was in the cosmogonic terms of a material Source, expressed in a variety of mythical forms. The great egg, the golden seed, the primeval man, the androgynous being are examples of such mythical explanations. Despite this rather complex early cosmogonic picture, elaborated even more in some Puranas later, Vedantic concern is quite simple—to give an account of the one self-existent Source from which all else derives. The second statement of the Brahma-Sutras puts this conviction succinctly: '[Brahman is the one cause] of the world's origin, etc'.

Almost all the non-Vedantic systems, both 'orthodox' and 'non-orthodox', were non-theistic in the early stages of their development. Yet all showed a tendency later to become theistic, or at least to include theism in some form. Even in Vedanta there was a very early movement from a monistic to a theistic emphasis. In part at least the theistic trend in Vedanta will have carried over into the other systems, in the course of the interplay of ideas. A devotional stress and belief in a single deity as the worthy object of devotion had become almost ubiquitous even before the Christian era. But this process was not one merely of unconscious influence. It must have become increasingly apparent to the non-Vedantic systems that they needed some satisfactory explanation of the origin of the universe. Vaiśeṣeka's 'unseen power' propelling the atomic elements; Samkhya's notion that there is a self-creative impulsion in Nature, perhaps concomitant with its (equally) inexplicable interplay with the selves (*puruṣa*); the Ritualists' idea that ritual action carries with it a power sufficient to perpetuate the world's existence; Buddhism's teaching that creation is merely a state of eternal flux, and that one momentary causal state has the potency to produce the next causal state—all these alternative theories seemed quite inadequate to Vedanta. In some cases they seemed inadequate even to their protagonists, so that they felt it necessary to introduce a 'Lord' who was sufficiently powerful and intelligent to initiate the creative process.

Such a Lord was, however, only an operative or efficient cause, whereas the tradition established in Vedanta was that Brahman should be both operative and substantial Cause. Here again we see Vedanta's concern for an immanental Transcendent. Brahman's two-fold causal role presented serious difficulties to both Sankara and Madhva, though for rather different reasons. They agreed that there can be no other independent causal power, or the supremacy of Brahman would be in jeopardy. Hence considerable space in the commentaries, following the lead given by the Sutras, is taken up by repudiating the Samkhya and other theories of the origins of creation. Vedanta cannot allow that there is any power inherent either in Nature, or in any constituent substances of the universe, that operates apart from the supreme Brahman's causal power. To be a supreme Being such an all-causal role was necessary.

Vedanta also intended to provide a superior and more satisfying theory at an *ontological level*, though 'superiority' here is largely a matter of presupposed perspective. The systems Vedanta contended with were all pluralistic in one form or another. Vaiśeṣika analysed the universe into its six basic Categories (*padārtha*) and its nine Substances (*dravya*); Samkhya(-Yoga) found a fundamental dualism of Nature and Souls; the Ritualists' system was initially based on the manifold character of the sacrificial acts; Jainism made a radical distinction of Souls and Matter, along with its seven other fundamental Entities (*tattva*); and Buddhism too, with its ineradicable causal links, and its refusal to recognise any substantial or essential ontic basis to this causal process, is diametrically opposed to Vedanta's single-substance ontology. It was this concept of Brahman as the one centre of being, self-existent, infinite, free from all imperfection, integrating all other existents into one universe, that proved to be the most convincing of these various ontological positions, at least to later Indian thinking.

In the case of those systems that moved into a (mono-)theistic position, such as Nyāya-Vaiśeṣika and Samkhya-Yoga, there was an immediate strain placed on the pluralist ontologies to which they were committed, a fact which must have contributed to the gradual loss of the inner coherence and strength of these systems. Perhaps the transition to theism itself indicates some loss of inner conviction. But having accepted the need for the 'Lord' to take an essential role as an explanation of the creative process and as a means to mental integration and eventual self-liberation, there must have always been the threat that this deity could not be accommodated to a role of one among many basic categories. Even in Vedanta of course not all deities assumed an all-inclusive ontological role, for polytheism was still retained as a second-order doctrine. For the supreme and perfect Brahman, however, there was no such secondary role. As the one integrator of all finite, dependent beings his otherness was assured. But by the same token so too was his immanental dimension. No utterly transcendent Being can function as the all-integrating, all-inclusive One.

A somewhat different kind of 'reason' for Vedanta's transcendent Brahman was the need to be faithful to *scriptural revelation*. The more conservative Vedantin may well claim that the witness of scripture to the perfect and unlimited character of Brahman is the sole binding reason why Vedanta should be so concerned about this transcendent dimension, in differentiating its position from other religious systems. There is a serious problem of interpretation here, however. Descriptions of a transcendent dimension are necessarily made with reference to some known entity. This immediately establishes some kind of relationship between the transcendent and that which it is said to transcend. The question is, how should the relationship be understood.

In the Gita the principal descriptive method is by way of inclusion. The supreme Being is *supreme* precisely because it includes all other beings not being exhausted by them. In the chapters leading up to the glorious manifestations of the Lord as containing the whole universe within his body, there are several passages declaring his immanence in all things. But we must note of what kind this is: 'Know me to be the eternal seed of all existences. [Yet] whatever states of being these may be . . . they are all from me alone. I am not in them, they are in me. By me all this universe is pervaded through my unmanifested form. All beings abide in me, but I do not abide in them.'[2] Even within this pan-en-theistic scheme, therefore, there are frequent negations used to describe the supreme Being; it is *not* identical with other beings, just as the self is not to be confused with the beings of the natural world, which are mutable, mortal, restlessly active, tainted by various kinds of imperfections, determined by karmic influences, and comprised of differing degrees of the three constituent qualities. The self is 'not of this kind'.

This *via negativa* was used even more strikingly in the Upanishads. Sometimes pairs of opposites emphasise this otherness as in the Bṛhadaraṇyaka-Upanishad:[3] 'That is called by Brahman-knowers the Imperishable. It is neither gross nor fine, neither short nor long, neither shadow nor darkness, neither air nor space. . . .' Elsewhere we find positive and negative characteristics brought together: 'That Imperishable is unseen but is the seer, is unheard but is the hearer, is unthought but is the thinker, is unknown but is the knower.'

Frequently there is merely a list of negations: '[That Imperishable] is unattached, without taste, without smell, without eyes, without ears, without voice, without mind, without radiance, without breath, without mouth, without measure, having no within and no without.' This way of negation of the qualities of finite beings seems most forcefully expressed in the famous saying 'Not thus, not thus' (*na-iti, na-iti*), repeated a number of times throughout this Upanishad. Commentators of an absolutist persuasion have taken this to mean that in an ultimate sense no directly positive statements can be made about Brahman's transcendence; merely figurative expressions of sheer otherness are possible if his radical infinitude is to be preserved.

But is this the predominant Upanishadic view of the nature of the supreme Self? Is it even the intention of texts emphasising most strongly his otherness? To give an adequate answer to such questions would require a far more thorough study than is possible here. Four general points, however, seem relevant to the issue:

1. In the great majority of passages in which the otherness of Brahman is expressed in extreme form, even in the negating passages, usually we find a complementary affirmation of his immanental, subtle form of being. Often this will be in terms of his inwardly controlling and knowing presence, as in an Upanishad[4] usually thought of as favouring a monistic view: 'Explain to me the Brahman that is immediately present and directly perceived, that is the Self in all things.' 'This is your Self that is within all things. . . . You cannot see the seer of seeing; you cannot hear the hearer of hearing. . . . He is your Self which is within all things.'

'He who dwells in the earth, is within the earth, yet whom the earth does not know, whose body the earth is, who controls the earth from within—he is your Self, the inner Controller, the Immortal.'

2. Conversely, in passages so starkly expressing Brahman's immanental dimension that they even seem to identify his being with universal being, further examination shows that there is rarely such sheer pantheism. Brahman is usually a transcendent being 'within' the universe, or identifiable by contrast with some part of the universe. One such statement begins 'Truly all this is Brahman' (Chāndogya-Up. 3.14.1). Then in the verse immediately following, Brahman is said to 'encompass all this'; he is infinitesimally small 'within the heart', yet 'greater than space, greater than sky, greater than these worlds'. Thus an initial statement of Brahman's immanence, expressed in extreme form, leads into an equally emphatic statement of his transcendent character.

When we take up these two points together it is clear that the Upanishads generally do not see transcendence and immanence as two contradictory dimensions or even contrasting polarities in the being of Brahman. It is true that later Vedantins, especially Sankara and Madhva, believed that the older Vedantic 'immanental' theory of the universe as the direct modification of Brahman posed a threat to the perfection of his being, so they felt it even more important to clarify his transcendent dimension than to continue to declare his substantial immanence. Whether there is an inherent flaw in the Brahman-modification idea or not, basically the Upanishads intend a transcendence that relates to and is expressed in terms of the immanental being of Brahman; and an immanence that is qualified by his otherness.

3. Another aspect of this 'otherness' should be noted. The Sanskrit prefix *para*, deriving from the same root as the English word 'far', usually means 'other-than', and is used in spatial, temporal and evaluative

senses. Thus it can signify any of the following: remote, beyond, other than, more than, former, later, superior, and even inferior in certain contexts. *Parama*, as in *paramātman*, is its superlative form, carrying the sense of 'the highest', 'supreme'. It is, in other words, almost invariably used with reference to some other, known entity. Even when negative prefixes are used to indicate otherness, they are always related to an entity that is known, that is part of the experienced universe. So that the intention of the transcendental statements of the Upanishads referring to Brahman as *tat* for example, is not so much to attempt to indicate some sheer otherness, a 'that-ness' which is entirely beyond all known categories, but a more-than-ness, a supreme dimension of being that cannot be exactly identified with any empirical categories, but which includes and goes 'far' beyond them.

4. It is usual to divide the Upanishads into two types—earlier Upanishads that are monistic, and later Upanishads that are theistic in their attitude towards Brahman. We have already seen how important the monist–theist distinction is to the Vedantic enquiry in general and to this study in particular. But it does not substantially affect either the Upanishadic concern for a Being that is transcendent to the empirical universe, or the essential relation of this transcendence to its immanental forms of expression. Monistically expressed, Brahman's transcendence tends to be identified with the transcendent character of the most inner self, though this inner self is not limited to the self within man. Theistically, Brahman's transcendence is mainly seen in terms of the supreme attributes of a personal Being; but this in no way precludes the most intimate 'locating' of that transcendence by reference to the being of the universe.

'Higher than this [world] is Brahman, the Supreme, the immense, the one hidden in all creatures according to their bodies, the one who envelops the universe; knowing him as the Lord men become immortal.'[5]

Commitment to treating such scriptural revelation, whether monistic or theistic in tendency, as the sole authoritative basis for a Vedantic system, provides another clear reason for the Vedantins' concern to express the transcendent nature of Brahman. At the same time they needed to provide a system which could properly include the immanental expressions of this transcendence.

4 The Analogy of Selfhood

In attempting to understand and elucidate within an immanental framework Brahman's transcendent being, all Vedantins were obliged to take their cue from those passages in their sources which point to selfhood as the most appropriate model for this. Many of these passages use the terms *Ātman* and *Puruṣa* (usually translated Self and Person) almost interchangeably with the name *Brahman.* No doubt the two Vaiṣṇava Vedantins, Ramanuja and Madhva, found this person-model peculiarly fitting to their theistic position, in that the name *Puruṣa-uttama*, the highest Person, is a favourite name for Viṣṇu. Thus their predilection for speaking of the divine transcendence in terms of supreme personal qualities arose naturally out of the doctrinal symbolism of their religious tradition. On the other hand, their concern that Brahman should be recognised as supreme Lord, distinct from all finite selves, made it impossible for them to think of him merely as individual soul writ large. Such crude anthropomorphism was even more impossible to Sankara, with his radical view of Brahman's transcendence.

All Vedanta, however, to some extent is analogical in the method by which the transcendent Being is understood and described. Knowledge of the inner, individual self in some sense is thought to lead to knowledge of the universal supreme Self. Thus the immanental dimension of his transcendence is also preserved. Among the six Indian systems, it is in Vedanta alone that selfhood is used as the model for grasping all Reality. Some other methodological assumptions were held in common. But in taking the self-model as the most significant point of reference in determining the nature of ultimate reality, Vedanta stands on its own. Samkhya does understand selfhood as a principle of transcendence; but the immanental power of the universe is distinguished absolutely from this, Nature's qualities being quite contrary to those of the pure Self. Though Vedanta accepts the self–nature distinction, even their contradictory qualities, the self must also in some way be able to 'include' the natural world.

The roots of Vedanta's analogical method are probably to be found in the Vedic idea of the innate correspondence between ritual microcosmos and the macrocosmos of the wider non-sacred universe. Then by the Upanishadic period the sacred power of the ritual was transferred to the inner self, probably as a result of its meditation upon the ritual's inner meaning and the belief that this was the means to transcendent liberating knowledge. Eventually the micro-macro-cosmic correspondence was found between inner self and supreme cosmic Power, the great Self, Brahman. The climax of this new insight was the pronouncement that *Ātman*, the inner self, is one with *Brahman*, the cosmic Self. This still leaves open the precise nature of the correspondence, but the basic Vedantic model for supreme Selfhood, and so for ultimate Reality, has now been established.

It may be useful to look briefly at the way in which this determining insight is introduced in the Chāndogya-Upanishad passage[1] usually called the *Sad-vidyā*, or knowledge of essential Being, which culminates in the pronouncement 'He is the Self; That thou art'. In this passage Uddālaka first attempts to identify the immutable essence of things, and calls it '*Sat*'. He then declares that this self-existent, irreducible Ground of all existents is also the Ground of the inner self, and in fact has the character of selfhood. So Uddālaka initiates his son into this knowledge: 'He [the essential *Sat* of all beings] is the Self: that thou art.' That is: 'Your selfhood is of the same essential nature as that Selfhood underlying all beings.'

Now there is no question here of Uddālaka merely deducing the nature of inner selfhood from the nature of cosmic selfhood; but neither does there seem to be a direct inference of cosmic selfhood from individual selfhood, though it is difficult to believe that the sense a person has of inner continuity and coherence of being, the ability to desire certain ends, and work towards those ends through a bodily existence that the self feels it somehow transcends—it is difficult to believe that this is not in some sense reflected in the concept of the universal Self. In any case there is an analogical relationship discovered between inner selfhood and supreme Selfhood.

Four major types of interpretation of the self-model can be identified. Each seems to take its stand on some distinctive feature of selfhood and interprets the supreme Self, indeed the whole of reality, by means of this distinct analogical perspective. Even doctrines that may appear to be held in common by all Vedantins, perhaps taken from a common Vedantic tradition, are found to be woven into the concerned system in subordination to the determining analogy.

1. The Vedantic type that is probably most 'primitive' takes the idea of *self-projection* as its interpreting principle, though in this system, which

must include Bhāskara's *Bheda-abheda* and Vallabha's *Śuddha-advaita*,[2] the self-model does not take quite such a clear-cut analogical role as in other Vedantic systems. Two strands of traditional thinking seem to lie behind the self-projection idea:

(a) There is the notion, common to virtually all Indian religions, that while the soul in itself is eternal and essentially unchanging, the action associated with it has the power to determine the kind of bodily existence that the soul is to enjoy in subsequent births. As it desires and acts, so it is born and experiences, by reason of its power of self-projection.

(b) One important strand of Upanishadic cosmology transposes this to the cosmic level. The whole universe, with its variety and plurality of beings, derives from the one Self. The great Brahman desired to 'become many', modifying and diversifying his own being in order to bring the universe into existence.[3] Thus in the system, such as Bhāskara's, following this strand of thought most closely, Brahman alone is universal cause, both substantial and efficient, in a real and unqualified way.

Bhāskara's *Bheda-abheda* system is the earliest extant expression of this type of Vedanta. Because he teaches that the one supreme Self, Brahman, is the cause of all finite beings by a process of real and direct self-transformation, both the oneness and the plurality of things are taken as equally and ultimately real. Hence the name *Bheda-abheda*—difference along with non-difference. And this Vedantic type of causal theory is known as *Brahma-pariṇāma*, or Brahma-modification, a theory explicitly taught in the Brahma-Sutras. According to this theory each finite being *is* the great Brahman, the one Self, though manifest under the self-limiting conditions of finite forms of existence. Thus the great text, 'He is the Self; That thou art', can be taken in a direct and literal sense to mean 'He is the Self [who has become all this]; that Brahman thou [as a real finite being] art'.

So the power of the eternal soul to project itself in various forms of psycho-physical existence was taken by this Vedantic school to an infinite degree in the case of the supreme Self. 'Brahman wills to be the manifold and becomes the manifold by his own infinite power of *pariṇāma* . . . the absolute by its immanent energising power transforms itself into the relative.'[4]

More than one modern commentator has described this system, rightly or not, as 'pantheism'. And even though Bhāskara and others of the school made serious efforts to avoid the conclusion that the supreme Self, by really becoming this universe, is necessarily subject to the changes and sufferings inherent in its life, and to defend the transcendent perfection of the supreme Self throughout this process, other Vedantins felt that the theory of direct self-projection disastrously compromised such perfection. It is because of this inadequate interpretation of the transcendental dimension of Brahman's immanence that I shall not take this Vedantic system as a representative type. In any case, it seems to me that between them Sankara and Ramanuja have conserved the most important aspects of Bhāskara's contribution to Vedanta.

2. *Sankara*[5] was one of the first Vedantins to recognise that while the idea of the self-manifestation of Brahman is clear enough in the Vedantic sources, the earlier accounts of this as a real and unqualified self-modification were untenable if Brahman's transcendence was also to be upheld. Sankara, therefore, took the state of *self-consciousness* to be immutable selfhood's most significant feature. On this basis he works his system out in a number of inter-related ways.

We should note in the first place that 'self-consciousness' does not mean for Sankara a person's sense of individuality, but the pure Consciousness lying behind all those mental states in which there is particularised consciousness of determinable objects. Even in each act of such objective knowledge, Sankara believed that there is an initial moment of indeterminate knowledge, when the object is presented without its particular characteristics. True selfhood is thus a state of utter subjectivity, in which the Self contemplates pure Selfhood without any subject-object relationship to confuse that consciousness. Even the existence of such an all-conscious supreme Self, argued Sankara, is established by the fact that the self within has unqualified, irreducible consciousness of its own existence. The *Ātman* is conscious of its existence, therefore *Brahman* exists.

By referring to the self's Consciousness, therefore, Sankara was intending to bring out the unqualifiable otherness of the supreme Subject in his transcendent perfection of being. Only as the Beyond is Brahman able to provide the release from this mutable, dependent world which Sankara saw as the aim of Vedanta.

The same transcendent perspective launched Sankara on his role as great high-priest of absolute monism. For in that such transcendent Selfhood, or pure Consciousness, is necessarily one, the sense of separateness felt by each finitely existent self must be due to the influence of objectifying mental processes. But this we shall take up more fully in the next chapter.

Dreamless sleep provides the clearest particular analogy of that pure Consciousness underlying every experience of the Self. Obviously, however, the direction of Sankara's thought makes a rather special kind of analogical method necessary. There is no question of making a direct analogy between some determinable feature of finite selfhood and the infinite Self.

Indeed, all 'knowledge' of Brahman, which is the aim of the whole Vedantic enterprise, is of a very special kind, according to Sankara. The supreme Self cannot be merely the object of knowledge to a knowing subject. This would be to diminish unrecognisably the transcendent nature both of the Self and of the experience by which that Self is 'known'. It is a matter of immediate realisation or direct vision of that which in reality is the eternal nature of things.

At times it seems that self-manifestation, which results in the creative process that in turn makes personal attributes necessary, is an essential aspect of Brahman's being in Sankara's thought. Yet all causal categories, all effected states, all determinable attributes remain ambiguous in his system. Like Samkhya he taught that the effect is implicit in its cause. But unlike Samkhya he was unable to allow that both are equally real. The dependent and determinable status of every effect meant that from the point of view of the reality of the Cause, which is pure Consciousness, the effect must be unreal. Thus the self-manifestation of the supreme Self is an apparent not a real process of change. There can be no real self-modification of transcendent Selfhood.

Nor can there be any direct verbal identification of the pure Consciousness of transcendent Selfhood. Thus while Sankara elevates the identity-texts of the Upanishads, along with statements of negation, to a special category of revelation, from which normative viewpoint all other 'secondary' texts are to be interpreted, even such definitive statements of the supreme Self's nature have to be stripped of all the finite connotations inevitable to them as verbal and therefore conceptual constructs. Even the great saying, 'He is the Self; that thou art', can only be applied to the supreme Self in a subtly indirect sense. The necessarily finite perspective of all words means that in themselves they do not have the power of probing the mystery of transcendent Selfhood.

In his concern to uphold the transcendent nature of the Self, Sankara adopted an analogical method that was ultimately exclusive in its outworking. The determining analogue, that is the pure Consciousness of transcendent selfhood, makes all other analogical statements entirely provisional in their significance. They do have the power to set the seeker on the path leading in the direction of the ultimate realisation, but that path of enquiry itself ends before its final destination, and all words, concepts, analogies, symbols, 'turn back powerless'. The pure Consciousness that is the ultimate destination can only be indirectly indicated even by the self, in its necessarily finite state, from which the analogy of consciousness is taken. Only intuitive realisation, which goes beyond all analogical understanding, can take the self from its finitude into the pure Selfhood of the infinite realm.

3. It was inevitable that a reaction to Sankara's radically monistic transcendentalism would come from the theistic side. *Ramanuja*[6] was the first to produce a notable counter-system, by taking the *self's relational* character as the determining feature by which to interpret the Upanishadic self-model. His argument was that just as each finite self is in an inseparable relationship with a particular body, so by analogy the supreme Self is inseparably related to the universe of spiritual and material beings. Without contradicting the ancient Vedantic thesis that all beings participate in the one Being, he defined that oneness in terms of its constituent relationships. Hence the name of his system, *Viśiṣṭa-advaita*, that is, 'Non-duality [determined by] distinctions'.

In the first place we should note that Ramanuja's interpretation is in direct opposition to Sankara's pure-Consciousness analogue. No doubt this is primarily because of the merely provisional character Sankara's interpretation accorded theistic experience, practice and doctrine. Ramanuja held that the relationship of finite self to supreme Person is one that can never result in identity of being, without on the one hand the annihilation of that individuality which constitutes infinite selfhood, and on the other a blasphemous diminishment of the lordly supremacy which constitutes the essential transcendence of Brahman. This same relational existence, argued Ramanuja, characterises the being of the whole universe. If 'consciousness' is spoken of there must be a distinct self that is conscious, or that has consciousness as an attribute of its existence. And if you speak of 'knowledge' of Brahman, then there must be a knowing subject. And what is known of Brahman must be the object of that knowing relationship, though in relation to the universe and its selves Brahman himself becomes the Subject. Do not the accepted means of all valid knowledge, that is perception, inference and testimony, function on this same relational principle?

Ramanuja goes on to argue that when scripture speaks of 'knowing' the supreme Self what is intended is devout meditative worship, for in numerous passages 'to know' Brahman is equated with such 'meditative worship'. Naturally Ramanuja finds the culmination of this meditative worship in the relationship of loving, trusting, serving devotion. It is in this relationship that the soul's ultimate liberation is attained, and the most significant aspect of the ignorance deluding the soul is its failure to recognise its essentially dependent nature. The finite self's eternal destiny is to serve the supreme Person, its glorious Lord, the highest Brahman.

Thus, far from excluding the glorious personal attributes of the supreme Self from his essential nature, Ramanuja found in them that

Self's truly distinctive character. His was an inclusive analogical method, in which he took such qualitative greatness as was evident in the finite being and applied it to the supreme Self to an infinite degree. Brahman's perfections, therefore, are not without direct analogical precedent in finite beings, but in him such perfections are realised super-eminently.

It was on this score that Ramanuja felt it necessary to criticise with some vigour the interpretation of the self-model made by Bhāskara and others. Ramanuja accepted readily enough the earlier Vedantic concept of the creative process as a kind of self-manifestation. The idea of a direct self-modification by Brahman, however, he found to be a serious threat to Brahman's perfection of being. To say that he is both the perfect supreme Self and this universe of change and suffering was, to Ramanuja, even worse in this respect than the teaching of the absolute monist about the character of the supreme Self.

Ramanuja therefore revised the traditional Vedantic theory of the creative process by saying that it is only the 'body' or relational aspect of Brahman's being that is changed. By his miraculous *māyā*-power the supreme Person is able to introduce quite real changes into those inseparably related finite beings which constitute his body, while at the same time remaining the immutable and perfect inner Controller of all.

This idea of the supreme Self's lordly inner control of the whole universe is clearly prominent in Ramanuja's mind when he uses the self-body analogy, just as it would seem to be when the same analogy is used in an important Upanishadic passage, in the Gita, and in other scriptures, all of which gave Ramanuja reason to think that his was a legitimate analogical approach.

Even the Upanishadic text, 'He is the Self; That Thou art', was interpreted with the help of the self-body analogy. It is, contended Ramanuja, neither a statement of absolute identity, nor does it require the stripping away of all literal connotations. It is rather a direct statement of the properly analogical relationship of supreme Self to all finite selves. While we should not confuse self and body ontologically, in everyday language we often quite legitimately identify the body by speaking of 'myself', 'yourself', etc. It is in this way that 'thou' is used here, according to Ramanuja. It refers to the finite self in its particular embodied form. At the same time it carries an analogical reference, for just as Brahman is the inner controlling Self of the whole universe, so he is the Self of each finite being.

This form of analogical identification of Brahman is taken even further. It is not only each finite self but every finite entity that has a similar analogical reference to the supreme Self, for it is the whole complex of such beings which constitutes his 'body'. He is the ultimate Referent indicated by all words, in so far as words indicate particular entities inseparably related to their inner controlling Self. Ramanuja is thinking here particularly of Sankara's theory that each word, even in scripture, needs to be stripped of its finite connotations before any understanding of Brahman's real being can be attained. Ramanuja on the other hand wished to apply all texts directly, even though he accepted that as the infinite, supreme Being, Brahman can never be exhaustively described by verbal statements. The direct meaning of all words can be included, even if transcended, when applied to the supreme Being.

How seriously, though, should we take Ramanuja's professed dependence on scriptural revelation, even though his determining analogy is clearly part of that revelation? (Just as was Sankara's determining understanding of Selfhood, which then, however, proved to be transcendent to all means of revelation, and was ultimately dependent only on intuitional grasp.) By basing his system on such an analogy, and taking this as his hermeneutical norm, does Ramanuja not commit himself to an analogical method that can operate independently of scriptural revelation? It seems to me that in fact his system operates between these two methodological poles. There was the given revelation (which precluded dependence on inferential argument concerning the Subject of that revelation), and there was the intrinsic correspondence between finite beings and supreme Self (and so an analogical method), as implied by the Self-body analogy provided by the revelation itself. So there is a continual interplay between these methodological procedures. That the 'revealed' analogy of the Self-body relationship carries a built-in inclusiveness makes a more general analogical procedure legitimate even within the restraining framework of a professed revelationist method.

4. Although *Madhva*[7] also was a Vaiṣṇava theist, he found it impossible to accept Ramanuja's exposition of the world-God relationship. In particular the concept of organic inseparability of supreme Person and finite universe seemed to Madhva still to compromise that supreme Person's transcendent perfection. Sankara's viewpoint was, of course, far more abhorrent to him, being described as 'robbery'. It robbed scripture of its primary intention to exalt the glorious personal attributes of the Lord; thus it robbed the Lord of his supremacy; and in so doing it robbed the soul of its true destiny.

Madhva, therefore, took the *self-determining will* of selfhood as the most significant feature by which the self-model is to be interpreted. We have already noted that this was a significant aspect of the doctrine of *karma*, and that the other Vedantins certainly gave some importance to the idea of determining will in their interpretations of the supreme Self. Only for the monists was the concept of causal will a problem, in that all particular determinations and the differentiation effected thereby seem to contradict their cardinal doctrine of the oneness of all things. Therefore determining will was thought of as operating only at the lower level of reality. It certainly cannot be the explanatory principle which Madhva makes of it. Ironically and unexpectedly, we shall find that there are some points at which the positions of Sankara and Madhva converge far more than do Sankara and Ramanuja.

These are some of the ways in which Madhva worked out his system on the basis of self-determining will as the self-model's most significant feature:

Perhaps first in theological importance is Madhva's ascription of omnipotent lordship to the supreme Self. He is the one self-determining Being, with all others being dependent on him, and determined by his supreme will. Madhva's is thus a fundamentally dualistic (*dvaita*) description of things, though the very opposite of a dualism which thinks of the two constituent categories as either ontologically autonomous, or in contradiction of each other. Every finite entity is thought to be under the controlling will of the Lord. He alone possesses the 'fulness' of being and infinite qualities necessary to be the one self-determining (*svatantra*) being able to govern all other-determined (*paratantra*) beings. In line with this position Madhva stressed the effective causality of the Lord more than any other Vedantin, extending that causality quite explicitly to include all action, all bondage, all ignorance, as well as creation and liberation. In whatever way other Vedantins may have acknowledged Brahman's supreme control of the universe, none of them took it to be the principle by which to interpret the whole Vedantic system as Madhva did.

Such an interpretation does, however, raise a problem for the analogical method I have taken to be implicit in Vedanta. I have suggested that Madhva took self-determining will as selfhood's most significant feature, and explicated the character of the supreme Self by applying this to an infinite degree in his case. But does not Madhva himself say that such self-determining will is the exclusive property of the suprene Self, and therefore cannot be arrived at by any kind of reference to the finite self? How could finite selfhood possibly provide the analogue for a Selfhood by whose sheer will the finite entity has come into being?

His interpretation of the great saying usually translated as 'He is the

Self; That thou art', would also seem to deny that finite selfhood can indicate something of the nature of supreme Selfhood. Madhva takes the text as a *negation* of any correspondence, reading it as 'He is the Self; That thou art *not*', which is in fact grammatically possible. Even apart from this one text, Madhva frequently contrasts the character of the finite self and that of the supreme Self, quoting from a wide range of theistic sources to confirm his interpretation.

As a consequence of his radical emphasis on sovereign will as the proper principle of interpretation, Madhva has to deny the traditional Vedantic doctrine that the universe derives from the *being* of Brahman. He can accept this neither in an essential sense, nor in a substantial sense, and certainly not in an illusory sense. The character of the universe, he claims, derives from the sheer will and activating power of the Lord. Its substantial being, its existence as a mutable entity, derives from certain eternal, uncreated Substances, such as Nature, Time, and Space. The inherent characteristics of these irreducible Substances, or the potencies determining the manner by which finite entities evolve, depend upon the all-determining lordly will. In fact, had the Lord so chosen, he could have created the universe without the use of any of these Substances. In any case, Madhva felt that to speak of a substantial relationship between the supreme Self and any other finite being was to threaten the supreme Being's perfection intolerably. The same concern led Sankara to teach that illusory *māyā* must be the 'substance' from which all created beings derive, though ostensibly he still accepted the doctrine that Brahman is both substantial and efficient cause.

In general, then, Madhva would contend that it is supreme Selfhood, as revealed in scripture, that is the determining point of reference in his system; the inner self surely cannot be the model for understanding the supreme Self. But there are hints at some points that the self's sense of subjecthood was taken more seriously than the structure of his system allowed Madhva to confess. Thus while he more usually contrasts finite selfhood and supreme Selfhood, he also allows certain similarities between them. In one passage immediately after asserting that 'the supreme Lord is absolutely distinct from the whole class of souls', he can say that 'the soul is spoken of as Brahman just because it has for its essence qualities that are similar to Brahman's'.[8] Rather like Ramanuja, Madhva regarded this soul-'essence' as being fully realised only after there has been release from the bondage of karmic effects. Madhva differs from Ramanuja, however, in claiming that devotion must as it were transcend itself so that it reaches the level of immediate, intuitive experience. Even in this transcendent state there is not an identity of

Selfhood, as in Sankara's system, but there is direct knowledge of the essential nature both of supreme Self and finite soul.

It is the supreme Lord who is to be meditated on as the Self, but here again Madhva describes the relationship underlying this in terms that suggest he is more indebted to the self-Self analogy than he likes to admit. 'The word "self" alone expresses the fulness of his attributes . . . being the receptacle of all the qualities that we find in different entities in the universe. Therefore the Lord should be worshipped under the name *Ātman* alone.'[9] It was necessary to his system that the meaning of 'selfhood' be determined by reference to the lordly Self, for the whole movement of his thought is explicitly from that supreme Subject to knowledge of subordinate finite subjects. Implicitly, however, even Madhva from time to time shows that his clues for that supreme Selfhood are derived from the lesser finite realm. There are intrinsic values seen in the inner self especially that can lead to an understanding of the supreme Self.

5 Individual Self and Supreme Self

There is good reason for beginning our detailed comparison of the three representative Vedantins with the question of how the individual self relates to Brahman, the universal Self. We have just seen that it is this inner self that provides Vedanta with its basic model for understanding the transcendental immanence of the supreme Self. In some revelatory texts it seems less an analogical relationship than an affirmation of sheer identity. So it is around just this issue that the major Vedantic debate revolves. If the transcendent Self alone is the ultimate reality, how can any finite being share its nature? If any existent does share that Being, is not its oneness lost and hence its perfection of being diminished? This dilemma leads the monistic branch of Vedanta to argue that the 'sharing' must either be illusory, or in reality must be a sheer identity of being. Thus any distinction within Brahman's fulness of being, or any extension of his simplicity of being, even the idea of any pervasive or participant immanence, is seen as a threat to its transcendent character.

So we find that the very doctrine comprising the basis of Vedanta is also the cause of the most deep division between the various Vedantic schools, and the issue on which they take up their distinctive postures. As we saw earlier, concern for ontological oneness was one of the chief issues dividing Vedanta from virtually all other systems. Of whatever school, all Vedantins have a belief in the individuality of the supreme Being, and in some kind of integrity of ultimate reality. Even those schools antagonistic to Sankara's style of monism usually retained the term 'non-duality' (*advaita* or *abheda*) as part of their nomenclature.

A crucial question in Vedantic studies is, therefore, what alternative forms of 'non-duality' are suggested by its theistic interpreters? If worship and devotion were to retain their ultimate value for the theists, clearly they were obliged to argue for the reality of the soul-Lord distinction and for the reality of the self as an individual. Equally clearly, this results in a supreme Being with very different dimensions of transcendence. What efforts did they make to protect this transcendent character and the integrity of Brahmanhood while at the same time arguing for such distinctions? From the theists' point of view, of course, it was precisely the loss of this distinction which seemed to threaten most seriously the perfection of the supreme Being.

SANKARA

In general we find that for Sankara the absolute oneness of the Self is the only proper expression of that supreme Being's perfection and transcendent nature. By the same token, the supreme Self cannot be thought of as in any way transcendent to the inner Self, for they are in essence identical. This inner Self, however, is not the empirical ego, but rather the transcendent consciousness underlying individuality. The soul, as an individual entity, shares in this transcendent Selfhood only in a distorted way; a variety of analogies and descriptive devices describe such distortion.

Sankara begins his commentary on the Brahma-Sutras by outlining what he sees to be the essence of Vedanta. In the first place, he contends, the true Self, the transcendent Subject, is in every respect in contradiction with the non-self, which includes all objective existence. It is the confusion of these two opposites which is the cause of all evil, and it is with 'a view to freeing one's self from that wrong notion and attaining thereby the knowledge of the absolute unity of the self (*ātma-ekatva-vidyā*) that the study of the Vedanta-texts is begun'.[1] Later, while arguing the case that knowledge of Brahman is the essential object of scripture, not action as taught by the Ritualists, Sankara first quotes such determinative texts as these: 'Being only was this in the beginning, one without a second'; 'In the beginning all this was Self, one only'; 'This is the Brahman without cause and without effect, without anything inside or outside, this Self is Brahman perceiving everything'; and the text of paramount importance in Vedanta, 'That thou art'.[2]

To argue as the Ritualist would, that such passages are meaningless without some action being intended as a result, ignored, says Sankara, the infinitely better result that does accrue from the knowledge of such texts, 'cessation of all pain, and thereby the attainment of man's highest aim. . . . For if the knowledge of absolute unity has once arisen there exists no longer anything to be desired or avoided, and thereby the conception of duality, according to which we distinguish actions, agents and the like, is destroyed.'[3] Again and again in this passage Sankara repeats his conviction that the true Vedantic goal is the knowledge that one's Self is identical with Brahman. Ultimately there is only one Self, one Being, one pure Consciousness.

Such an emphasis leaves us in no doubt that Sankara's principal concern was with Brahman's transcendence. The one Self, the Beyond, is not to be confused with the many finite souls. And because of its transcendent nature, the knowledge of this 'unity of Brahman . . . is a secure fortress inpregnable to logicians . . . inaccessible to persons of shallow understanding'.[4] Being the Self's immediate presentation (*sākṣātkāra*) of its own consciousness to itself, naturally this knowledge is beyond all external proof. But to what extent has Sankara been able, or even concerned, to express this transcendent Being in immanental terms?

From one point of view Sankara could claim to give more prominence than any other Vedantin to the immanental dimension; for is not the great Brahman identified with all selfhood everywhere? Thus 'Brahman is not something to be obtained by a person, for Brahman constitutes the very self of that person. Even if the supreme Being were altogether different from a person's self, it would still not be something to be obtained. For as it is omnipresent, its nature is to be ever present to everyone, just as all-pervading as space is.'[5]

As the Self of all, ever present to all beings, Brahman is also said to be the illuminator of all, being essentially 'self-luminous'. This is how Sankara comments on the Upanishadic statement that the Self is the 'light within the heart': 'The self is called light because it is self-luminous, for through this light, which is the self-luminous Self, the body with its sensory organs sits, goes out, and works, as if it were intelligent. This is like a jar that shines when placed in the sun, or a gem when placed (for testing) in milk.'[6] He goes on to say that the intellect is first to be illuminated by the self, then finally the whole sensory organism—indeed the whole universe. 'Because it shines, everything else shines; this universe shines through its light.' Thus 'the Self, the Person, being all-pervading like the ether, is an infinite Being. Its self-luminosity is infinite because it is the illuminator of everything, though it is not illumed by anything else.' Elsewhere this is described, less metaphorically perhaps, as the ground-Consciousness underlying all individual conscious minds, and as that bliss-source from which all particular experiences of joy derive.

The immanental dimension is, therefore, not lacking in Sankara's exposition of Brahman's relationship to the individual self. But it is subject to a variety of rigorous qualifications. Perhaps the most obvious is Sankara's insistence that immanence is to be taken in a non-spatial sense, that is, in a transcendental sense. Texts speaking of Brahman as 'entering into' all finite beings, thus suggesting he pervades them in a spatially limited sense, or which refer to him as being 'obtained', or as the 'goal of going'—such texts should not be taken literally. If the soul really 'goes to Brahman', it would mean both that Brahman and soul are initially distinct and separate from each other, and that he is spatially locatable. But this is quite an inadequate idea of the highest of Brahman's immanence: 'Transcendent Brahman is present everywhere, within everything. It is quite impossible that such a Brahman should ever be the goal of going. For we do not go to what is already reached.'[7] Being 'omnipresent and eternal like space', he is 'the self that is within all'. 'Reaching the highest', therefore, must simply mean 'realising the Self'.

In a similar way, the soul cannot properly be called either a part or a production of Brahman. There are revelatory passages that suggest just such relationships between the soul and the Supreme, but they should be taken in a metaphorical sense only, with an 'as it were' added.[8] Again, such passages should be recognised as motivated by practical considerations, not as statements of ultimate truth. Describing the soul's relation to Brahman as similar to that of sparks to fire implies that in some sense the soul participates substantially in his being, in the manner of part to whole, as the Sutra recognises. But Sankara takes more seriously other revelatory texts that the supreme Being is 'without parts'. Any such divisibility of his being would make him subject to change and thus non-eternal, according to monist thought.

Much of the argument about 'parts' occurs in the context of discussing whether Brahman has actually become 'effect' in the creative process. One suggestion to be answered was that only a part of Brahman was thus involved; part of his being remained untouched and properly immutable. But to Sankara this rather crude division of Brahman into parts threatened his perfection as much as if his whole being were involved in the changes of the creative process.

Sankara does offer another explanation of these non-transcendent scriptural statements with their idea of 'differences depending on time and space'. They refer, he suggests, to the non-transcendent, qualifiable, personal Brahman. But we shall take up this question of Sankara's 'two Brahmans' in a later chapter.

Another way Sankara qualifies the immanental aspect of Brahman's being is much more central to his system. Now it could be argued that if Brahman, as the universal Self, is immediately present to all, why is there so much confusion about his being? Why is this universal transcendent Self not recognised by all as one with the individual self? How, in fact, does Sankara account for the general assumption that one's self is distinct from the supreme Self, if in reality there is the oneness of pure Consciousness? Various principles of distortion are introduced:

The idea of the superimposition (*adhyāsa*) of features of the non-self upon the Self is one prominent explanation of how the Self fails to recognise its own true character.[9] This occurs because the mental faculties, which stand as it were between the inner Self and the objects of sensory experience, are sufficiently close to the person's inner being to act as a kind of mirror for the Self. Unfortunately, it is the characteristics of mental life, with all its objectifying and determining powers, that get reflected—and the inner Self is confused by what it sees. The unreal is projected on to the real. From the point of view of ultimate Selfhood all the distinctions of 'I' and 'you', 'mine' and 'yours', are not real. Similarly unreal from that absolute vantage point is the whole cognising process with its distinctions of knowing object, known subject and means of knowledge. All agents of action, even scriptural revelation and the actions it expects, are likewise devoid of ultimate reality (*pāramarthika*), however necessary they may appear from the practical point of view (*vyāvahārika*). The Self's transcendence, then, is so absolute that there is nothing else which can be said unambiguously to share its being.

The difference between Self and non-self is put in the following way in one passage[10] discussing the mutual superimposition of self and body. The disciple suggests that in this theory each respective superimposition will lead to a relation of constant conjunction with each other, like pillars and bamboos (in a house construction). This the Teacher agrees should be avoided, on the grounds of the possibility of the Self existing for the benefit of another (*parārtha*) and being non-eternal; whereas in reality the Self is pure consciousness, is independent (*svatantra*), exists entirely for itself (*svārtha*), without serving another's purpose as in the relation of servant to master, and hence is changeless and eternal.

Immutability and independence are, to all Vedantins, necessary characteristics of a perfect being. To the monist this means that the inner self too must have no necessary reference to any thing or any being outside itself. It must exist purely for its own sake. Dependence signifies to the monist a vulnerability implying mutability and unreality, all of which result in suffering. But even the very memories of pain and misery are eradicated by the knowledge of the inner self's impeccable oneness with the supreme Self.

Underlying the confusion of Self with non-self is the soul's fundamentally distorted understanding of its existence, keeping it deluded about its proper status. Sankara's system stands or falls upon this notion of an inexplicable Ignorance (*avidyā, ajñāna*) inherent in the soul's embodied existence.[11]

This inherent Ignorance is inexplicable in two ways. It cannot be defined as either real or unreal; nor does Sankara attempt to locate it either in the supreme Self, or in the finite soul. His silence on this point did not deter later monists from attempting so to locate it and give it a relatable basis. Indefinable though its ontological status may have been to Sankara, there is no doubting its importance in his system. It is the essential principle of explanation for the discrepancy between the oneness posited of transcendent Reality, and the multiplicity of common experience. In other words, this inherent Ignorance is Sankara's method of interpretation by which the inclusiveness necessary to any valid Vedanta becomes possible even in his more exclusive transcendentalism. All that is not one with that transcendent Being can be included on this basis. The soul's various perceptions and cognitions, the fruits of its actions, even its sense of distinction from the supreme Being—all appear real to the soul as it views things through the veil of its inherent Ignorance.

Sankara even seems to ascribe a creative function to this nescient principle. It so screens the soul's consciousness that the objective world is, as it were, created for that soul. But his account of this process is not entirely consistent, and in any case he more often explains creative activity be means of the illusory power of divine *māyā*, a cosmological principle related to and operated by the supreme Lord. But such an anomaly is only apparent; it is the soul's fundamental Ignorance that leads it to believe in such a distinct creator Lord.

From the soteriological point of view, therefore, the significance of this inherent Ignorance is unquestionable. If the soul's most fundamental need is to have its veil of Ignorance lifted, it follows that nothing new can be gained by the inner self. Recognition of what in reality already exists, and realisation of (*anubhava*, literally 'becoming with') that already existing transcendent state, is all that will be required. This, precisely, is Sankara's thesis.

Sankara makes considerable use of yet another technical term in his attempt to explain why objective experience is invariably distorted, though it does not seem as essential to his system as is the soul's Ignorance. Distortion is there also because finite conditions are inevitably subject to 'limitation' (*upādhi*). Only the infinite, unconditioned being of the supreme Self can be free of the distortions resulting from such limitation. The finite soul is irrevocably associated with this conditioning process, has become subject to the limitations of 'name and form' and has thus become conditioned by distinctions that are ultimately unreal. Though such limitations are entirely extrinsic to the transcendent inner Self as such, they are inherent to the whole finitising process, and thus have a universal range of operation.

> When the (unconditioned Self) is related to such limiting conditions (*upādhi*) as the body and its organs, which are characterised by Ignorance, it is called the embodied individual soul. When its limiting condition is the power of eternal and unlimited knowledge, it is called inner Ruler (*antaryāmin*) and Lord (*Īśvara*). The same soul (*ātman*), being by nature transcendent, absolute and pure, can be called the immutable and supreme Self. Similarly by this limiting finite connection . . . the gods, different species, individuals, men, animals, spirits and so on, the Self assumes [as it were] those particular names and forms (*nāma-rūpa*). The difference between these things, therefore, is due to the difference of the limiting conditions and to nothing else. For all the Upanishads conclude that there is 'One only, without a second'.[12]

The ideas of improper superimposition, inherent Ignorance, and the limiting conditions of finitude are confirmed by a variety of analogous situations and experiences in life. In addition to the reflection metaphor and the idea of magical illusion (*māyā*) there are two other metaphors to be noted. Firstly, just as the coiled rope is mistaken for a snake, or the shell for a piece of silver, so the objective world in general is mistakenly cognised; it is taken as having the character of ultimate reality, because the Self is deluded by the mental and physical organs with which it has become conjoined. This is not merely saying that things are more than what they seem. From the transcendent Self's viewpoint the universe is just the opposite of what it seems: all the qualities and distinctions presented to the mind in this apparent world are positively deluding. We cannot call them totally non-existent, for this would be Buddhist voidism. But any reality external objects possess is dependent upon the objectifying viewpoint. From the transcendent Subject's point of view they are quite unreal.

Then, the experience of deep, dreamless sleep[13] also gave the monist further confirmation of the changeless, unconditioned character of the transcendent Self, as we noted previously. The joy of waking from a disturbing dream indicates something of the contrast between the unreal and the real. Although dreams can predict events that are able to take place in the future, dreams as such are illusory, analogous to the soul's delusion by the world. In dreamless sleep, however, the soul anticipates its true character of pure Consciousness; it participates in the pure Bliss of Brahman's infinitude. There is no consciousness of pain or misery. But consciousness does persist, as is shown by the awakened soul's awareness that there was no dream during the sleep. In so far as it does not possess the perfect knowledge of the fully liberated soul, dreamless sleep can be called an anticipatory analogy of that final Bliss.

Sankara also found it impossible to accept the full reality of the soul's embodied state, and the continuous cycle of birth and rebirth in which the soul is said to be caught up. He contends that it cannot really be the individual self's action which has brought about this embodiedness, nor can any action be the cause of that self's release. It is solely by an immediately intuited understanding of the self's oneness with the supreme Self that the instantaneous removal of all the fear and pain experienced in this embodied life can be accomplished. Thus 'it is not possible to establish this state of embodiedness upon anything else but wrong knowledge'. For the 'embodiedness of the Self is [not real but] caused by wrong conception, and hence the person who has reached true knowledge is free from his body even while still alive'.[14] He then gives an apt quotation: 'As the slough of a snake lies on an ant-hill, dead and cast away, thus lies this body; but that disembodied immortal self is Brahman only.'

It is the individual's preoccupation with his external, finite conditions that makes it impossible, except by way of inner enlightenment, to recognise the essential Self beneath these externals; until then not even the difference between the supreme Self, the [lower] Lord and the individual soul is realised. In essential reality there is only one unchanging Self; in conditioned existence it appears under innumerable 'names-and-forms', the peculiar marks of embodied existence. But there are other marks invariably accompanying it—misery, pain, fear, mutability. Just as the cause of all this is the one fundamental mis-conception of the Self's oneness, so the solution is the supreme and simple realisation of that oneness.

From the theistic point of view the most serious issue raised by Sankara's absolute identity of the individual and the supreme Self is the resulting loss of the Lord's distinctiveness of being and the soul's relationship of dependence on that supreme Being. In the Vedantic debate this appears in more than one form. One question is put thus: 'How can you make this assertion [that the world's creation, and so on, proceeds from an omniscient, omnipotent Lord] while all the time you maintain the absolute unity and non-duality of the Self?'[15] In other words, is your supreme Self really the Lord of the world and its souls? Sankara seems to answer this clearly enough: 'The Lord's being a Lord, his omniscience, his omnipotence and so on, all depend on the limiting conditions whose self is Ignorance; while in reality none of these qualities belongs to the Self whose true nature is cleared, by right knowledge, from all limitations whatever.... The Bhagavad-Gita also ... declares that in reality the relation of Ruler to ruled does not exist.' It is not difficult to imagine how offensive such a position was to convinced theists.

A corollary to this, rather paradoxically, is the Self's gaining of, or realising, its attribute of lordship, once it has realised its oneness with Brahman. Here Sankara must mean that there is an intermediate state of experience before the soul realises that highest state where lordship of any kind is eliminated. Here is an illustrative passage: 'Because the Self is the ruler of all, therefore it is the Lord of all.' This is described as 'keeping the different worlds apart, distinct from one another.... Therefore in order to keep the worlds apart, the Lord, from whom the self-effulgent self is not different, acts as the embankment.'[16]

One who knows this becomes 'the controller of all', which is said to be an important 'result of the knowledge of Brahman'. We are here reminded of an aspect of early Vedantic thought and Tantric practice, which is often neglected—that an important goal of esoteric knowledge was the attainment of control over things. To the theistic Vedantin, however, such omnipotence was an attribute unique to the supreme Person, the highest Brahman, and in him alone was it an ultimate reality.

RAMANUJA

The term *Viśiṣṭa-advaita* was not used regularly to describe Ramanuja's system until some four centuries after his death. It is, however, a remarkably apt name, especially if the full force of the grammatical relationship is brought out and we translate it as 'monism determined by distinctions'. Ramanuja was certainly concerned about the integrity of universal being, but he insisted that this oneness must be interpreted in the terms of the distinct entities it includes.

Much of his writing on this issue is, naturally enough, directed against

Sankara's absolute form of monism. But his assertion that the supreme Being should be 'distinguishable' is not merely a matter of polemic. It is quite basic to his viewpoint that some kind of distinction should be made between three eternal realities—the supreme Self, the individual self, and the material universe. And by describing the oneness in terms of 'inseparable relationship', Ramanuja was asserting that the self embodied in the individual and the Self embodied in the universe are not absolutely one.

For what reasons, then, does Ramanuja so adamantly reject the concept of absolute non-duality? In general his polemic takes two forms: some arguments are aimed at the logical structure of the absolute position, while others are based more on theological affirmations or scriptural interpretation. In the long opening statement (*mahā-siddhānta*) of his Great Commentary (*Śrī-Bhāṣya*) it is in this order that the arguments are put forward, whereas in his systematic treatise the more theological affirmations dominate from the beginning. This chapter follows the latter order, leaving some of his logical argumentation for the next chapter.

First we may note the positive ways in which Ramanuja interpreted identity texts such as 'That thou art', drawing on the exposition in his systematic summary of Vedanta, Vedārtha-Saṃgraha. In Brahman's case the two terms 'That' and 'thou' can be brought into a relation of 'appositional identity' primarily because 'Brahman is the Self of the embodied individual self', and therefore can be given 'the same name as that individual soul'.[17] The term *tād-ātmya*, often used in Vedantic discussion to indicate the oneness of Brahman and other beings, means literally 'whose self is that (*tat*)', which is exactly how Ramanuja interprets their oneness, while denying any absolute identity.

Another ground for such relational identity Ramanuja finds in the supreme Self's incomparable causal power. 'The word *tat* refers to Brahman as the One who is the cause of the world, the abode of all perfections, the immaculate and untransmutable One. . . . So it is said that the words *tat* and *tvam* both apply to the same Brahman but under different aspects. And in this manner all the various perfections of Brahman . . . are preserved, and not one is made incompatible.'[18] Many other passages also stress this kind of integrity of being resulting from the fact that Brahman is the one Cause, both in an effective and in a substantial sense.

Ramanuja further elucidates this 'appositional' construction by pointing to Brahman's role as 'inner Ruler of the individual soul'. Similarly in the passage we have been considering, it is declared that there is nothing contradictory in saying that 'the supreme Brahman, who is the cause of the world, is also the soul of the individual soul in as much as he is its inner Ruler'. Elsewhere Ramanuja often takes this idea, which is quite central to scripture and Vedantic thought, as his ground both for repudiating any absolute non-duality, as well as for advocating a oneness of inner being. Thus he can even allow that 'Brahman is to be meditated on as being the Self of the devotee'.[19] And the ground for such an identification? 'As the meditating soul is the self of its own body, so the highest Brahman is the Self of the individual soul. This is the proper (and ancient) form of meditation.'

The quite natural corollary, then, of this concept of Brahman ruling the inner Self of all is to describe the universe of souls and material nature as the supreme Self's 'body'. Taking Ramanuja's writings as a whole it becomes clear that this self-body analogy is the key to the interpretation of his system.[20] In the debates with various other schools that arise during the course of his Vedantic commentaries, after pointing out what he sees as logical flaws in the opposing viewpoint, he repeatedly turns back to this analogy of the self-body relationship to clarify the distinction between his and the other systems.

Ramanuja defines a body's relationship to the self as follows: 'Any entity that an intelligent being is able completely to control and support for its own purposes, and the essential nature of which is entirely subservient to that self, is its body.'[21] This brings out clearly his conviction that the body, that is the universe of souls and material nature, is entirely dependent upon and subservient to the supreme Self. It also means that the universe is instrumental to the purpose of its Self, as Ramanuja states quite explicitly. There are three other ideas implicit in this definition:

1. The Self is essentially transcendent to its body. From a practical point of view it is quite possible to identify the two. A person speaks of his body as his 'self'. But the point of view that identifies them in an ultimate sense is merely deluded, both in the case of the soul-body relationship and in the case of the self-Brahman relationship. An essential distinction must be maintained if the transcendent perfection of the supreme Self is to be preserved. Even in the state of perfect liberation, 'the soul's essence is to be subservient to another'.[22]

2. Equally important to Ramanuja in using this analogy is the 'inseparable relationship' (*apṛthaktva*) he finds between the supreme Self and the universe which is his body. (Another definition[23] of the body actually includes this term.) The inner inseparability of the three eternal and fundamental substances (*tattva-traya*) of Ramanuja's system sug-

gests to many Vaiṣṇava commentators an organic and dynamic complex of being. Certainly there is the implication of a 'communication' of being between the supreme Self and all other entities held together in this inseparable relationship, similar to the communication between self and body.

While this analogy does suggest the accessibility of the supreme Self to other beings within the relationship, at least in one place Ramanuja denies that the participation is by virtue of an innate identity of being. It is rather due to the imparted and infused presence of the Self to those finite beings dependent upon this Self's controlling support. Such thinking, however, is really more typical of Madhva's system, as we shall see.

3. Ramanuja also uses the self-body analogy to corroborate his view that the universe, with its multiplicity of distinct beings, is real in an absolute sense. This includes the finite self with all its individual particularity. It is because the universe relates to the supreme Being as body to self that it partakes of the reality of that Being. In an organically dependent relation with this supreme Reality, substantial character is communicated to every 'part' included in the divine 'body'. And as the supreme Self, according to Ramanuja's understanding of the self-body relationship, the body is 'included' in the self, in the pan-en-theistic manner suggested by the Bhagavad-Gita. One of Ramanuja's definitions of the body states that it 'abides in' the self, being 'included by' the self for its own purposes. This need not be taken as contradicting his other soul-doctrine which declares it to be atomic in form. For all its atom-like character, its potency is thought to extend throughout the body, thus transcending the body and in a sense gathering into itself the body's being.

Lest it be thought Ramanuja takes the self-body relationship too literally, we may note at least one way in which he admits the analogy not to be applicable. As far as the self and body are concerned, there is a kind of inter-dependence; the soul needs the body for the accomplishment of its purposes. This does not, says Ramanuja, apply in the case of the supreme Self's relationship to the universe, for as the Lord asserts in the Gita, 'I am the supporter of all beings; they are of no help to me at any time'.[24] In an exaggerated way Ramanuja says here that the universe of creaturely beings is not *necessary* to the supreme Self. There is, however, no doubt at all about the reality of those 'unnecessary' beings, any more than about the compassion their 'supporter' has for them.

That souls and material nature are the 'dependent types' (*prakāra*) of the supreme Self is another doctrine of Ramanuja's, almost inseparable from his self-body analogy, though less clear-cut in meaning. *Prakāra* is usually translated 'mode', which sometimes makes for confusion (especially when used in close proximity to a word (*pariṇāma*) with a very different connotation but translated 'modification'). Ramanuja usually expresses the relationship of the self-body analogy to *prakāra* by saying that as a result of nature and souls being the body of Brahman they aslo constitute his *prakāra*. Occasionally this is put in a slightly different way—'Because it is the *prakāra* of the soul, a body is a definite thing.'[25] He further defines this relationship by saying that 'bodies are the *prakāra* of their souls, since they are attributes qualifying these souls'.

Here Ramanuja shows one reason why this *prakāra*-idea is so important to his system. It is another form of saying that pure substances with no distinguishing qualities are ontological (as well as epistemological) non-entities. And this applies equally to the archetypal substance of Brahman's being. It too is always manifest along with innumerable and perfect qualities, a substance without any kind of distinguishing features being impossible to cognise or conceive. These qualities, however, are not only the super-eminent perfections necessary to the supreme Being. As 'archetype' of all existence the most prominent 'ectypes' which eternally typify his Being are those of souls and material nature—the dependent *prakāras* to which he is necessary *Prakārin*.

The comment on Brahma-Sutra 1.1.13 discusses this at some length. Against possible monistic objections Ramanuja argues that it is 'not a question of whether it is a quality, generic characteristic, or substance that determines whether it is possible for it to be predicated of a certain substance. . . . It is rather its being a *prakāra* of some substance that makes it possible. . . . [This] means having its existence, persistence and conception inseparably connected with the substance of which it is the *prakāra*.'

We have now seen the three essential characteristics of this *prakāra*-existence. It is eternally and necessarily *dependent* on its *prakārin*, its originating substance; it is *inseparably related* to this *prakārin*; and it is typified by distinct characteristics. When Ramanuja looked for the most exact illustration of this *prakāra-prakārin* relationship, he found it ready to hand in the analogy that was so eminently scriptural, that was simpler to apply and elucidate, and that became even more basic to his system—the self-body relationship. To Ramanuja the body is by definition 'that which is entirely dependent on and controlled by the self'. Its inseparability from the self was even more axiomatic. It is par excellence that 'dependent type' of 'ectype' which cannot exist but by its relationship with the self.

Four other kinds of relationship are employed by Ramanuja to re-iterate the soul's dependence on and inseparability from the supreme Self. The *Principal-accessory* (*Śeṣa-śeṣin*) *relationship* is probably the most important of these. The Ritualists had used the former to describe the subordinate part of the sacrifice, and the latter to indicate the principal purpose it is intended to serve. Ramanuja's use of the terms is sometimes in the context of debate with the Ritualists. To some extent he accepts the meanings suggested by them, but significantly he personalises the relationship, making the Principal-accessory relationship equivalent to that of master and slave. Thus, from the point of view of devotional religion, a welcome dimension has been added to the relational ideas discussed above.

In the closing section of Vedārtha-Saṃgraha the definition of the soul as a serving subordinate entity is challenged, and a text (from Manu's book of Social Law) thought to contradict the idea is quoted: 'All dependence on others is unhappiness; all self-dependence is happiness.' Then: 'Service is called a dog's life, so give it up.' Ramanuja replies that this is a false desire for independence of the body, not the soul, and is merely looking for its gratification. 'The proper nature of the soul, however . . . is to be a subordinate entity (*śeṣa*) to some other being', meaning of course the supreme Being.

In the Gita commentary[26] this service is expressed in terms of the worship which it is the delight of the devotee to offer his principal, his Master. In that the Lord is the real doer of actions, the devotee should act in everything as though the Lord were acting. Then all acts are to be an offering to the Lord, in that he is the supreme Master (*Śeṣin*). And there is one phrase of Ramanuja's, repeated several times, which captures so exactly the devotional spirit of the Gita: 'Since you are controlled by me, your sole essence (*rasa*) and delight (*rati*) is to be my subordinate (*śeṣa*).' Thus by means of this analogy, Ramanuja has been able to bring out more clearly the intimate personal relationship of devotees with his Lord, not only the general one with the universe as a whole.

Then in his comment on the opening verses of the glorious vision of the Gita's eleventh chapter: 'I have heard of your immeasurable greatness, which consists of your being eternally the Principal of all intelligent and non-intelligent beings, in your being superior to all by virtue of the host of glorious qualities such as universal knowledge and untiring strength that are yours alone, in your being the Ground and Support of all, and in being the One who causes all things to function.' It is, in fact, this role of principal Being or Master which seems to be inseparably linked with the divine Lordship in Ramanuja's thought. 'This truth of God's being the Lord of all and the principal Person of all is declared in a number of texts. . . . To be the Lord means to be the Controller, and to be the principal Person is to be Master.'[27]

Then Ramanuja describes the relationship of supreme Self and inner self in the less complex terms of Brahman as the Support (*ādhāra*) with all other beings as dependent (*ādheya*). To a large extent this merely elucidates a little further the self-body relationship. Brahman alone is the ultimate Ground of all other existents. To convey the idea that he is the one self-subsistent Person, Ramanuja invariably uses this analogy in conjunction with other more personal terms.

This Support-dependant relationship, however, does take on a new aspect when the relationship is that of the Lord with those souls devoted exclusively to him. For their part there can be no other thought than that of complete dependence on his supporting power and forgiving grace. The feeling that he alone is their support is most intense in their case. This is their 'essence' and their 'delight'. 'Because of their intense love for me, they find that it is impossible to support their souls for even an infinitesimal part of a second without singing my praise, striving for me, and worshipping me.' And the dependence can never be reciprocal, even though there will be some mutuality about the soul's relation to its body. 'My existence is not under their control. . . . I am the supporter of all beings; they can be of no help to me at any time.'[28]

And yet, following the Gita's own suggestion, Ramanuja describes a remarkable change in the Lord's attitude towards his dependants, when their devotion is so intense that they feel 'unable to sustain their souls without worshipping me, and when this worship is their sole aim'. For in such cases, even the Support feels that 'without him [that devoted soul], I cannot sustain my soul'; 'I treat them as if they were my superiors'.[29] Clearly this is not an ontological statement on Ramanuja's part, though it does have considerable theological significance.

A more personal, though somewhat similar analogical relationship is that of the *Controller* (*niyantṛ*) *and the controlled* (*niyāmya*). Although these have an original sense of restraining and being restrained (hence the use of *niyama* in yoga), Ramanuja more often seems to intend a positive governing and directing on the part of the supreme Self. This is 'his precise name for one of the essential aspects of God's essential lordship (*īśitṛtva*), which means, also, of his supremacy (*paratva*) over his creation'.[30] It is rather overshadowed, however, by the more prominent scriptural title with which it is often linked, the 'Inner Controller' (*antar-yāmin*). One example of the way Ramanuja uses these two titles together will suffice: 'The controller (*niyantṛ*) is the "ruler over all" in that he enters within as the inner Controller.'[31]

Another pair of terms of great importance in Ramanuja's system is that of *Whole* (*aṁśin*) and *part* (*aṁśa*). This description of the soul as a 'part' of Brahman has probably been more criticised than any other aspect of Ramanuja's teaching. The most obvious objection to such a part-whole form of relationship to describe the inner self's relationship with the supreme Self is that Brahman's perfection is thereby jeopardised; 'all the imperfections of the soul are Brahman's also'. But Ramanuja specifically rejected the idea that the soul is a divisible piece of Brahman. Any such spatial, quantitative extension of Brahman in the soul would naturally implicate Brahman in the defects of the soul, as Ramanuja himself readily admits.

Nevertheless, Ramanuja boldly disallows the concessional 'as it were' sense with which Sankara had interpreted the Sutra declaring the soul to be a 'part' of Brahman. To Ramanuja this declaration was a direct contradiction both of any theory which takes supreme Self and inner self as entirely different, as well as of those who take the self as Brahman, either erroneously perceived, or distorted by the 'limiting conditions' of finitude. The Whole-part concept, says Ramanuja, is intended to make clear that both kinds of scriptural statement, those declaring non-difference and those declaring difference, must be taken 'in their primary, literal sense'.

His first concern is to show that sheer non-duality is precluded: 'The fact that the soul is created by Brahman, is ruled by it, constitutes its body, is subordinate to it, abides in it, is preserved by it, is absorbed by it, stands to it in the relation of a meditating devotee, and through its grace attains the different ends of man'—in other words all those theistic indications of the 'distinction of the soul and Brahman'—all these are essential to the Vedantic revelation, not 'mere reiterations of differences established by other means of [non-transcendent] knowledge'.[32]

Ramanuja then suggests a number of examples in which being a 'part' of something does not mean being of identical nature with it. Light is part of a luminous body; generic characteristics are part, by being attributes, of the species to which they belong; the body is 'part' of the embodied self again in the sense of belonging to it. But in none of these cases is there identical nature of whole and part. In many cases, contends Ramanuja, the distinguishing attribute (*viśeṣaṇa*) will be the part, and the distinguished entity (*viśeṣya*) the whole. To show differences of essential character is just what is necessary in distinguishing one thing from another. In the case of the supreme Self also there is a difference of character from the soul which forms 'part' of it.

Equally important is the fact of the part's *inseparability* from its whole.

It is quite impossible for the attributive parts of a 'thing distinguished' to maintain any separate existence of its own. They are 'ultimately bound to the substance which they distinguish'.

To what extent, then, according to Ramanuja, does the 'That thou art' text attribute identity of being to Brahman and soul? Just as the soul can be 'identified' with the supreme Self by virtue of his supreme Selfhood and the soul's inseparable dependence as that Self's 'body', so every life-soul, even every creaturely entity, refers ultimately to its inner Self, the supreme Brahman. This idea emerges out of Ramanuja's systematic exposition of the *Sad-Vidyā* passage we noted in Chapter 4.

He first asserts, in reply to the monist's interpretation of the text 'This real being was alone in the beginning, one without a second', that the other part of the text contradicts the view that only the cause is real, all manifestations of difference are unreal. For it is also said that 'All can be known when the One is known'. But this is only tenable, says Ramanuja, when 'that "all" has reality of its own by having the "one" for its soul'. For this One, 'whose essential form is comprised purely of knowledge, bliss and perfection, whose greatness is immeasurable, who possesses boundless, unequalled, countless perfections ... [is] the supreme Brahman himself, whose body is constituted by intelligent and non-intelligent beings in subtle state'.[33] A further description of Brahman's self-manifestation follows, using the Upanishadic analogy of the lump of clay and its products which are marked by a variety of names and forms.

Then comes a rather unexpected application of this train of thought. Just as 'the living soul is itself ensouled by Brahman ... all non-intelligent matter becomes definite things (*padārtha*) when the living soul ensouled by Brahman enters into it, and then all substance assumes name.... Hence it follows that all words which denote some definite thing ... actually denote the entire composite entity; the body, the individual soul represented by it, and finally the inner Ruler of that soul, the supreme Person in whom that entity terminates.' In this way the whole universal process, originating from, dependent on and consummated in the supreme Person is 'summed up and applied to one specific individual soul in the statement "That thou art"'.[34]

Although Ramanuja cannot allow that the soul is identical with the supreme Self, he frequently suggests their *similarity* of character. Even when free from the bondage of *karma*, the soul 'cannot become one with the highest Self'. For 'one substance cannot pass over into the nature of another, but merely leads him who meditates on it, and who is capable of change, towards its own nature (*ātma-bhāva*), in the same way as the magnet attracts iron'. This means, he says, that the one imparts to the other 'a nature like his own . . . for the attracted body does not become essentially one with the body attracting'.[35]

There are, of course, a number of qualities which the soul possesses in common with Brahman. In later Vaiṣṇava thought one such list of these includes inward individuality, consciousness, spirituality (*ātmatva*), and agency, but there are other lists of common attributes. Ramanuja himself, following the Upanishads and Vedanta-Sutras, arrives at the following list of the soul's 'defining attributes'—truth, knowledge, bliss, purity and infinity. This clearly includes more potentially transcendent qualities than the previous list mentioned. But while these rather exalted attributes can be applied both to the supreme Self and the inner self, we should note an important distinction: in the soul the bondage of *karma* is able almost to obliterate, certainly to obscure, these divine qualities. Nor is the soul able to realise such qualities just as Brahman does.

Ramanuja does accept, however, that there are many scriptural texts which declare the necessity and the possibility of the soul's real recovery of their true nature, when it is fully released from the fetters of karmic influence. 'Of him who has freed himself from his ordinary name and form, and all the distinctions founded thereon, and has assumed the uniform character of intelligence, it may be said that he is of the character of Brahman. . . . His being is the being, that is the nature, of Brahman.' But this does 'not mean absolute oneness of nature'. Its 'non-difference from the highest Self' is of a qualified kind; there can be no obliteration of individuality, even in that ultimately exalted state. Rather, because all the differences of embodied existence have been removed and the soul has realised its 'essential nature of uniform intelligence', the soul can now be described as 'no longer different from the highest Self'. And it is still because 'as inner Ruler he is the Self of all and all things constitute his body', that there is no one separate from him.[36]

In other words, whatever qualities may be attributed to the inner self, they are always derivative, dependent on the supremacy of the highest Self. The soul's bliss is an example of this. 'This is the meaning of the text "Brahman is bliss". . . . In that Brahman is essential delight, a person is happy when he has attained Brahman. That supreme Person, who is happiness of incomparable excellence by himself and in himself, also becomes happiness to others, since there is no limitation to the nature of his happiness.'[37]

This contrast between the soul's limited qualities and the supreme Self's sheer abundance of perfections will be drawn in more detail in

Chapter 8. Meanwhile, we may note that such features as are shared in common have this fundamental difference: they are essential and eternally perfect in the supreme Self, but merely derived and potential in the finite self. They are derived from the self's participation in the supreme Being, in whom they are pre-eminently and infinitely realised. They become realised in the finite self only by means of devotional meditation on the supreme Self. In this way the devotee is set free from his bondage and 'obtains the realisation of Brahman, which makes him become like Brahman'. The loss of this Brahman-like character is real, and its recovery is dependent upon the devotee entering into a relationship of trust and love with the supreme Self. But it was the self-body analogy, elaborated by a rich variety of other relational analogies, and suggesting a substantially intimate relationship between the supreme Self and the finite soul, that provided a convincing basis for the soul's intimate dependence on the Supreme, though without submerging the soul's individuality of existence or the permanence of its devotional subservience to that Being.

MADHVA

In recent years a number of Madhva's followers have made vigorous attempts to defend the authenticity of their Teacher's interpretation of the Vedantic tradition. This was made necessary by the rather brusque treatment he has received at the hands of writers on Indian religious philosophy in the past 100 years. Only one, however, going against the stream of interpretation followed even by fellow Madhva-scholars, has tried to establish that Madhva's system is 'the culmination of Vedic and Upanishadic Monism'.[38] More usually his system has been recognised as radically dualist. In view of such variety of interpretation, it will be helpful to examine just what kind of oneness, if any, Madhva intended in his teaching on the individual soul and the supreme Self.

It is not merely because certain texts refer to a unity of being that Madhva too found it necessary to incorporate it in some way into his system. His distinctive theological outlook also made some kind of universal oneness a necessity. Undoubtedly it was his intention to establish an integrated monotheism. Like Sankara and Ramanuja, however, he had no intention of completely excluding the underlying polytheism of the Vedic tradition. Indeed, as we shall see, a functional hierarchy of deities became quite prominent in his system. He was also to some extent indebted to the pluralistic thought of other Realist schools.

However, the 'dualism' by which his system is normally defined is at least in part a corollary of his doctrine of the incomparable greatness of the supreme Lord, from whom all other existents have to be distinguished. Of course, every Vedantic system was faced with the problem of accounting for and including in some way the 'second-order' aspects of existence. And a system that is seriously monotheistic in intent, despite its inner need to provide a coherent system integrated around the supreme Being, will also have to cope with certain special strains. How can the finite participate in the infinite Being, as Vedanta demands, and at the same time ensure that this finite and necessarily 'other' existence is both real and dependent, as monotheism demands? Madhva's system boldly attempts to meet this challenge.

In his Viṣṇu-Tattva-Nirṇaya the following question is posed: 'What is the significance of the statement, "Of all forms of being he is non-dual"?' To which Madhva replies: 'There is non-duality (*advaita*) in respect of the highest Reality. He alone is the supreme Reality over all. . . . He alone has non-duality [which] only signifies that he has no equal or superior.'[39] A similar explanation is found elsewhere: 'Revelatory texts sometimes describe souls as non-different from Brahman by virtue of . . . the outstanding prominence and ontological independence of Brahman.'[40] Such descriptions should not, however, be understood literally, in terms of any identity of essence between them. This idea that Brahman's supremacy of being accounts for such declarations of non-duality is sometimes reversed; the 'difference' of Brahman from all else which is declared in scripture signifies his being 'defectless', not characterised by the flaws found in all other beings..

Such 'oneness' is also an expression of the perfect harmony between the various attributes of the supreme Lord. No kind of mutual contradiction and hence no difference exists between his attributes and his actions, manifestations, or even essential being. To account for this perfect integrity of attribute and essence Madhva introduces, in this same passage, the principle of 'intrinsic distinction' (*viśeṣa*), by which each distinct attribute in any substance by its very constitution is enabled to exist and function in harmonious separation from other attributes. The Lord himself has introduced this system throughout the universe, but it operates most perfectly within his own being. Hence it can be said, 'There is no plurality here', or, 'Only one, without a second'.

The oneness expounded in Madhva, then, being principally a declaration of the supremacy of Brahman, led to doctrines completely at variance with the monism of Sankara. The transcendence of the supreme Being in Madhva's system was not that of Self over non-self, but the transcendence of the supreme Self over the inner self, and all other existents. Not even Ramanuja expresses this otherness so uncompromisingly.

Madhva also allows a oneness of reality resulting from Brahman's supreme creative power. As we shall see more fully in Chapter 7, all that exists derives from the supreme Lord. The one Lord is able to create this manifold universe even though it would be impossible to anyone else. Moreover, it is 'because the "One" is dominant . . . and because Viṣṇu is the cause of all' that the knowledge of the 'One' also gives knowledge of the 'all', as scripture declares.[41]

Madhva, however, diverges rather radically from the other Vaiṣṇava theologians on the nature of creation, and in particular on what constitutes the substantial cause of the universe. He does not accept that Brahman, in subtle, unmanifest form, himself comprises this substantial cause (*upādāna*) of all creaturely existents.

Thus he also rejects the doctrine of Brahman's creative self-manifestation (*pariṇāma-vāda*) almost as fiercely as he rejects Sankara's doctrine of illusory manifestation (*vivarta-vāda*), asserting that 'whatever is incompatible with the divine sovereignty should be rejected. Inconsistency with the divine majesty is itself the criterion of what is unworthy of acceptance'.[42] Self-transformation into this finite and defective universe constitutes such a compromise, according to Madhva. Thus the kind of 'oneness' of being shared by supreme Self with the inner self and all other entities was, in Madhva's system, very different from that understood by both Ramanuja and Sankara.

The analogy most favoured by Madhva to describe the Brahman-soul relationship was that of original and reflection (*bimba-pratibimba*). This may seem unexpected in a radical theist like Madhva, especially in view of Sankara's use of the same analogy. In Sankara's case it seems to fit neatly into his whole scheme, suggesting as it does the impermanence and even unreality of the objective universe. For a reflection obviously has no reality of its own, and exists only so long as the original continues to project its image. And the idea of 'projection' is precisely what Sankara used to describe the relationship of Self to non-self. Ramanuja, on the other hand, avoided the reflection metaphor in his Śrī-Bhāṣya by interpreting this Sutra as 'fallacious argument'.

This was how Madhva developed his reflection theme, taking it in a sense quite divergent from Sankara's: 'Equality with the Lord or his manifestations cannot be predicated of the soul because it is but a reflection of the Lord, as described in the text, "the souls stand as so many reflections with regard to different forms of the Lord".'[43] Using the Sutra's other description of the soul as a 'part', which in its literal sense was an unacceptable term to Sankara, Madhva asserts that both finite souls and special manifestations or Avatāras of the Lord can be called 'parts of the Lord'. But the difference is that souls are parts only in the sense of reflections; they are not of the original substance. The Lord's special manifestations, on the other hand, are 'essential' parts, really sharing in his substantial being.

So an important contrast emerges in the usage to which Madhva and Sankara put the same analogy. Madhva intends to point out the essential difference between the soul and the Lord, and the fact that the reflection is totally dependent upon the original. Sankara, however, points to the essential identity of the two, any differences being accounted for by distortions of the mirror or vehicle of reflection. In Madhva's interpretation there is no place for any such medium of reflection, just as there is no 'limiting condition' such as we find in Sankara's monistic view of finite existence. Clearly Madhva uses the analogy in a rather special sense.

Another analogy used by Madhva at first sight would suggest even more strongly just such a minimising of the reality of finitude. When an Upanishad describes this life as the shadow of the person, Madhva applies this to the self's relationship to Brahman; it is the shadow (*chāya*) of the supreme Person. 'The Lord is immeasurably more than and superior to the souls, as the substance is greater than its shadow. The shadow is there because of the Substance. It is bound to the Substance; but not vice versa. The dependence is thus unilateral and not reciprocal. [Also] the shadow is outwardly similar to the Substance. . . . The Souls have the same form of reality, consciousness and bliss, resembling Brahman's.'[44] It is just this total dependence with the secondary idea of a limited similarity, that Madhva intends by referring to souls as reflections. However, when souls are likened to 'puppets' it is clearly the dependence rather than the similarity that is dominant.

We noted above that, unlike Sankara, Madhva gives no place to any medium of reflection between the supreme Self and the soul. One reason for this is that it suggests an impermanent, even illusory relationship between the two, perhaps with the reflection being taken back into the original, as in Sankara's doctrine of identity. For Madhva, the souls exist eternally as reflections: such is their essence. When pressed, however, Madhva eventually allows that there is a kind of 'medium' for the Lord to use—the essential nature of souls themselves, each equipped as it is with its own 'intrinsic distinctions'. To explain this Madhva uses another simile, that of the sun and the rainbow. The sun's rays shine through the raindrops, which have the power to change these rays into the various colours of the rainbow. Thus to the notion of total dependence as an essential characteristic of the soul Madhva adds another dimension—it also has potency, luminosity, and other Upanishadic qualities such as consciousness, bliss, and so on. But only when there is perfect realisation of the more contrasting quality of dependency will those qualities which manifest similarity with the supreme Self also be realised. Once this stage has been reached, there is the possibility of what Madhva calls *Bimba-aparokṣa*, the immediate vision of the Original. Here again we find Madhva adopting terminology and suggesting concepts that are nearer to Sankara than to Ramanuja, though in fact he can be distinguished from both.

Madhva's most characteristic description of Brahman refers to his controlling Will. He is primarily the Ruler, the One on whom all existence depends, whose Lordship is essential to his being. Thus *Sva-tantra* and *para-tantra*, the Self-determined and the other-determined, are his favourite descriptive terms distinguishing Brahman from created existence. The more usual translation is 'Independent' and 'dependent'. But Madhva does not here intend to suggest Brahman's existence in separation from all other existents, which the more negative *in*dependent could imply. The dependent nature of everything other than Brahman is the necessary corollary of the declaration of Brahman's *Sva-tantra* nature. He alone is self-determining; his existence depends on no other source, and his willing depends on no external compulsion. And although this dependent existence of the universe which arises out of Brahman's self-existence is not one of 'inseparable relationship' in quite the substantial sense asserted by Ramanuja, it can in Madhva's view be described as a relationship of inseparable contrast. Brahman's is the necessary self-existence and self-determining that provides the controlling ground for all other existence. Much as it may have been necessary to redress a certain anti-Madhva imbalance in Vedantic study, and to show Madhva's intention to integrate all beings into a single universe, it seems doubtful if this system can be taken as an implicit monism. We must give sufficient weight to Madhva's own insistence on the dual character of reality. He asserts quite conclusively: 'There are two orders of reality—the Self-determined and the other-determined.'[45] This can hardly be translated as 'two ways of presenting truth'.

It is to the dependent order that the soul belongs, as Madhva never tires of insisting while opposing the monistic view of Vedanta. Thus: 'There is no equality of experience between the Lord and the soul; for the Lord is all-knowing, all-powerful and self-determining; while the soul is of little understanding, of little power, and absolutely dependent.'[46] Again, commenting on a later Sutra, he quotes from a minor Upanishad: 'The Lord indeed is most High, self-determining, highest in excellence; the soul is of limited power, dependent, humble.' The contrast between the two orders, the self-determining and the other-determined, is such that all dependent creatures only find a place in scripture 'in order to declare that everything rests on the support of the supreme Lord'.[47]

Madhva finds it necessary to clarify any ambiguity concerning the role of *karma* in relation the Lord's will, and in some ways defends the dynamic of the divine will more successfully than does Ramanuja. He says that even though the soul's embodied state is determined by that soul's previous action, it must not be forgotten that 'the very existence of *karma* and other things depends on the Lord'.[48] Similarly, 'the very existence and operation of Nature (the vehicle of *karma*'s potency) are the gift of the Lord'. The soul's involvement in such a changing embodied state is a 'necessary attribute of the intelligent soul' and a further sign of its 'state of dependency': immutability being accepted by all as the necessary characteristic of transcendent perfection and independence, though in the case of the theists, not of reality.

The Upanishadic passage so dear to the monists, 'In the beginning all this was being only, one without a second', culminating in 'That thou art', is interpreted by Madhva on the same principle that the soul's utter dependence on the Lord is the ultimate truth to be revealed to the soul. It was this new knowledge of his difference from and dependence on the Supreme which, according to Madhva, in the Upanishadic passage in question, destroyed the seeker Svetaketu's initial pride, and prompted in him the liberating spirit of true devotion.[49]

Though Madhva stressed the transcendent character of Brahman so persistently, there is what may at first appear to be surprising importance given to his all-pervasiveness and omnipresence. Translators of Madhva tend to use these two terms interchangeably, whatever the original. Strictly speaking, to 'pervade' all things, implying presence 'within' all, poses slightly more difficulties for the strict monotheist (and the monist) than the presence-with that is suggested in 'omnipresence'. But the distinction should not be pressed, in that both spatial terms 'with' and 'in' imply some kind of transcendental immanence. More important is the recognition that a system which rejects the notion of a single substantial origin, and yet which is bound to a view of the supreme Self's inner control of all, will necessarily stress the all-pervading action of that Self. Like Ramanuja, Madhva found the Upanishadic name 'inner Controller' useful for explaining the identity texts. 'Texts like, "I am Brahman", "What I am, that he is".... "That Puruṣa who is in the sun is myself", and "It is I who am he", have significance from the standpoint of the inner Ruler of all.'[50] And whatever may be the actual derivation of the name Viṣṇu, Madhva frequently takes the title 'All-pervading' as the most significant name for Viṣṇu, claiming that this is its etymological basis. He attributes the same meaning, among others, to the name *Ātman.* But the individual soul must, he contends, be distinguished from the Lord in this case; for (as Ramanuja argued) the soul is atomic in form, and not all-pervading. Then in his comment on the very first Sutra he takes the three syllables that comprise the first two words, *a,ta,tha,* and in each case gives an esoteric interpretation meaning pervasiveness, so arguing that here is a veiled reference to the all-pervading Viṣṇu.

Rather like Ramanuja, Madhva understands this inner pervasiveness of the supreme Lord to be the means by which he accomplishes his control of the universe. 'The supporting of the whole universe is predicated of that which is within . . . and the greatness of his glory is to be found described in the passage, "He is supreme Lord of beings".'[51] Madhva even makes limited use of the concept so dominating Ramanuja's thought—that the universe is related to the supreme Self as the body is related to the soul. Commenting on the Upanishadic saying that the earth is like the body of Brahman, Madhva writes: 'From the Will of Viṣṇu such a real world decays every day, and being present everywhere in this world, the perfect Lord is most blessed. Hence this world is spoken of as his body . . . there is nothing inconsistent in speaking of the world as the Lord's body.'[52]

Madhva's main thought here is that without the Lord's life-giving presence within, the universe could not function. 'Lifeless matter having a dependent existence and as such resembling a body, only the Supreme Lord who dwells in and rules this Nature-Origin (*Pradhāna*) is to be taken as the Unmanifest. . . . [Nature] is dependent on him and is guided by him, and is consequently like unto a body of the Lord.' But Madhva is careful to emphasise that the Lord indwells this 'body' only in a subtle form. There is, he asserts, no question of such gross presence within the material universe as to call into question the Lord's immutability or eternal perfection.

More specifically the Lord indwells the *soul,* guiding and controlling its every action. 'With the supreme Lord seated within as a guide, the soul enters the womb along with the Lord, is born with him, and guided by him he does *karma.* . . . Him indeed they call Lord of the self.' Then in an earlier Sutra: 'Viṣṇu, though all-pervading and so unlike the soul, is to be contemplated as abiding in the narrow heart, and is ruler of the senses. Further, omnipresence is consistent with residence in a point of space as in the case of space itself. So then, "Viṣṇu is Lord of all senses. As such he dwells in all beings."'[53]

Although the terms *jīva* and *īśvara,* soul and Lord, are brought together usually by way of contrast, the various scriptural terms for the individual, such as living soul, self, and so on, are sometimes read as meaning the supreme Lord. Thus, for example: 'Viṣṇu is said to be "living soul" (*jīva*) because he always sustains the senses. He, the all-pervading One, enters the great elements . . . enters the bodies, both unmoving and moving, and sets the individual soul in motion from one bodily state to another, this self being defined by its eternal distinction from the Lord. It is by the presence of Viṣṇu that the individual becomes glad even if he has to become embodied as a tree.'[54]

In other cases Madhva interprets soul or self as the highest Lord merely because the terms are used in contexts ascribing to them qualities which can only belong to the highest Lord. So, 'the term "living soul" (*jīva*) is used in the sense of the highest Self in the passage which says: "This verily dies if deserted by the soul; the soul does not die." The individual soul cannot be the ultimate sustainer of life.'[55] Similarly the term 'self' (*ātman*) in the great saying which Madhva reads as 'That thou art *not*', is said to denote the supreme Being. Then Madhva goes on to quote another Upanishad: 'Hari is primarily the "Self" (*ātman*) because he is infinite and because he is the knower and creator. All others are reflected selves. Their attributes are limited.'[56] This canon of interpretation of texts can, and sometimes does, lead to some strained exegesis. But then, purely objective exegesis has very rarely marked the interpretation of scripture, historically speaking, in any religious tradition.

There is another way in which the soul was understood as Brahman in Madhva's scheme. In general his system of meditative worship (*upāsanā*) was somewhat more elaborate than Ramanuja's, and what may seem surprising is that in some aspects its aim seems nearer to Sankara's thought than Ramanuja's. Interestingly enough thay all take Sutra 4.1.3 to mean that the individual self is to be the object of meditation in some way, disallowing the view of the 'first objector' that such an interpretation contradicts the theistic position. But of course Madhva suggests a rather special way of avoiding any such 'blasphemy'. Firstly, 'whenever the self (*ātman*) is contemplated as Lord, the attribute "Brahman", that is, "perfect", should be added to the self.' In this way Madhva intends that there should not be meditation on the self as though it were Brahman, but rather meditation on the only perfect Lord, using the self, and indeed a variety of other symbols (*pratīka*) to this end.

Madhva also allows, as we have seen, some degree of essential *similarity* between the Lord and the soul. On this account too the soul can be spoken of as Brahman. He can assert categorically that 'the Supreme Lord is absolutely distinct from the whole class of souls. . . . It is plain the soul is separate from the Lord, not one with him.'[57] Yet this is how he comments on the next Sutra: 'On account of having for its essence qualities that are similar to those of Brahman, the soul is spoken of as Brahman.' There is clearly a distinction here between the soul's essential being (and the qualities belonging to it), and the soul in its actual embodied state. At this point Madhva is close to Ramanuja's teaching. The essential qualities become fully manifest at the time of release from the bondage of karmic effects. So in that condition in particular the soul can be said to 'enter into Brahman' and become 'one with Brahman'. 'Just as the virile power which actually exists in the child becomes manifest in youth, so also the blessedness and other qualities forming part of the soul's essence become manifest on release.'[58]

We may note in passing that Madhva regards the properly devotional relationship with the Lord and his gracious self-manifestation as the only means by which this 'essence' is realised. Or, as he puts it in an impressive verse: 'Having come to the supreme Light, [the soul] stands revealed in its own form.' This self-realising experience, however, is sometimes expressed in terms which would be suspect to some theistic systems. 'Just as pure water poured into pure water acquires a common nature with it, so the man of wisdom shakes off merits and sins and as a pure soul attains to the highest similarity.'[59] There is also fairly frequent reference to the need for 'immediate realisation' of the Lord, a direct knowledge of his essential nature.

Despite these occasional suggestions of inherent oneness, however, Madhva generally denies any identity of nature between the Lord and the soul. 'The unity of the soul and the Lord consists in sameness of thought, or it may mean dwelling in the same place. . . . It is not unity of essential being. For even the realised soul is different from him. The difference between the two lies in the Lord being independent and infinite, and the individual being finite and dependent.'[60] In a previous passage he had described it as 'conformity of mind and will'.

To explain the text, 'He who knows Brahman becomes Brahman', Madhva quotes a theistic text: 'O Viṣṇu, you transcend all measure and limitation. You are boundless and complete. . . . No one can attain such greatness as yours. . . . Just as all minor lights, existing separately in their own forms, enter into the overpoweringly effulgent sun at day, so all Brahmans called "souls" (*jīvas*) enter into the supreme Brahman in the state of liberation, even though they have their own distinctive essences.'[61]

The analogy of sleep, so dear to Sankara, is also used by Madhva, though in a limited way. When scripture says the soul 'goes to Brahman in sleep', Madhva takes it to mean that the heart is the Brahma-realm (*loka*), or the 'retreat' of Brahman during times of deep sleep, when the soul is not conscious either of external objects or of its dependent relationship with Brahman. He uses the simile of the bird roosting in its nest: 'So does the individual self enter Brahman during deep sleep and release, even though it is different from him always.'[62] Madhva also insists that embodied conscious life as well as the presenting and withdrawing of cognitions in dreams, are all 'brought about by the supreme Will of the Lord alone', dreams being indicative of the good and evil to come. And Madhva takes the Lord's withdrawing of dream-cognitions and the state of dreamless sleep as an anticipation or analogy of the ultimate release to come. He concludes: 'For in his gift lies the release of the soul from bondage.'[63]

Despite Madhva's preference for the reflection analogy, and an unexpected stress on the soul's need for 'immediate realisation' of the true being of the supreme Self, there can be no doubting the conviction with which he also declared the reality of the soul's distinctive character, and its corollary, or perhaps its basis, the supremely distinctive being of the Lord of all. Indeed, he stresses equally often that the soul's fundamental ignorance concerns these two basic realities—the soul's true nature, that is its dependence, and the Lord's true nature, that is its independence. But the soul's dependence is based more on the sheer independence of the supreme Self, rather than on any sharing in that supreme Self's ultimate being. It is only as long as the 'Original' wills the existence of the 'reflection' that it can continue to exist. Such sheer ontological dependence certainly gives sufficient emphasis to the transcendent being and will of the supreme Self. But by denying an intimately substantial union, a real participation in the being of that Transcendent, has not Madhva's position moved that much nearer to the very absolutism he was intending to refute?

6 Ways of Knowing

Vedanta seems to pose an epistemological dilemma for itself at the outset. Brahman is declared in some Vedantic sources to be essentially unknowable, or beyond knowledge; yet many other texts speak of the need to know this transcendent Being. To know the unknowable is the whole point of the Vedantic enquiry. Should it be assumed that he is unknown only prior to the Vedantic enquiry, anti-transcendentalists would argue that there would not even be the 'desire to know' him were he absolutely unknown.

It is clear that all Vedantins, in one form or another, have to accept that there are different levels of knowing. All agree that the supreme Being cannot be known by means of empirical experience acquired through the senses. They disagree considerably, however, on the extent to which these types of knowing should be contrasted. If Brahman is to be known by means of trans-empirical experience, does this mean a complete divergence of normal cognition and Brahman-knowledge? The fact is that the Sanskrit word for perception (*pratyakṣa*) can be used of both levels of knowing. Usually sensory perception is intended; but not infrequently it also means a direct vision of the Transcendent. Thus it includes both basic types of knowledge recognised by Vedanta; that acquired through sensory perception, and that given through the transcendent revelation, whether given in scripture, or in intuitive perception. In general it is said that scriptural revelation initially evokes the desire to know Brahman; and this knowledge culminates in the transcendent experience of him.

SANKARA

Sankara takes to the extreme the two ideas that Brahman is both unknowable (in a cognitive sense) and knowable (in an intuitive sense). He is quite prepared to acknowledge that in the ordinary sense of the word 'it is possible to know only that which can be the object of sense-perception', and 'the unseen is to be known through the seen'.[1] But in that ordinary cognisance is entirely dependent upon such sense-perception, or on the mental activity related to it, knowledge of Brahman which has any kind of cognitive and conceptual reference can only be of a qualified, limited, and so provisional kind. When Sankara says that our knowledge of the seen is the basis for our knowledge of the unseen, he is not meaning the unseen supreme Brahman. In addition to the fatal flaw of inherent Ignorance, there are also those limiting conditions that distort all empirical knowledge, and even knowledge of God. Thus he says: 'Even when you know Brahman under the finite limitations of the great deities, even this divine spirituality is minimal because it is limited by these conditions.'[2] From the finite and human standpoint the supreme Being is unknowable in his true infinitude.

In the course of Sankara's writings[3] answers are given to various objections that can be raised in response to what seems a bleak view of the supreme Being's knowability. He argues, for example, that even the name 'Brahman' does not signify the reality of his being, until the sound is accompanied by the necessary enlightenment regarding the Being indicated. To an extent the other Vedantins agree with this non-literalism. But when Sankara goes on to claim that no name is able to convey the reality of this supreme Being, for it is quite inconceivable, the objector retorts that unless we take this word 'Brahman' to indicate a conceivable, real entity, what possible grounds are there for enquiry into his being?

Sankara's reply is that in himself Brahman, who is properly so named by virtue of his pre-eminent greatness, is an existent, ascertainable entity (*pratipanna-vastu*). In the first place his existence is indicated by the testimony of scripture. A further indication of this Being, perhaps to Sankara even more reliable, is the universal sense of self-consciousness, which in its transcendent subjectivity is nothing less than essential Consciousness. Thus Brahman, though beyond all finite description, is not inconceivable in the sense that the contradictory phrase 'a barren woman's son' would be. On the basis of such a self-contradiction no enquiry is possible at all. Moreover, though the immediacy of the awareness of self-being ('I am') indicates the Brahman's self-evident character, there are so many misconceptions of this self-evident Being that enquiry is needed to clarify its proper meaning, and so to make it known in a self-liberating way.

A further doubt is raised: if one's own self is identical with this transcendent Being, why is the self not always and immediately conscious of such identity? Why do we have to depend on the Upanishads to be told of this? Sankara's reply suggests that the self is the witness of 'That', the ultimate Reality, but there is no question of his being known as some other external object can be known. The self is 'conscious of' Brahman in the sense of realising oneness with Brahman. And it certainly cannot be known from scriptural passages concerned with what man has to *do*, any more than by means of 'a whole army of logical argument'. The subtleness of the self's 'consciousness' of Brahman is such that 'it cannot be denied, for of that very person who denies it it is the self. Neither can it be striven after, nor avoided, since it is Self of all.' Thus the presence of the supreme Being is so subtle that both his knowability and unknowability are quite different from any normal epistemological process.

Should such a subtle 'presence' be objected to on the grounds that it has been said in scripture that 'the whole world is its manifestation', Sankara acknowledges that Brahman is manifest by the universe, but qualifies it by saying that the world of name and form cannot possibly reveal the essential nature of that which transcends all such limitations. Thus he interprets the Gita's claims for the ineffability, in an extreme sense, of supreme Being. 'It is not manifest. It is inaccessible to any of the senses. It is unthinkable. It is a wonder, an unseen and strange thing. To all beings the supreme Reality is night.'[4] Even the possibility of doubting and denying Brahman's existence is 'due to the fact that Brahman is beyond all sensory experience. . . . There is room for doubt that it does not exist just because it is devoid of the usual conditions of existence and [yet] is common to all alike.'[5] The Self, then, is only to be known through the Self: '[The Self] is known through every state of consciousness, so it is truly known. There is no other way of knowing this inner Self.'[6] Thus the Self cannot be known but by means of its own self-revelation in transcendent Self-consciousness.

If this Self is such a self-revealing being, an 'established fact', 'never unknown to anybody', why is there the need for enquiry into its being? If this Being is already 'established', on what ground is the enquiry begun? Even if it is said that it is the essential being of which we are so ignorant, there is still the problem of how there can be any 'desire to know' something that is essentially unknown. And in any case is it not a conviction of Vedanta that this supreme Being is made known by scriptural witness?

Sankara replies to these inter-related questions by pointing us to the distorting veil of Ignorance accompanying human existence. A person is unaware that he knows the Self, or rather *is* the Self. Even the scriptural witness can only provide a preliminary knowledge, which still requires sustained exegesis of the texts in order to ascertain the real nature of that supreme Being to which they point. For example, the *that* of '*That* thou art' has to be frequently repeated until its full meaning is known. Whatever the means provided to acquire this knowledge, there will always be the need for a stripping off of this veil of Ignorance, until eventually in an intuitive leap the pure Self in its self-revealed, self-established character is clearly seen.

'Hearing' the great sayings of scripture will invariably precede immediate realisation (*anubhūti*). But hearing and revelation can never be more than provisional pointers to this realisation of the Self's oneness with Brahman. Nothing can either mediate or reveal it in a direct sense. Thus, after 'knowing' Brahman, scripture has no further validity.[7] In fact no 'means' to such knowledge is more than an expendable step, even though necessary, to the goal of direct Experience. 'Knowledge', therefore, has a rather special sense in Sankara's usage.

We are now in a position to trace the steps by which the transition from 'unknown' to 'known' is made. At the initial level of enquiry, when desire to know Brahman is first awakened, various provisional descriptions (*adhyāropa*) of Brahman can be made. The teacher begins at the seeker's own level of understanding, describing Brahman in terms the seeker can grasp at whatever stage he has reached. In one passage[8] Sankara calls this the Arundhati method. When a person who knows where this very small star is situated wishes to point it out to someone who does not know, he begins by indicating the Great Bear, to which it belongs. Then he points out a particularly bright, easily identifiable star that is quite near to Arundhati. At each stage, he may say 'there it is', though it is not really the thing indicated. Something similar to this method of initiation does seem to have been quite common to the Upanishadic teachers. Some monist exponents quite openly compared it to the need temporarily to tell children untruths in order to coax them into accepting some more important idea. Just such a provisional approximation of the supreme Being was also the basis of the monists' system of meditation. The image, whether mental or physical, is only to be taken *as if* it were Brahman. Each step of progress along the path to full realisation enables the initiate to see more clearly that the image is not in fact the supreme Brahman.

In a similar way all words can throw some light on the thing to which they refer, though always on the basis of a relationship, and so only in a qualified, limited sense. This relationship between word and reality is of four kinds—species, action, quality or connection. Thus things are identified by being one of a certain species, such as a man; or because of engaging in a certain action, such as teaching; or by reason of a distinguishing quality, such as being tall; or because of connection with something else, such as being the son or teacher of such-and-such. In each case the supreme Being differs from this normal kind of word usage. He is not one of a species, not limited by specific action, not qualifiable, and being 'One without a second' is unconnected in any way. (This is part of his comment on the Gita's assertion[9] that 'Brahman cannot be expressed [even] by words such as "Being"' (*sat*).) Only objects, such as pots and jars, can be fully described by words, so Brahman is never fully describable. This would imply a quite unacceptable limitation in his being. While such descriptions must be attempted from a provisional point of view, from the absolute point of view it is equally necessary to recognise them as imperfect approximations.

Sankara suggests three different types of indirect statement, according to their 'less or more remote connection with the word's direct literal sense'.[10] Thus he says that we should 'distinguish those cases in which the indirect meaning is not far remote from the primary meaning and those in which it is remote', whereas his opponents, Ramanuja in particular, claimed that scriptural statements never need to have their direct meaning stripped away in this manner.

The most theologically significant kind of statements are those which both partially exclude and partially include the direct meaning of the words. This method of indicating the supreme Being has been compared[11] to the Thomist method of analogical predication based on the common characteristics of being, or the *analogia entis.* Sankara also says that beingness (*sattā*) is common to both, which should mean that certain terms can be applied to both finite and infinite in a properly analogical way, with a relationship that is neither merely external nor purely metaphorical. But it seems to me questionable whether Aquinas' general distinction between self-existent Being and causally dependent being corresponds significantly to Sankara's distinction between absolute (*pāramārthika*) Reality and the limited, pragmatic reality (*vyāvahārika*) of finite beings, which are persistently described as 'unreal' from the absolute viewpoint. Thus direct communication between finite creature in his finitude and infinite Self seems precluded. However, further analysis and comparison is needed here.

Of all scriptural statements about Brahman, Sankara takes the great sayings of the Upanishads as the hermeneutical norm by which to interpret all scripture. The statements of negation we have already considered. There are also the identity statements and statements which seem to be definitive predications. In both these there is some use of the principle of indicating the supreme Being on the basis of similarity with as well as difference from the literal meanings of the words used. We shall return to these uses of theological language.

The next stage in understanding the truth about Brahman is best summed up in the Upanishadic spiritual discipline, 'Hearing, mental reflection, and inward meditation'.[12] The great sayings of scripture, in the initial stages at least, have to be heard repeatedly, especially as taught by a Guru. Indeed Sankara seems to regard the 'grace of the Teacher' as more essential than the grace of the Lord in guiding the initiate along the path towards enlightenment. At this stage the seeker needs to reflect on the conceptual content of each text, perhaps considering the context in which it occurs and comparing it with other relevant texts—in other words applying reason to aid his understanding of its meaning. The seeker needs, however, to move beyond these initial stages and on to meditation at a transcendent level, contemplating its import within his inner Self. Thus *dhyāna* or meditation which is beyond all intellectualising is essential if the text's inner intention—only indirectly indicated by the words used—is to be reached.

We might look briefly at the text 'That thou art' as an example of this process. The reality underlying this statement is an already established fact, but the hearer is ignorant of such an identity, and therefore needs to hear it repeatedly stated, so that eventually there will be an intuited realisation of the true nature of the inner Self. Before this, however, there is the need for examination of the context, so that the seeker can understand what is the 'That' being indicated. When he discovers that the omnipresent absolute Self is being indicated, he also realises that certain elements in the *concepts* of both 'That' and 'Thou' have to be discarded. All but the pure, infinite Self in each determinant has to be excluded. The identity that remains will then be absolute and unqualifiable, and it is on this that the inner Self will meditate. Subject to the proper method of 'hearing, reflecting, and meditating', therefore, such identity statements provide the seeker with a potentially valid knowledge of the nature of Brahman. 'The oneness of Brahman and Self which the identity statements express is not that of non-essential combination [but] is a fact based on the interconnection of words at the transcendent level in "That thou art" and similar statements.'[13]

So the third stage in the process of 'knowing Brahman' is to *negate* (*apavāda*) certain connotations in all descriptions of this transcendent Being. Whatever potential communicative power there may be in the great sayings, in their direct sense they can never be more than provisional pointers. Sankara was obviously greatly impressed by the

'*Neti, neti*' method of progressive negation as well as that of double exclusion—'neither this, nor that'—which the Upanishads employ. But in all the Vedantic sources perhaps the most startling negation is the Gita's paradoxical statement, 'the highest Brahman . . . is not being (*sat*), nor is it non-being (*asat*)'.[14] Sankara comments as follows in a series of objections and replies:

> OBJECTION: How can the 'unknowable' be described as 'neither being nor non-being'?
> REPLY: As he is inaccessible to speech, the knowable Brahman is defined in all the Upanishads just by the denial of all distinctions.
> OBJECTION: Only that which is spoken of as being can be said to exist. If the knower cannot be spoken of as 'being' (or 'existence'), then it cannot exist as knower . . .
> REPLY: But neither is it non-being, since it is not an object of our consciousness of non-existence.
> OBJECTION: But every state of consciousness is either consciousness of existence or non-existence. The 'knowable' therefore. . . .
> REPLY: Not so, for it is beyond the reach of the senses, and thus is not an object of consciousness accompanied with the idea of either being or non-being. . . . As such it can only be known through the means of knowledge called testimony; it cannot be, like a jar, an object of consciousness accompanied by the idea either of existence of non-existence.

The process of negation is in effect a process of conceptual purification. Sankara defends the need for the repetition of scriptural texts about knowing Brahman on this basis. It is not because the actual knowledge of Brahman is unable to effect immediate release, but because 'by again and again repeating a sentence which on the first hearing had been understood only imperfectly, all misconceptions are gradually removed and a full understanding of the true sense is arrived at'.[15] Elsewhere he says explicitly that the 'knowing' involved in these progressive acts of mental purification 'is merely a preliminary antecedent to the [true] knowledge of the Self'.[16]

There are in scripture, however, a number of texts that Sankara believes are intended to reach the essential being of the Transcendent. His interpretation of these definitive texts is probably the most subtle aspect of his system. Again we should note his insistence on the impossibility of defining Brahman in the absolute sense, for he is the 'indefinable'. 'Only a particular distinguishable thing (*viśeṣa*) can be defined; and every such particular thing is a changeable thing (*vikāra*). But Brahman is not a changeable thing, being the source of all changeable things. . . . Just because it is undefined (*nirukta*), it is not an abode of attributes'.[17]

The words used in what appear as definitive statements, however, do not all carry the same intent. In particular, verbal statements can be made in either a primary or direct sense (*mukhya-artha*), or in an indirect or implied sense (*lakṣaṇā-artha*). The same word even, used in different contexts, can carry both senses. For example:[18] The word 'self' (*ātman*) is primarily applied in secular usage to indicate the self, and in this sense is subject to notions of differentiation. When these are set aside by the 'not this, not this' process of elimination the term becomes fit indirectly to indicate the supreme Being, even though the latter is beyond the reach of the word as such.

The name 'Brahman' has a similar double reference.[19] Its primary meaning is from the root 'to grow' and hence denotes something great. By 'implication' it can be applied to the supreme Being to mean the absolutely Great. But the indirectness of application must not be overlooked.

Here follows a metaphor of a king in military procession. The cry may go up, 'There goes the king', even though he is in fact hidden from view at the time. By a process of elimination people come to realise that the king is the one not in view, and so 'the idea of the king is properly secured'.

Such key-terms as 'inner Ruler' contain the spatial notion of 'abiding within', and the relational concept of 'ruling another', which have to be discarded before the term can directly indicate the supreme Being. Neither does the great saying, 'One only, One without a second', escape the same purifying process. It can only be taken in an indirect sense because 'One' can signify merely the first in a numerical series, whereas it is intended to indicate Brahman's incomparable transcendence.

Even that other great saying,[20] 'Reality, knowledge and infinity is Brahman', which may appear to be unqualifiably definitive of the absolute Essence, proves to be subject to the same procedure. It is introduced by declaring that 'the knower of Brahman (*Brahma-vit*) attains the Highest'—terms which an objector is able to interpret as meaning 'the attainment of one limited thing by another limited thing'. No, replies Sankara, it is only realisation that is intended here, as when a man forgets to include himself in adding up the number of people present, then corrects this when he 'realises' or 'discovers' his own self to be the missing number. It was merely temporary ignorance that caused the non-realisation. And the reminder about Brahman which follows in the Upanishad is intended as 'a definition capable of indicating the intrinsic nature of that Brahman that was referred to briefly as "knowable"'. As he is regarded as knowable, he is the 'distinguishable substantive' in the sentence, and the terms 'Reality, knowledge, infinity', stand in apposition to the substantive. In this way Brahman becomes marked off from all other nouns, just as a particular lotus is known distinctly 'when it is described as blue, big and sweet-smelling'.

This clearly leaves Sankara open to the charge on his own premises that his Brahman has become a qualifiable, non-transcendent Being. The objection is raised that nouns and their distinguishing adjectives only become meaningful when there are a number of equally distinguishable nouns belonging to the same class, and a number of different adjectives possible, from which the relevant ones have to be chosen. But there is supposed to be only one Brahman, with no others from which he can be or needs to be distinguished.

Sankara's reply to this is the assertion that the terms 'Reality, knowledge, infinity', are not used as qualifying adjectives but as uniquely attributed definitions. Each one can stand alone; thus 'Brahman is reality, Brahman is knowledge, Brahman is infinity'. 'Reality' indicates the immutability of Brahman, and so 'distinguishes Brahman from unreal [because changeable] things'. 'Knowledge' means the consciousness of Brahman. 'Infinity' means subject to no kind of finite limitation. But each of these definitive terms, while not being dependent on the others, yet has a significant mutual reference to the others. For example, it could be equally well said that Brahman is knowledge which is immutable and without any limitation and so on. Thus each definitive term helps to purify the meaning of the others, should they be wrongly understood.

Having acknowledged these terms as definitives of the essence of Brahman, Sankara goes on to conclude that it would be quite wrong to use them as direct descriptions of Brahman. Each of these terms can only 'indicate' his real being. The word knowledge, for example, could mean that Brahman is an agent of knowing, which would make him subject to the objects of his knowledge. Knowing also implies a kind of activity, in normal usage. The supreme Being itself is subject to none of the limitations of such usage. Thus, it can 'only be indirectly indicated, not directly described' (*lakṣyate, na tu ucyate*). In itself that supreme Being is 'ineffable' (*avācya*). But by means of these terms which 'serve to define and delimit each other by being placed one immediately after the other, and by means of their implicit meaning, they become definitives (*nivartaka*) of Brahman'.[21]

Underlying this rather complex hermeneutical method of Sankara's is the conviction that ultimately Brahman cannot be conceptualised, but only intuitively realised. This is a direct form of knowledge (*aparokṣa-jñāna*) that transcends all mental cognitions, all verbal descriptions, all subject-object relationships. Hence 'words turn back, having lost their power'.[22] They cannot probe to the mystery of that Being who is pure Consciousness, pure identity of Selfhood. For such transcendent knowledge the leap of intuition at some point becomes necessary, and revelation is superseded.

There is no denying the determination with which Sankara sets out to protect the absolute nature of the knowledge of Brahman. The skill and the consistency with which he maintains its transcendent nature is impressive. The question is, however, whether this does not result in a loss of viability as a theological descriptive method. He can allow no statement about that supreme Being to stand without radically stripping it of all those positive meanings normally associated with such statements. Here at least that now famous criticism of theological statements that they all die 'the death of a thousand qualifications' seems justified. His 'indirect meanings' establish so subtle a relationship between the cognitive meaning of each description of the Supreme and the reality they are intended to indicate, his comparisons are so hedged about by negation, there seems such discontinuity between scriptural revelation and intuitive experience, that nothing in such descriptions can be more than provisional in nature.

RAMANUJA

Ramanuja's treatment of the knowing process, including knowledge of Brahman, diverged sharply from that of Sankara. It may well be that some of the formal features of his epistemology derive from the realism of the Logicians and the Ritualists. But his ontological and theological positions differ greatly from these other realist schools, and in Ramanuja's system ways of knowing are of a piece with forms of being, especially the being of the supreme Person. Four aspects of Ramanuja's distinctive view of the knowing process, including the knowing of the supreme Being, may be mentioned here.

The Logicians had allowed a distinction between initial indeterminate perception and the fully determinate perception which follows. The Ritualists too agreed that there is some such distinction in the stages of our perceiving process, but at least some of them claimed that even the initial, apparently indeterminate stage before all the particular features can be distinguished, is still sufficient to promote action on the part of the cogniser. This of course fits in neatly with the Ritualists' essentially functional view of things.

While Sankara had seized on the Logicians' analysis of initial perception as indeterminate to bolster up his view of the undifferentiated, unqualifiable character of Reality in itself, Ramanuja's position was closer to the Ritualists. He defines this initial moment of perception as 'the apprehension of the object while destitute of some but not all differences'.[23] This initial cognition has definite structure (*samsthāna*) and is sufficient to form the basis of later fully distinguishable cognitions of the same object. Then the relation of the first cognition to subsequent ones can be made, precise identity established, and eventually action taken on the basis of this knowledge. The initial perception can certainly not be called the only true one, undistorted by later differentiation, as the monists would claim. Some even defined all true perception (*pratyakṣa*) as immediate awareness. As it stands in its naked 'thisness', indeterminate perception is, according to Ramanuja, neither true nor false. Later investigation has to reveal its reliability or otherwise. Nor, being a cognition of the self, and so an object of the self, can it be the pure consciousness monism argues for. In fact, as with the Ritualists, Ramanuja sees an unbroken continuity between initial perception and later determinate perception—an epistemological position that exactly reflects his ontology.

On the question of 'mistaken identity', which Sankara took to illustrate the fundamental flaw in the self-object relationship, Ramanuja favoured a theory of 'real-perception' (*sat-khyāti*). When for example, the sea-shell appears as a piece of silver, the element of silver should be taken as real, just as the shell is real. In other words the silvery element in the shell was (mistakenly) allowed to dominate the perception. In all other respects there was a correct perception. For there is a certain givenness in the perception of all objects external to the self. Even the sometimes fantastic content of dreams should not be taken as sheer illusion. Dream-material, he contends, is given by the Lord for some specific benefit to the dreaming soul. Here again Ramanuja's theological realism leads him to find reality in all kinds of perception. At the same time there are certain specially given perceptions, perhaps yogic insights, which suggest that some perceptions are of greater benefit than others, though their reality does not differ. This opens the way for the very special 'divine-perceptions' granted graciously by the Lord, in which the knowledge of himself is given directly as the culmination of all other knowledge.

Such continuity extends, in Ramanuja's system, even to the relation of visual mediate perception to intuitive, immediate knowledge. Even in the monist's vocabulary the term 'perception' can refer to both. But in so far as any perception becomes mediated (through the senses, thought-processes, etc), just so far does the immediate experience become distorted. Ramanuja, on the other hand, not only asserts that whatever is perceived is just as real as immediately realised knowledge, he even describes that immediate knowledge in clearly cognitive terms, or in terms of cognition-plus. One protagonist of Madhva's theism considers it a serious flaw in Ramanuja's thought that there is no 'distinctive state of *Brahma-aparokṣa* or . . . immediate intuitive perception of God, *in this life*, other than the mental image conjured up by the devotee through constant flow of meditative recollection. . . . This means that the highest kind of direct experience of God open to man is mediate (*parokṣa-vṛtti*).' He finds it 'difficult to see how a meditative cognition can be said to attain a vividness of presentation equal to that of an actual immediate presentation'.[24] Ramanuja himself claims that mediate meditation 'can be so clear as to be almost immediate'. And in another place he writes that 'knowledge of Brahman which is understood as meditative worship is . . . in intuitive clarity not less than direct intuition'.[25]

The difference here between Ramanuja's emphasis on the need for experience, even 'direct experience' of the supreme Being, to be mediate, and the absolute immediacy advocated by both Sankara and to some extent by Madhva is not one of divergent meditative techniques. These they largely share in common. What is at issue is the relation of the supreme Person to the universe in general and to souls in particular.

Ramanuja's self-body analogical interpretation of this relationship has already been discussed in some detail. One further aspect which seems relevant here is his description in realistic terms of the universe as the 'manifestation' of the supreme Person's glory and lordship. Ramanuja's writings[26] reveal a considerable range of usage for this term *vibhūti*, but the central idea is clear. The universe is the finite manifestation of the transcendent Lord, through which he exercises his powerful will and pervades all beings as Controller. His *vibhūti* is the realm in which he manifests his glory. In effect this concept makes more dynamic Ramanuja's body-soul relationship as an interpretation of the supreme Person's penetrative relationship with his universe.

According to Ramanuja, then, Brahman's glorious transcendence is revealed most convincingly in his immediacy to his whole creation; as soul to body, as the Lord in relation to his great 'manifestation', he is eternally related to it and thus accessible to it. Because the supreme Reality is so intimately related to this universe, it too partakes of reality.

This is the theological and ontological ground of Ramanuja's epistemology. What is perceived in mediate visual perception is real, just as Brahman and the knowledge of Brahman is real. There is an immediacy intrinsic to the mediating character of the whole universe in Ramanuja's system. This is certainly one reason for his lack of insistence on the immediate knowledge of Brahman as found in the other Vedantins. He finds such immediacy already present especially in meditative devotion.

At this point we may note again Ramanuja's assertion, made on the basis of Brahman being the inner Self of all beings, that the various names denoting these beings all refer ultimately to their ensouling, supreme Being. Van Buitenen summarises the idea thus: 'Just as the body terminates in the soul, so the soul terminates in the inner Soul. Consequently all the words which describe the body ultimately refer to the soul, and all the words which refer to the soul ultimately refer to God.'[27] This can be broadened to include every entity in the universe, for all comprise the supreme Self's body. The implication is, then, that there is an analogical indication of that supreme Self in all existence, for he is their ensouling Principle, their inner Ruler.

Ramanuja, however, makes it quite clear that within his pan-entheistic system knowledge of the supreme Person, Brahman, is not automatically acquired. Quite the reverse; for with all Vedantins Ramanuja accepts the fundamental Ignorance afflicting the soul due to its karmic bondage. The soul is in need of enlightenment of the knowledge of Brahman's glorious Being and of its own dependence on that Being. And the relationship of loving devotion is to be equated with the desired knowledge of Brahman. Very early in his Great Commentary—in its 'small doctrinal statement', in fact—Ramanuja argues that it is those who constantly devote themselves to the Lord with worship and love, who receive that knowledge by which they are able to attain him, knowledge by which they are liberated from their bondage. At this point he quotes appropriate verses from the Bhagavad-Gita. He then describes this knowledge of the supreme Being as having the character of 'immediate presentation' (*sākṣātkāra*), even though the devotional relationship remains intact, and the God-soul distinction remains unblurred.

For it is Ramanuja's contention that all knowledge is necessarily relational. Whether visual perception of external objects or direct vision of spiritual reality, whether the testimony of one person to another, or the highest revelation of scripture, at every level Ramanuja believes that a similar process takes place as far as the communication of knowledge is concerned.

He argues[28] that each of these 'means of knowledge' functions on the assumption that there are distinct characteristics possessed by the objects they make known. Even the knowledge of the supreme Self cannot be established without such differentiation. There has to be distinguishable character, or there can be no reliable basis for making claims about the supreme Being. Without this, how can he be known in any way—all knowledge being necessarily of a qualifiable and relational character? The knowledge communicated in testimony, for example, is invariably comprised of words related to each other in a particular sequence. Each word conveys a special meaning distinct from that of the other words in the sentence. Nor can there ever be 'perception' of being unqualified by any kind of distinct character.

When the monist allows that empirical knowledge may be of this kind, but knowledge of Brahman must be pure consciousness, which is entirely self-luminous and does not require any kind of knower-known relationship, nor any kind of validation from, or limitation by sources outside itself, Ramanuja offers an analysis[29] of the way consciousness functions.

To say that consciousness is never an object is contradicted by the fact that one person's consciousness can be the object of another person's. If this were not so there would be no possibility of communication, even by Guru to disciple. We also frequently experience past consciousness as the object of present consciousness.

Two possible definitions of consciousness are then suggested. If it is said to manifest itself to itself or to prove its own object by its own being, the subject-object relationship seems to be avoided. But Ramanjua re-interprets these definitions in the following way: 'The essential character of consciousness or knowledge is that by its very existence it renders things capable of becoming objects—to its own substrate—objects of thought and speech. This consciousness . . . also called knowledge by the use of various terms, is a particular attribute belonging to a conscious self and related to an object. As such it is known to everyone on the testimony of his own self—as appears from ordinary judgements such as "I know the jar".' So he concludes that self and consciousness are not one, that consciousness itself always operates in relation to objects different from itself, the self alone is permanent and unchanging, and that all conscious states are attributively related to this inner self.

Ramanuja is then accused of confusing the pure self with the ego, the knowing 'I'. The self is 'absolutely non-objective', 'pure homogeneous light'; the 'I' is 'the objective element. . . which is established through its being illumined by the self'. Ramanuja makes a simple analysis of the concept 'I know' as his first argument against this idea. It is the 'I' which provides the subjective basis for 'knowledge' to exist; so the relationship is one of subject and attribute. And if this 'I' is not the real self, then 'the inwardness of the self would not exist; for it is just the consciousness of the "I" (as Sankara himself argued) which separates the inward from the outward', the subjective from the objective. Even the desire for eternal release would soon evaporate if it were not the conscious self which is to attain endless bliss, but 'some consciousness different from me', and a consciousness too which is dependent on the 'I' for its existence. For 'when that connexion is dissolved, consciousness itself cannot be established, any more than the act of cutting can be established when there is no person to do the cutting and nothing to be cut. Hence it is certain that the "I", that is the knowing subject, is the inward self.'

Thus the experience 'I know' establishes the existence of 'the I itself', while it is through that I's consciousness of the 'not-I', objects other than itself, that such objective existence is established. 'Hence to say that the knowing subject, which is established by the state of consciousness, "I know", is the not-I, is not better than to maintain that one's own mother is a barren woman.' Nor is the 'I' dependent for its 'light' upon some other inner illuminating entity. The 'I' itself is self-luminous, 'for to be self-luminous means to have consciousness for one's essential nature. And that which has light for its essential nature does not depend for its light on something else. The case is analogous to that of the flame of a lamp or candle . . . the lamp being of luminous nature shines itself and illumines with its light other things also.' By analogy, Ramanuja argues that the 'self is essentially intelligent [possessing consciousness], having intelligence as its quality. To be essentially intelligent means to be self-luminous.'

Sankara's doctrine of inherent Ignorance was also given a fairly exhaustive critical examination by Ramanuja. For the monist's concept of absolute identity stands or falls on the validity or otherwise of the idea that apparent differences are not ultimately real. They are made to look real by a defect in the person observing them.

Ramanuja agreed that the soul often does live at a deluded level, both in confusing its materiality with the soul's eternal nature, and in falsely imagining that it can exist independently of the supreme Self. Obviously some theory of the soul's ignorance is necessary, not only because scripture refers to it, but also to explain why as a matter of fact the vast majority of souls fail to recognise their proper relationship with the supreme Self. In his Seven-Objections[30] Ramanuja argued with some force that the monist's concept of inherent Ignorance is quite unacceptable:

1. It has no proper locus or basis, as neither Brahman nor the soul can be in such a relation with it, without radically distorting their true nature.

2. On the monist's own reckoning Brahman is self-revealing consciousness, which cannot possibly be obscured by any such negating entity as hypothetical Ignorance.

3. To say that its nature is neither real nor unreal also raises problems. If it were real, clearly this would undermine the non-dualist position entirely. But if it were the unreal cause of an unreal world, this would in turn require some other false cause, and so on *ad infinitum*. To say that this inherent Ignorance is revealed by Brahman is equally impossible; for Brahman is eternal, and the result of his revealing such Ignorance would be eternal bondage.

4. To call it 'indefinable' puts it outside the possibility of being experienced. For all experienced things are either real or unreal.

5. Its existence is not supported by any of the acceptable means of knowledge. Scripture does speak of a principle of delusion, but this is quite different from the monist's theory. Scripture's '*Māyā*' simply means the wonderful, but real, world-creating power of Brahman.

6. The idea that it is knowledge of an absolutely unqualifiable Brahman that can immediately remove such Ignorance is equally impossible for reasons already listed.

7. The theory that such knowledge of Brahman, as distinct from the wholly transcendent Brahman in itself, is done away with in the pure state of release, just as a fire destroys itself after destroying a forest, is also untenable. In the case of such a fire, there will in fact always be ashes remaining! And as anything separate from pure-Brahman is ignorance, then the liberating knowledge itself becomes an ignorance that is bondage, and final liberation becomes unattainable.

Ramanuja's basic objection to this absolutising of ignorance is that there can be no such all-enveloping principle operating in distinction from, certainly not with the collusion of, the supreme Self. It is not only that it is brought in to bolster the theory, disagreeable to Ramanuja, of the non-reality of the universe. He sees it also as a threat to the supremacy and integrity of that Brahman it was supposed to protect.

Ramanuja himself interprets the Ignorance referred to by scripture in terms of the creative and potentially deluding power of *karma*, and Nature, which is the principal instrument of *karma*. The soul's true existence, in particular its proper condition of eternal dependence on Brahman, can be obscured by reason of its embodied state, as determined by that soul's previous deeds. To account for this deluded state, therefore, it is quite unnecessary, in Ramanuja's opinion, to bring in any further category, inexplicable and indefinable, such as Sankara's inherent Ignorance.

Ramanuja takes his realism here to the extent of contending that not even the knowledge of Brahman, whether mediate or immediate, can fully release the soul from its bondage while it is still in an embodied state. Release in this life (*jīvan-mukti*) as taught by the Monists, Buddhists, Jainists, and Samkhya-followers, is equal to saying 'my mother was childless', according to Ramanuja. Being joined to the body certainly has its positive values, but is nevertheless a mark of bondage. Release means, among other things, being set free from bodily existence.[31]

His extensive argument[32] against any inferential knowledge of Brahman is also of considerable importance. All Vedantins ostensibly based their system on scripture as providing the sole revelation of Brahman, and all were expected to deny that inferential argument could be a basis for belief in Brahman's existence. Strangely enough, both Sankara and Madhva, despite their stressing the need of special direct knowledge of Brahman, as well as espousing the Vedantic theory that scriptural revelation must be the basis of such knowledge, make very little effort to argue against the inferential treatment of that knowledge attempted by the Logicians.

Only the more important of Ramanuja's arguments need concern us here. The two main contentions put forward by the Logicians that he felt to be invalid were: (1) Just as we infer from the existence of a living person's body that non-sentient matter is inhabited and animated by an intelligent principle, so by analogy we can infer the existence of Īśvara as supreme Self from the empirical fact of the universe of non-sentient matter. (2) The existence of causal Being can also be inferred from the 'world's being an effected thing'. For common experience tells us that an effect is always produced by an agent who has sufficient know-how concerning the various other causal factors. That Ramanuja rejects both arguments is highly significant, for did he not have a vested interest in supporting the analogical bases on which they stand? In other contexts he himself makes use of the 'inseparable relationship' both of body and soul and of cause and effect. This could explain why he felt it necessary to give such full treatment to these questions. But the only explanation of his rejection of the Logician's arguments must be his uncompromising belief in the trans-empirical character of the supreme Being, even though that transcendence is seen as much in his accessible immanence as in his incomparable otherness.

Ramanuja brings forward a number of counter-arguments to show that on no count does the soul-body analogy provide the kind of proof for which the Logicians attempt to use it. The universe, for example, does not look like a normal animate body; even such motion in the universe as we see need not be explained by the existence of a single animating, supervising principle, such as Brahman. Ramanuja seems to consider the self-body analogy as much a matter of revelation as is the nature of the supreme Being to which it points.

The argument that the idea of a creator or causal agent, if taken as comparable to agents such as are known to us in experience, would mean that this Creator works by means of his body, and hence must be a non-transcendent being, was first put forward by the Jaina anti-theistic logicians. Ramanuja, again surprisingly, uses this same argument, though not with the intention of proving there can be no Creator, nor that the idea of a divine body is untenable and implies lack of transcendence. On both counts he has an interest in establishing just the opposite.

What he found objectionable in the Logicians' method was their assumption that causal activity on the empirical level is in itself sufficient guide to understanding the divine causal activity. Ramanuja could hardly reject their contention that volitional action can take place quite apart from association with a body. He did find improper their idea that *inference* directly leads us to the theory that there is a supreme intelligent agent, called the Lord . . . [who] is without a body, and through his mere volition brings about the infinite expanse of this entire universe so variously and wonderfully planned'.[33] Ramanuja even accepted that no body is essential to Brahman's being or necessary to his action. But for him Brahman is not merely the *effective* cause, which is the kind of causal agent the Logicians attempt to prove as necessary to explain that which is observable in the material universe. For them, the interaction of the atomically constituted causal substances is sufficient to account for the substantial being of the universe. Thus the universe (i.e. the 'body' which needs an animating explanation) is substantially self-existent, though its particular form brought about by the movements of the atomic substances requires the Lord's will as at least one of the contributing causes.

Ramanuja, on the other hand, with his conviction that Brahman alone is the substantial as well as effective Cause of the universe, regarded the relationship of Brahman (the Soul) to Universe (the body) in a more organically dynamic way.

His rejection of the Logicians' argument from *effect*-state to explanatory cause is even more fundamental. Indeed, we have already seen that it is really this inferential approach to the supreme Being's existence that underlies the above argument against the inanimate-body-requiring-intelligent-soul theory. Even if the universe were thought of as an effect, says Ramanuja, it cannot be validly inferred from this that it is the supreme Person who is its originating cause. Some of the polemic guns he fires off are clearly lifted straight from the armoury of the anti-theists, and it is not clear if Ramanuja was entirely serious in putting forward all of these arguments. There is, however, no such doubt concerning his attack on the Logicians' attempt to argue from finite effect to infinite Cause.

Even though he would agree that the universe is an effect, its effected status can only be used for proof regarding its cause when that effect is capable of being produced, and when the causes for that production are unquestionably known. But the only causal agents of which we have such unquestionable knowledge, such as can provide a basis for perception and inferential argument arising from this, are finite, even material bodies, which have to make use of various implements to carry out their causal intentions, and in any case are 'not endowed with the power of a supreme Lord'. Thus the basis of inferential argument concerning the Lord's existence is not applicable to his trans-empirical Being, however valid it may be in the realm of empirically observable cause and effect. Along similar lines he complains that 'qualities not met with in experience are attributed to the subject about which something has to be proved'.[34] In fact the world could be said to look more like a number of effects, which would suggest either a succession of causal acts, or a number of different producers. Then Ramanuja goes on to argue that you cannot infer a supreme Cause which is outside the karmic process if you are arguing on the basis of a cause-effect sequence which always operates within this karmic process.

Ramanuja's logic in this whole debate is remarkably forceful, and in some respects anticipates the logic used against arguments in the West for the existence of God. But there are more fundamental theological reasons that lie behind this insistent rejection of the Logicians' inferential method. In the first place the supreme Being seen by Ramanuja as the Cause of all effected existence differs considerably from the Logicians' 'Lord'. Though a divine Being of 'infinite merit', extraordinary power, eternally free from the limitations of embodied existence, and consequently a fitting object for the soul's meditation, the 'Lord' is still but a *primus inter pares*. He lacks the transcendent as well as the immanent dimensions Ramanuja looked for in a truly supreme Being. Hence this Lord's protagonists found no difficulty in attempting to prove his existence on the basis of the inferential method they used so effectively in areas which are properly subject to logical argument.

Secondly, although Ramanuja attacks the Logicians' position by using the same logical method by which they intended to establish the Lord's existence and causal activity, he accepts in total the Vedantic view that it is only scripture that can provide knowledge of the supreme Person—knowledge which is entirely reliable and subject to none of the uncertainties of reason. 'Thus the inference of a creative Lord which claims to be in agreement with observation is refuted by reasoning which itself is in agreement with observation, and we hence conclude that scripture is the only source of knowledge with regard to the supreme Person.' He concludes: 'What scripture tells us of is a being which is different in character from whatever is cognised by other means of knowledge.'[35]

Despite this revelationist posture, however, we should note that just as Ramanuja teaches the inherent knowability of things (by virtue of their ultimate reality and because knowledge is an essential attribute of the self), so he suggests the essential knowability of the supreme Being. Brahman is essentially the highest Person, endowed with cognisable if not empirically comprehendable perfections. It is these glorious qualities which provide the most important basis for the soul's knowledge of the highest Person.

'Knowledge', therefore, understood as an intimate acquaintance that has clear conceptual content, is a prominent feature of Ramanuja's Vedanta. But in that this knowledge is best seen in the inseparable relationship of individual self and supreme Self, both of whom are knowers and known, subject and object, then its fullest expression is seen in the devotional relationship of mutual love. At this level, though still mediated through the relationship, knowledge has the quality of immediacy, 'the clarity of direct intuition'. Ramanuja, moreover, sees no intractable contradiction between all forms of indirect knowledge and ultimate knowledge that is immediate. Both the relational ontological structure of his system and, even more important, its devotional or grace-oriented theology, make such a mediated immediacy of Brahman-knowledge possible without denying its transcendent nature.

MADHVA

Madhva's realism in epistemological matters was in many respects similar to that of Ramanuja; especially in its opposition to any notion of the unreliability of our cognition of the objective world. The whole point of the recognised means of knowledge, says Madhva, is that they 'comprehend the objects of knowledge just as they are'.[36] All knowledge, whether obtained by perception, inference, or testimony, always has the same validity. In some matters, however, the two theists' positions are not identical.

More than Ramanuja, for example, Madhva stresses that there must be no malfunctioning, no 'flaw' between the senses and the objects in the case of perception; the reasoning process must be flawless in the case of inference; the verbal witness must be flawless in the case of 'testimony'.

He also differentiates between the quality of knowledge experienced by the Lord, that experienced by Lakṣmī, by a yogi, and by a non-yogi. In each case the knowledge acquired is quite real, but the grading is also significant. The Lord's knowledge is always 'essential' (*svarūpa*); the knowledge of a non-liberated soul is 'functional' (*vṛtti*). Then again, Madhva tends to stress the veiling effect of Ignorance on the soul, obscuring its functioning as a knower. Unlike Sankara, he asserts that this obscuring is quite real, not illusory. It is real because it is directly caused by the Lord himself.

When, however, the proper conditions for knowing things are adequately met, there is no possibility of the cognition of illusion. Like Ramanuja, Madhva develops some quite forceful arguments against the monists' concept of illusory perception. He says, for example, that if the objects cognised by means of visual perception are false (*mithyā*), then the knowledge gained through all the accepted means, including scriptural testimony, becomes invalid, and 'the world is robbed of its light'.[37] For scriptural testimony as a method of knowing operates on the same basis as all other testimony, and this in turn is 'supported by perception'. Nor does the perception of the objective world bear any essential resemblance to the illusory experiences of dreams, as the monist contends.

Like Ramanuja too, Madhva found quite unacceptable Sankara's idea that scripture's statements about Brahman are merely indirect indications of his essential nature. If Brahman is held to be inexpressible except by means of figurative statements, then he must be inexpressible altogether, even by such statements.[38] Even the material of dreams is real, being given specially by the Lord, as Ramanuja argued.

Like Ramanuja too, Madhva dismissed the idea of a primary 'indeterminate perception'. Knowledge of the essence of a thing is invariably a distinctive knowledge of something 'unique and different from all else'.[39] Nor is there any such thing as pure knowledge independent of a knower and an object that is known. Any such knowledge would be 'merely an empty void' (*śūnyata*).

Even Sankara's theory that knowledge of the objective world is real, but only at its own pragmatic and relative level, is found by Madhva to be untenable. The monist argues that the perceived world is real enough, and its perception valid enough, up to the moment of higher enlightenment, when it becomes superseded by that higher knowledge. Madhva claims that if a perception is valid at all, it remains valid; or to put it the other way, if it is once shown to be invalid, then its validity must always have been questionable. Validity is not a question of value at a particular time. Once the validity of some body of knowledge is properly established, it can never be found to be false without denying its previous validity also. In any case, if validity at a particular stage of knowledge is the important thing. This applies to the validity of all scriptural texts, even those that are claimed as the basis of the monist's position. What is to prevent them also from being negated at some later stage? And 'if the experiences of the joys and sorrows of life can be regarded as illusory at any stage, how is one to be certain that the identity texts, which are taken as declaring that the soul free from pain becomes Brahman, might not be equally susceptible of error?'[40] If the one experience is thought to be unreliable and unreal, statements concerning the other experience are equally suspect.

Monistic statements are particularly vulnerable because they do not have the intrinsic support of the accepted means of knowing, such as testimony, perception, and inference. Madhva argued,[41] rather like Ramanuja, that all these *pramāṇas* function in a way that makes it impossible for them to communicate knowledge of an unqualifiable entity, one whose being is absolute non-difference. On the other hand, texts that declare Brahman to be a distinguishable Being have a special invulnerability, having as they do the full support of all the valid ways of knowledge.

Madhva, then, aligned himself categorically alongside the theistic realists in opposition to the monistic view of the way in which Brahman is described in scripture and made known to the inner self. It seemed nonsense to Madhva to speak of scripture's 'indirect indications' of the supreme Being by virtue of that Being's ineffability. What is entirely ineffable cannot even be expressed indirectly. Indeed, such an attitude towards the essential being of Brahman undermines the whole enquiry into that being. At the outset of his commentary on the Sutras Madhva characterises this Being about which the enquiry is to be made as 'devoid of defects, the valid object of knowledge, and the goal of attainments'.

He goes on to elaborate on this by saying that part of the perfection of Brahman is that he is 'perceivable' and eminently 'knowable', though like Ramanuja, Madhva took 'not thus, not thus' to mean the supreme

Person is never exhaustively describable. His greatness is always 'immeasurable' in the sense that his qualities are immeasurably greater than those found in his creatures. To this extent he is incomparable. Nevertheless, such 'negation' of known qualities is only from the point of view of the enquirer and his limited knowledge. 'A real subject like Brahman cannot be a mere void. It is essentially qualifiable.'[42] That he is not knowable by sensory perception is precisely what makes the enquiry necessary, though his trans-empirical character should not thereby bring his very existence into question. But a necessary prerequisite for the enquiry into Brahman is that he be distinguished by his great qualities. Madhva even goes on so far as to agree with Ramanuja that the supreme Being should not be thought of without any kind of form or definite character. When scripture describes him as 'formless', it simply means that he is 'of transcendent form'. As a parting shot he asserts that even a negation says something distinctive about any person.[43]

Madhva agrees further with Ramanuja in allowing virtually no positive role to reason and inference in establishing valid knowledge of the supreme Being, as would be expected in view of his generally transcendental outlook. Scriptural revelation alone is the source of such transcendent knowledge. He even derides inferential logic as a 'harlot', quite capable of use by anyone, partial to no particular position. Nowhere, however, does Madhva subject the inferential approach to the knowledge of the supreme Self in the searching way that Ramanuja does. One point he does make is that the case for non-duality is just as much incapable of being established by reasoning as is the existence and transcendent character of the supreme Lord. And the reasoning process at least points to the need for a distinguishable Being.[44]

The Vaiṣṇava idea that all words contain an inner reference to the supreme Self, in that all entities are ensouled by that Self, also finds an echo in Madhva's writings.[45] But at this point we begin to see some significant differences in the outlook of the two theistic Vedantins. Madhva agrees that it is because 'the Lord Hari is the inner Ruler of all' that every name signifies that highest name of the Lord; just as every good quality in the universe ultimately signifies his most excellent qualities. Even the personal pronouns and their various case terminations point beyond themselves to this inner Ruler, 'the import of all persons'. But now we see how Madhva differs from Ramanuja: the primary reference of these words is to the inner Lord; they refer to the various individuals and other entities only in a secondary sense. There are two reasons for Madhva to put the relationship in this order, as we now see.

The ground for this primary reference of all words to the Lord is 'because he is the Independent'. We discuss this immensely important Madhva concept in the next chapter. Here we may merely note that it is certainly not due to any inner relationship, either substantial or essential, that words can be found to refer to the supreme Being. Just the reverse is the case. It is the utter dependence of all named things, their lack of all character and definite existence apart from the determining will of the Lord (though their substantial being is given by nature) that results in their names referring primarily to the Lord.

Moreover, all names are said to have a veiled reference to the highest name of the Lord. Thus we find a much more esoteric interpretation of the many names, including what appear to be quite innocent pronouns, particles and even syllables within words. Madhva goes to great lengths, sometimes straining etymology rather, to discover one or other of the divine names hidden in these words of scripture.

In particular, he is anxious to show that whenever there is mention of some transcendent quality, or wherever the name Brahman occurs, which he translates as 'the Perfect', it must be Viṣṇu who is intended. For Viṣṇu alone is held to possess such high qualities of transcendent excellence. Thus throughout his commentary on the Brahma-Sutras most divine names are taken to refer to Viṣṇu, or to one of various synonyms.

Madhva also gives words of a feminine gender a special significance. Nature (*prakṛti*) is personified in Viṣṇu's intimate consort, Śrī or Lakṣmī. In this indirect sense Nature, and thus all words of a feminine gender, can be taken to signify the supreme Being, just as the term Person (*puruṣa*), and all terms of a male gender, refer to that Being. He also makes this point on the grounds of the Lord's causal being and the dependence of all other beings. 'The state of being Nature consists in being the immediate means of bringing forth. . . . The male is the mediate cause. . . . Such is the distinction between the connotation of male and female. The one Lord Vāsudeva [Viṣṇu] the perfect Person, being both of these, is declared to be both Nature and Person, or male and female, by all words. Thus all things are designated under his name by reason of their being dependent upon him.'[46] Thus the affinity of Madhva's thought here to that of Ramanuja on the question of words finding their culmination in the supreme Being now looks less clear.

Closely related to this is the issue of words taken from secular usage being attributable to the highest Being, and consequently the whole question of that Being's describability. Firstly, Madhva recognises[47] the need for such words to be used of the Highest—and in fact he finds this a reason for claiming that there must be distinction within that essential Being, as does Ramanuja. Each word has its distinct meaning. So a combination of such distinct meanings to describe the Lord makes a clearly distinguishable being inevitable.

Like the other Vedantins, he does not accept the Ritualists' claim that this verbal form of scripture confirms their view of its essentially injunctive nature. Words and sentences, argues Madhva,[48] are not used primarily with some action in view. In teaching children to speak, for example (the example in fact used by the Ritualists to establish their case for the injuctive character of language), words are used principally to name things; they are descriptive and indicative. So, as Sankara also argued, scripture's principal intention is to indicate what already is; that is, the 'established fact' of Brahman. Scripture first informs us about his supreme being; the actions that are required in view of that supremacy are secondary. As we shall see in the tenth chapter, Ramanuja tends to give a more important role to the actions enjoined by scripture as a fitting acknowledgement of that supremacy.

Madhva also finds a greater anomaly than does Ramanuja in having to ascribe to the transcendent Being words which have a specific meaning in finite, secular experience. This further confirms the suggestion that the doctrine of all words referring primarily to that supreme Being is based on quite different grounds from that of Ramanuja's teaching. It does seem to set something of a limit to the applicability of secular words in this realm of supreme Being. The name 'Brahman', for example, which he takes to indicate 'greatness' and 'perfection', when used of the supreme Lord can indicate his transcendent being only very inadequately. Likewise that word of such significance in Vedantic thought, 'bliss' (*ānanda*), or 'enjoyment' (*sukha*), when used of the eternal Bliss of that transcendent existence has a very different import from its use in the context of worldly enjoyment. But Madhva sees no absolute incompatibility here. He finds a sufficient basis of similarity between the two realms for words from the secular level to be used meaningfully at the level of supreme Being. Nor is the signification merely figurative or indirect, as in Sankara's scheme. For, as we saw, Madhva argued that if the supreme Being really is inexpressible, it cannot be expressed indirectly either.

On this question of Brahman's knowability also we find Madhva taking a somewhat different line from Ramanuja, despite the various similarities already noted. Both acknowledge that there is always more to be said than can be said. The supreme Being is 'not only thus but more'.[49] Madhva, however, refers more frequently to 'incomprehensible' dimensions of that Being. He even claims that in his essential nature the Lord is 'non-manifest', though here he refers more to his manifestation in visible form, a somewhat different issue.[50] It is only by his transcendent grace that such manifestations are granted, and those only to his devotees. Even in such cases, however, his essential being always remains somewhat obscured to the embodied soul's understanding.

A concept that is very prominent in Madhva's system, and elaborated there in a most original way, is that of the 'inner witness' (*sākṣin*). This term is quite common in some other schools, notably Samkhya and Advaita, where it is intended to describe the knowing capacity of the self, its ability to comprehend the finite universe without becoming affected thereby.

Madhva's 'inner witness', however, gives to the self a more positive role than this in its function as a knower. Madhva obviously felt that unless there is some final arbiter whose judgement was absolutely infallible, the evidence derived from the variety of knowledge-sources could not be reliably sifted, weighed up and pronounced impeccably valid. This 'inner witness' is also called the self's 'essential sense-organ' in that it is not, like the mind, based on the material-organs. Madhva does not intend to deny that visual and other perceptions are reliable. We have already noted his stress on their validity. But when a fact is known, by whatever means, the inner witness has to grasp that fact in its immediacy of presentation and establish absolutely its validity. Though it functions only with the materials presented by perception, reasoning and testimony, it also serves as an instrument of 'immediate presentation', and can thus be called the self's 'intuitive faculty' (*sākṣātkāra*). 'It is only when intuited by the witness, with or without the aid of tests, that the true nature of validity comes to be clearly and fully realised and manifested. It is, therefore, absolutely necessary to draw a distinction between ordinary sensory, mental and other forms of knowing and the judgements of the witness.' Thus, 'perception by the witness is that in our experience which cannot be superseded and which is decisive in character. . . . What is established by the flawless verdict of the witness is true and valid for all time.' Nor would it ever be possible to commit ourselves to action without the inner conviction provided by this arbiter within. 'For any organised life based on unwavering efforts cannot be carried on merely on the basis of vague presumptions of validity, or of doubtful cognitions.'[51]

One aspect of the working of the inner witness concerns the criterion for judging between conflicting sources, even when one of these may be scripture. If, for example, there is a text suggesting the absolute identity of the Lord and the soul, and this is found to be contradicted by perception and other valid evidences, including experience which shows a variety of very marked differences, then final arbitration will be made by this directly intuiting faculty. Perception will be given the greatest weight in this process, being referred to even to 'explain' scriptures, for 'perception is the supporter of all sources of knowledge'; but even perception is dependent on the inner arbiter.[52] Thus while Madhva often stresses the finality of the knowledge provided by scripture, at least in matters pertaining to the supreme Being and the liberation of the soul, ultimately all scriptural statements are subjected to the infallible scrutiny of the inner witness.

The power of immediate perception makes the inner witness, for Madhva, the link between two other doctrines of considerable import in his system; the individual qualities intrinsic to each soul on the one hand, and the immediate and transcendent experience of the supreme Lord on the other. We discuss these ideas later. Compared to Ramanuja, Madhva refers much more often to such immediate and intuitive knowledge, as well as to transcendent experience as a basis for valid knowledge, such primacy of experience applying to knowledge of secular matters as much as to knowing to Lord.

7 The Supreme Cause

We now come to the issue most prominent in Vedântic polemics—what is the cause of the cosmic process? How can a perfect and transcendent Being be such a cause? And what is the nature of causal relations within this process? All Vedantins, following in general the lines laid down in the Brahma-Sutras, were at one in opposing a variety of causal theories which did not attribute the world's origin solely to the creative power of Brahman. In particular Samkhya's causal theory was felt to be a threat—perhaps because of its plausibility, perhaps because it was able to point to a number of supporting texts in the Vedas and Upanishads. What Vedantins saw revealed in scripture, however, was that only Brahman should be regarded as the all-powerful, self-existent Cause of the whole universe. But they also recognised problems which such a causal claim poses—problems concerning the transcendent perfection of Brahman. It is the difference in the Vedantins' response to these problems that accounts for the serious divergence in their descriptions both of Brahman as Creator and of the internal working of causal relations.

There is, however, an important aspect of Brahman's causality in which they are all agreed. Although it is invariably the case that every causal action produces a re-action, and thus binds the agent of the action to the cause-effect chain, it is said that the creative action of Brahman has not involved him is such karmic bondage. All Vedantins accept that Brahman did not act from any sense of need to attain a particular end. Creation was by means of the 'disinterested action' (*niṣ-kāma-karma*) of which the Bhagavad-Gita speaks.

The analogy used in the Brahma-Sutras,[1] and expounded by each Vedantin, is that of a king who, having no desires left to be satisfied, engages in something as sheer 'sport' (*līlā*). As Sankara writes: 'Analogously, the activity of the Lord may be supposed to be mere sport, proceeding from his own nature without reference to any purpose. . . . And if in ordinary life we might possibly, by close scrutiny, detect some subtle motive even for playful action, we cannot do so in the case of the Lord's actions, for all his purposes are fulfilled, as scripture says.' The implication is that Brahman created all things just because of his essentially creative nature—one way of emphasising that he is transcendent to the process. There is in the supreme Person no constraint to conform to a particular line of action because of some purpose outside his own being as it were. Neither is he compelled by some desire, as yet unfulfilled, which would be like an inner necessity, driving to action because of some benefit to himself.

As the Gita briefly suggests, and the Vedantins' commentaries amplify, creation brings no possible benefit to the supreme Being, though it is of great benefit to the creatures. Creation 'is performed for their welfare',[2] presumably providing all creatures with the opportunity to exhaust the karmic load that weighs them down, and eventually to attain freedom through the knowledge of Brahman.

Then along with the *līlā*-doctrine the Vedantins also emphasise that it was with conscious reflection and decision that Brahman created everything. No doubt Samkhya's idea of evolution from unconscious Nature is the immediate reason for this emphasis on conscious creative action. But is it also not another way of saying that Brahman is himself transcendent to creation? The non-reflective nature of the sporting analogy could lead to a view of creation as though by some unconscious inner necessity. This idea of intelligent decision preceding creation helps to counter any such potential danger. As an act of thought and will, it implies that Brahman is in himself transcendent to creation, and is able to direct the process intelligently.

Vedanta's contention that creation is intended for 'the welfare of the creatures' does, however, raise a number of questions, one of which is the precise role of *karma* in the causal process. At first glance, it seems odd to say that the beginningless actions of individual souls determine their particular embodiments and also to claim Brahman as supreme Cause. But we should remember that beginningless *karma* is only a concomitant cause in the creative process, and that too by permission of the supreme Lord of creation on whom it depends.

Whatever answers may be attempted by the various exponents of Vedanta, they themselves would confess some measure of inexplicability or mystery in the relationship between the perfect Brahman and the creative process with its imperfections. Thus they all make use of the term *māyā* to describe the creative act. But the extent to which they find creation an enigma varies greatly. Hence the very different meanings with which they interpret the *māyā*-character of the universe, again reflecting their divergent understanding of the nature of Creator-Brahman's transcendence.

SANKARA

In Sankara's writings there is no dearth of references to Brahman as the sole Cause of all. Commenting on the second Sutra for example, he says: 'The full sense of the Sutra therefore is: That omniscient, omnipotent cause from which proceed the origin, subsistence, and dissolution of this world . . . that cause, we say is Brahman.'[3] This definitive statement about Brahman is referred to a number of times throughout the commentary.

Sankara at first seems to accept this as proof that Brahman is the substantial as well as the operative Cause of everything. So he allows, as the Sutra puts it, that Brahman's material, immanental causality is by way of 'modification' (*pariṇāma*) of his potential, unmanifest causal form.[4] As the source of all beings, Brahman is endowed with the attributes necessary for such supreme creativity, such as being all-knowing, all-perceiving, all-powerful. It is Brahman's creative agency which is responsible for the entire world of effects. He does not acknowledge any eternal substances, distinct within the causal Being as Ramanuja does, or separate from this Being as Madhva does. This leads some interpreters to see a doctrine of *creatio ex nihilo* in Sankara.

In that Brahman is said to be the Cause of all, he himself requires no cause, according to Sankara. His being is characterised by self-existent 'Being', not by the cause-effect process of becoming. The very fact that he has caused this world of effects means that *he is*, and his existence cannot be doubted. 'It is a matter of common experience in this world that anything from which something is produced does exist—for instance, clay, the cause of jars, and seed, the cause of shoots. . . . If effects, such as names and forms, had originated from nothing, they could not be perceived because of not having their own existence (*nir-ātmakatvāt*); but they are perceived, so Brahman does exist.'[5]

There is then no possibility of an effect without the prior existence of Brahman as Cause. All existence is entirely dependent upon Brahman as Cause. And although, according to Sankara's fundamental thesis, the non-difference of cause and its effect must be maintained, this is not a reciprocal non-difference. For the effect, being dependent on Brahman's causal being, cannot be identical with the Cause in the same way in which the Cause is identical with its dependent effects.

Having described these very positive statements which Sankara makes about creation and Brahman's role in it, all of which show that he very carefully steered clear of that school of Buddhism which attributed the basis of everything, even *Nirvāṇa*, to the ultimate Void, we still have to reckon with the other pole of his dialectic. For in general Sankara was even more anxious to point to the ultimate unreality of all effected existence, whatever its relative reality. This is, of course, the inevitable corollary of his principal thesis that reality has the character of absolute non-difference.

Sometimes, though, he can make this same doctrine the basis for claiming Brahman as sole cause: 'There is no other substance from which the world could originate', Brahman being 'One only, One without a second'.[6] He goes on: 'It is at the same time operative Cause of the world, because outside Brahman as immanent Cause there is no other ruling principle.' Or again, 'The Omniscient creates the universe by virtue of his oneness with the materials, or names and forms, which are identical with himself.'[7] To assert such an identity, however, in Sankara's system presumes first the unreality of those 'names and forms'.

In other places the status of created effects becomes much more explicitly ambiguous. Sankara clearly regards all such effected existence as being quite incapable of sharing the ultimate reality of the Cause itself. We can see this by following through some of the more important points he makes in debate with the Samkhya school, as outlined in his Brahma-Sutra commentary. Before this, however, we should note the remarkable number of features which the monism of Sankara and the dualism of Samkhya share in common. Some scholars even claim that Samkhya was monistic in its earlier form, though this is entirely conjectural.

If we take as normative the classical Samkhya expounded by Īśvarakṛṣṇa in the fourth century, we find that Sankara, or the Vedantic tradition he represents, has not only made extensive use of the details of the cosmological process as described by Samkhya, but more particularly the description of the Self, both in its transcendent and individual psychological aspects. Whereas classical Samkhya was pluralistic in its view of the Self, Sankara is monistic as far as the transcendent Self is concerned. Nevertheless, their common idea of the self's passivity and immutability, of its distinction from the empirical life-soul, of the 'limiting conditions' of individuality, of the active object's attributes being superimposed upon the passively witnessing Subject, of that Self's release from a distorting object-world by means of discrimination and realisation of the true Self-essence, of the possibility of attaining this state of release even while in an embodied state—these are only some of the points of affinity on quite central issues that are significant for our understanding of Sankara.

One of those common features which is relevant to the question of causality is the inactive nature of the Self, a doctrine unacceptable to both Ramanuja and Madhva. Sankara denies that a Self can ever really engage in action,[8] for activity implies impermanence and change; it is preceded by desire and results in misery. The idea that the Self is an agent of action in the world is part of the deluding effects of Ignorance. Action requires all the qualities of the phenomenal level of existence; a mental organ to make distinctions, a body to operate through, and so on. The Self must be transcendent to all such.

Having noted these common features shared by Samkhya and Sankara, we can now move on to the polemic that arose between them.[9] Samkhya first argued that Brahman cannot be the material cause of the universe because the world is so different in character from that which is supposed to be its cause. Sankara replies: On the empirical level we do in fact find instances of effects arising from causes which appear to be different in nature, as with animal life-forms coming from non-intelligent dung, and hair and nails coming into existence as the effects of intelligent humans. In any case, there is an important common characteristic between Brahman and the world—their existence (*sattā*). But this should not obscure the more fundamental fact that causal being must be very different in character from effected being. So we cannot rely on perception and inference for our knowledge of the Cause of all, as Samkhya does.

Here Sankara outlines in brief some of the arguments that Ramanuja was to develop so effectively later, as we have already seen. In that Brahman is transcendent to effected being, asserts Sankara, he cannot become a mere object of perception as an effect can be. And because inferential argument is based on our perception of effected things, it is no more reliable as a means of knowing causal being's nature. Brahman's existence is to be known from scripture only, and by means of intuitive experience. But when reason is employed in a subordinate role, it will lead to confirmation of the Self's transcendent nature. The great Cause will be understood as pure Being with a nature quite different from that of the effected world; and yet it will be realised that the world cannot exist in separation from this supreme Self, in that the effect is non-different from its cause. and exists in the cause (as Samkhya also taught).

Should it be argued that intelligent Being cannot become non-intelligent effect, then Samkhya's opposite claim that the world (with its intelligent beings) originates from non-intelligent Nature is equally invalid. If moreover the apparent difference of cause and effect leads to the denial of Brahman as cause, it could equally well lead to the denial that the effect exists in the cause and is thus the same as its cause. In fact, to assume an intelligent Cause as taught by scripture is the only possible course.

Then comes a more peculiarly Sankaran doctrine. The reason why there can be no transference of qualities from cause to effect or the reverse when effect states are reabsorbed into causal state, is that the qualities of the effect 'are the mere fallacious superimpositions of Ignorance'. Here Sankara brings in his ideas of illusory *māyā*, dream-experience, and mistaken identity, though it is more by way of analogy in its use here:

> As the magican is not at any time affected by the magical illusion produced by himself, because it is unreal, so the highest Self is not affected by the world-illusion. And as a person dreaming is not affected by the illusory visions of his dream because they do not accompany the waking state and the state of dreamless sleep [in which the ultimately real state of pure Being is signified]; so the one permanent Witness of the three states [of creation, preservation and re-absorption, in which cause becomes effect, and effect returns to its causal state] is not touched by these three mutually exclusive states. For that the highest Self appears in these three states is a mere illusion, not more substantial than the snake for which the rope is mistaken in the twilight.[10]

Sankara goes on to acknowledge that the Samkhya system has a good deal of well-founded reasoning in it, but in that they do not teach the causal being of Brahman, and his perfect uniformity of character, their method is 'devoid of release'. Perfect knowledge has just this nature of non-duality, because 'it depends on accomplished, existing things'. And only that which is permanent, unchanging and of one nature is a real thing. Anything changing, like an effect, cannot be ultimately real.

Samkhya then argues that the origin of the world from Brahman, and its oneness with him as in the identity of cause and effect, is unacceptable because it contradicts all experience. There is a well-established distinction between 'enjoyers and objects of enjoyment'. How can we allow that these two are really one? Is it not better to acknowledge that scripture has no authority in such a sphere of empirical experience?

Sankara counters this argument first with another example ('waves, foam, bubbles and other modifications of the sea') from the empirical order showing that it is possible for something which is in reality one to change to states in which there is every appearance of two or three things existing separately.

But his principal argument is that 'in reality the distinction [between enjoyer and enjoyed object] does not exist because of the identity of cause and effect that is understood. The effect is this manifold world . . . the cause is the highest Brahman.'[11] To show that these are essentially one, Sankara then expounds the text: 'As, my dear, by one clod of clay all that is made of clay is known, the modification [i.e. any article made of clay] being a mere name which has its origin in speech.'

This is taken to establish his doctrine that 'these modifications or effects are names only, they originate from speech only, while in reality there exists no such thing as a modification. In so far as they are names [distinguishing particular effects], they are untrue; in so far as they are clay, they are true . . . the entire body of effects has no existence apart from Brahman.'

Sankara then takes a little further his idea of the unreality of the effect from the point of view of the Cause. To say that 'only the highest cause is true' (which is scripture's claim) implies 'the unreality of all effects'. So he goes on: 'For him who sees that everything has its self in Brahman the whole phenomenal world with its actions, agents, and results of actions in non-existent.'[12]

He then turns to some of the problems felt by the non-monist because of his claims for the sole reality of pure Being. He denies that this undermines the functioning of the usual bases of knowledge, or the communication necessary to the Teacher-seeker relationship (arguments used against monism by the theists). Although there is no ultimate reality in the differences assumed by these means to the goal of pure oneness, argues Sankara, they continue to be valid as long as a person is still on the path towards that final goal. It is similar to the experience of dreaming: 'The phantoms of a dream are considered to be true until the sleeper awakes.' And this applies equally to all the activities expected of a person in the world: 'As long as true knowledge does not present itself, there is no reason why the ordinary course of secular and religious activity should not be carried on undisturbed.'[13]

Pure Consciousness is the only state which is not superseded or invalidated when all other effects thought to result from such activity have been shown to be unreal. In the case of a person dying because of a falsely imagined snake-bite, it is not the bite or the death-effect that is real, but only the consciousness of them. Only this consciousness of dreaming remains intact after the dreaming person has woken up. Such consciousness (of the pure oneness of the Self) is neither useless, for it effectively removes all ignorance, nor is it erroneous, for there is no further knowledge which can invalidate it. And by it 'the entire course of the world which was founded on the previous distinction is made obsolete'.[14]

The theme of Brahman not really being subject to any kind of modification is then stressed again, though we noted earlier that as a mere concession to the soul's ignorance about the effect-world (and because the Sutra declares it quite clearly) such modification of Brahman was allowed. In reality, however, Brahman is immovable and changeless (*kūṭastha*). No such immutable Being could be the directly related basis of such varying attributes as are found in the world's three effect-states (creation, preservation, and dissolution). The Upanishad's negation of all attributes (in the 'Not thus, not thus' passage) is said fully to establish Brahman's changeless nature. In any case, what possible benefit is there from any supposed real self-transformation into this changing world? Those who maintain (as Bhāskara did) the reality of both such a transformation and the oneness of Brahman, can show no special 'independent result' accruing to the soul from the Brahman-modification side of their doctrine.

This evokes a final objection to Sankara's position: if there is no real modification of Brahman into the world (for it is *māyā* that in reality is substantial cause), then it cannot be held that Brahman is the real cause of the world, and all his causal qualities like omniscience, omnipotence, and so forth, are equally unreal. 'The doctrine of absolute unity leaves no room for the distinction of a Ruler and something ruled.'[15] Sankara dismisses this objection with a nonchalance that must have been greatly irritating to his opponents. All such talk of a Brahman related to the world, by way of his omniscience and omnipotent rule, immediately introduces those 'germinal principles called name and form, whose essence is Ignorance'. Necessary as such an 'omniscient Lord' may be for the creation of all this world of name and form (an undeniable existent from the phenomenal point of view), Sankara can only see such a view as based on 'the unreal projections of Ignorance'.

To define such distorting Ignorance is itself impossible, for it has neither being nor non-being. To this extent we cannot say that creation and the Lord's actual causality is without any degree of reality. So Sankara goes on to describe 'the entire expanse of this phenomenal world' as the mysterious illusion (*māyā*) and power (*śakti*) of the omniscient Lord. His illusory power is distinct from the Lord himself, and functions by means of creation's limiting conditions, the individuating dimensions necessary to finite existence. 'To the person who has reached the state of truth and reality the whole apparent world does not exist . . .

in reality the relation of Ruler and ruled does not exist; though all those distinctions are valid as far as the phenomenal world is concerned.'[16]

Even when we assume the real existence of such phenomenal effects, we see clues to the ultimate non-difference of cause and effect. For effects are seen to exist only when there is an existent material cause. No jars will be seen unless there really is some clay; no cloth unless there are threads. Such an invariable conjunction of existence itself implies non-difference. Scripture, moreover, makes it clear that all effects have their being in their causes and that there is absolute non-difference in the causal-state. 'Hence as there is non-difference before the production [of the effect], we understand that the effect even after being produced continues to be non-different from the cause. As the cause, that is, Brahman, is throughout neither more nor less than *that which is*, so the effect also, that is, the world, is throughout only that which is. But that which is one only; therefore the effect is non-different from the cause.'[17]

Although Sankara has now brought us back to an almost Thomistic view of the common character of 'being' found in both the supreme Cause and the world of his creation, it has become clear in the course of the debate that he finds causality, in anything other than a purely potential form, extremely difficult to fit into his concept of the transcendence of the supreme Being. In his system as a whole there is 'inapplicability of the notion of causality to the ultimate reality'.[18] To give some kind of explanation for this causal enigma Sankara was obliged to make use of the concepts of 'illusion' (*māyā*) and 'limiting conditions' (*upādhi*) as cosmological principles. Or perhaps it should be put in another way. The *māyā*-character of the world refers to the inexplicable mystery of the causal process. With his contention that everything but the pure causal state cannot be ultimately real, it only becomes possible to maintain the identity of cause and effect by calling the effect-state a modification of Brahman in his enigmatically illusory aspect—even the result of inherent Ignorance. Thus the 'modification theory' has become an 'appearance-theory', the 'effect-exists-in-its-cause' theory has become the doctrine that only causal Being really exists, and the substantial cause of the world is *māyā*, not Brahman himself. Only thus did the transcendent perfection of the supreme Being remain intact to Sankara's satisfaction.

RAMANUJA

For Ramanuja, the causal process holds little of the ambiguous character we find ascribed to it in Sankara's writings. With Sankara, Ramanuja follows the Vedantic tradition in describing all Brahman's creative action as done 'in sport', devoid of any intention of benefiting himself thereby. In so far as this *līlā*-metaphor attempts to bring out the essential creativity of the supreme Person, his sheer delight in causing the universe to come into being, then it might be said to fit more naturally into Ramanuja's cosmological scheme. Should it be thought to illustrate that there is no real connection between Brahman and his creation, then it obviously fits more neatly into Sankara's system. But Ramanuja recognises that monists used the metaphor to confirm their theory of illusory creation and replied rather caustically: 'Only people not in their right mind would take pleasure in unreal play.'[19]

Ramanuja's consistent realism enables him to take such sutras as 'That from which the origin and so forth, of this [world proceed]' in their direct and literal meaning. Commenting on this sutra he argues that the characteristics typical of such divine activities as creating, sustaining and dissolving the universe present us directly with the real character of the supreme Person. Because he is called 'Brahman', 'we already know him as possessing supreme greatness and power of growth'—both qualities being included in the meaning of the root. We also know them from scripture which says that 'Brahman is that which is the root of the world's origination, preservation and dissolution, those three processes sufficiently indicate Brahman as that entity which is their material and operative cause; and as being the material and operative cause implies greatness manifesting itself in various powers, such as omniscience and so on, Brahman thus is something already known; and hence origination etc, of the world are marks of something already known.'[20] In other words, even if this reference to Brahman is not a primary definition of his essential being, such an action-based description is entirely valid. 'For taken as attributes, these descriptive words indicate Brahman as something different from what is opposed to such attributes.' And except in so far as there is difference of time in the three stages of Brahman's creative action, there is no need on the basis of such a description to imagine plurality in this essential Being.

It is in a similarly realistic way that Ramanuja interprets the *māyā*-concept. Rather than trying to show an obscuring of Brahman's real Being in the creative act, Ramanuja sees the term as a description of the uniquely mysterious power of Brahman, the supreme Magician who is able to perform wonderful creative feats. Nowhere in scripture, he argues,[21] does *māyā* mean that which is indefinable, neither real nor unreal, as Sankara claims. Nor does it mean any kind of falsehood or deluding power. When it is equated with primordial Nature it merely 'denotes that which produces various wonderful effects', or that from unmanifest Nature 'manifold wonderful creations' come into being. And the supreme person is called the One who possesses *māyā* just because he is both the operative and immanent Cause. Even things which appear in dreams are the equally wonderful creation of the supreme Person, and thus can be called *māyā*. The individual soul is not capable of such creations for himself; only the supreme Creator 'who can immediately realise all his wishes', is able to create such experiences in others. Though such special creations may appear but for a short while, they need not be considered illusory.

Like Sankara, Ramanuja recognised the danger of the older Vedantic theory of Brahman's self-modification as the explanation of the creative process. In fact, though he so vigorously rejects Sankara's reinterpretation in terms of *Brahma-māyā*-modification, at one point[22] Ramanuja condemns those who would implicate Brahman in the soul's bondage to its endless series of embodiments as teaching a doctrine more dangerous even than the monists. It is to his body-self analogy that Ramanuja resorts in order to explain how Brahman can provide the substantial being from which all creation originates, and yet in essence remain unchanged by this 'modification'. In other words he teaches a Brahma-body-modification, with eternal souls and primordial Nature providing that inseparable though not essential part of Brahman that undergoes the change of the creative process. In that the body-metaphor is used in scripture of the universe in relation to Brahman, it is not surprising that both Sankara and Madhva make some reference to the world being 'like the body of Brahman'. It is surprising, though, to find Sankara in one or two places using the metaphor to explain how it appears that Brahman is associated with evil qualities. It is, asserts Sankara, only in 'his bodies' (that is, those finite distortions of his being in which this Self appears) that such blemishes are located, not in his essential selfhood.[23]

Like Sankara, Ramanuja makes some use of many of the features found in Samkhya's description of the creative process. Some scholars have remarked on Ramanuja's relative lack of interest in such cosmogonic details. Others seem to assume that his picture of the cosmic process is taken over from Samkhya with no significant change, apart from his attempt to reconcile Samkhya's dualism with the Vedantic Brahman. In general it is clear that Ramanuja has more of an intrinsic interest than does Sankara in describing such a process, for he takes it to be a real process. In comparison with Samkhya, however, the most significant feature in the limited use Ramanuja makes of that school's 'enumeration' of creation's origin is the consistent way in which he subordinates the whole process to the will and the inclusive being of the supreme Person. By explaining it as the body of this supreme Person he provides it with a distinctively new Ground, and at the same time provides the innate but inexplicable teleology of Samkhya with a convincing End. Cosmological principle thus becomes compatible with soteriological aim; both being understood as dependent upon that supreme Person. This is certainly more than a peripheral change of outlook.

As in the section on Sankara, we shall attempt to appreciate Ramanuja's interpretation of the causal issues by following through the more important points in his debate with Samkhya.

Ramanuja first denies[24] the validity of Samkhya's inferential method, as did Sankara in a somewhat cursory way. Some of Ramanuja's argument here resembles that which he employed against the Logicians. While they argued for the existence of an intelligent Creator on the basis of (among other things) the world's status as an effect, Samkhya used a similar inferential method in trying to prove that any universal Cause could not possibly be intelligent, merciful and in every way perfect. Basic to this argument is their theory (formally accepted by Ramanuja just as by Sankara) that all effected states are implicit in their previous causal states. Therefore the affinity of cause and effect must, argued Samkhya, be so close that the nature of the cause can be inferred from the nature of the effect. Given the unintelligent and pain-ridden character of the effected world, Samkhya felt that primordial Nature herself must be the most likely candidate for the role of substantial cause. It cannot be Brahman, for intelligent being as cause will not become devoid of intelligence when in effect-state. Cause and effect must be recognisably identical, 'and in this way the promise that through the knowledge of one thing all things are to be known is able to be fulfilled'.[25]

Ramanuja had already argued that Brahman's being as transcendent Cause, both substantial and effective, establishes him as the definitive category by whom 'all things are known'. Now he argues that this one-many principle is not reversible, reminding Samkhya that while the effect is not something essentially new, neither does it have a relationship of completely reciprocal non-difference with the cause.

Samkhya's understanding of the operative cause is not quite so clear, reflecting the inexplicability which Samkhya finds in the souls' relationship to Nature. Souls are essentially passive, yet just as the magnet is able to attract iron and cause it to move, so the very 'proximity' of the souls to Nature brings about the initial imbalance of the three strands of

Nature, and creation is initiated. *Karma* associated with souls seems to be the means of this attracting ability. There is another inexplicable instrumental cause called 'concomitant power' (*sahakāri-śakti*) needed to activate the causal state, just as seeds need to be crushed in order to obtain oil from them. The oil is present there in the seeds, but will not be 'manifest' until the crushing takes place. Other concomitant conditions such as place, time, and the form and constitution of a thing are also required for the one primordial Nature to be able to produce particular effects from particular causes.

Commenting on the fifth Brahma-Sutra Ramanuja had claimed that Samkhya's account of the creative process is immediately disproved by such texts as 'It thought, may I be many. . .'. Non-intelligent Nature is quite incapable of this kind of reflection prior to engaging in creative action, argued Ramanuja, along with the other Vedantins. The argument here is not mere scriptural fundamentalism. When he contends that 'in all sections which refer to creation the act of creation is stated to be preceded by reflective thought', Ramanuja is asserting that an intelligent purposive supreme Person is the most convincing and intelligible Cause of the creative process. Classical Samkhya, on the other hand, never provided a satisfactory explanation for the innate teleological tendencies it asserts. So, having listed a number of texts which declare the world to have sprung from the supreme Lord', Ramanuja concludes 'that the supreme Person, Nārāyaṇa [Viṣṇu], free from all shadow of imperfection, and suchlike evil, is the single Cause of the whole universe'.[26]

Of course a number of the arguments Ramanuja employs against Samkhya are taken over from Sankara, or more likely from a common Vedantic tradition. He says, for example, that there are instances in which the features of the effect are quite different from those of its causal state; scorpions out of dung being one such case. But in any case, he argues, the theory of effect-in-cause merely says that an effect cannot be so different from its cause as to provide no basis for their real and substantial continuity. It does not intend to say that cause and effect must exhibit precisely the same nature in every respect.

It is when Samkhya replies that any such substantial continuity involving Brahman in both causal and effected states must result in Brahman carrying all the defects of this effected state, that is, a world of change and suffering, that Ramanuja's analogical doctrine of the universe as only the body of Brahman is introduced. For Ramanuja, this seems to be the only valid way of protecting the essential perfection of Brahman. The universe, he claims,[27] with its misery and mutability, is not the essential Self of Brahman; it is his body. This fails to convince Samkhya, however, and a lively debate ensues. First we hear a series of objections from Samkhya: a body is made up of an aggregate of the five elements, as determined by the *karma* of that person, which immediately excludes Brahman from any such role; nor can souls and nature together comprise any such body; nor can a body be 'an abode of fruition'; embodiment, moreover, implies an 'enjoying subject', which would make Brahman subject to pleasure and pain just like a living soul. This all adds up to making Brahman in no essential way different from other souls—if the universe is held to be his body.

In reply, Ramanuja suggests that there are instances 'in ordinary life' (here following the ancient Vedantin, Dramiḍa) of people who are able to subject others to pleasure and pain without themselves being in any way affected by their actions—rulers, for example. Then Ramanuja denies that painful experiences result from embodiment as such. It is only *karma* that causes the soul to suffer, and Brahman is certainly not subject to the law of *karma*. Indeed he is the Lord of *karma*, who, himself quite independent of its influence, has 'arranged the diversity of creation in accordance with the different *karma* of individual souls'.[28] It is his creative action that makes the 'fruition' of the soul's *karma* possible.

It may not be possible to agree that Ramanuja has made clear 'the exact relation in which the perfect Brahman stands to the deeds of the souls',[29] or that he has completely removed the ambiguity of *karma* in relation to creation, and the subsequent question of who is ultimately responsible for karmic bondage. But there is no doubt that Ramanuja 'consistently upheld the perfect nature of Brahman' as Lord of *karma*'.

There is, of course, a close causal connection between *karma* and embodiment in Ramanuja's teaching. Without *karma* there would be no need for embodiment. And without embodiment, there would be no possibility of the 'fruition' of *karma* and its eventual exhaustion. But it is *karma*, he contends, not embodiment as such which results in the soul's miseries. This is made clear by the status of released souls. 'The person who has freed himself from the bondage of *karma* and becomes manifest in his true nature is not touched by a shadow of evil while all the time he has a body.'[30] Most probably he means that while the soul may not be fully free on earth the one wholly devoted to the Lord can be quite untouched by anything other than that *bhakti*-relationship. Elsewhere[31] he does say that the devoted soul 'by ruling the body, supporting the body and by having the body completely dependent to it, becomes the great lord in relation to the body'. Such freedom from the body amounts to the self's 'true nature being manifest' and being 'untouched by a trace of evil'. In any case, Ramanuja is consistent enough in upholding the distinction between the body as *karma*-determined (which will inevitably be accompanied by suffering), and the body as potentially able to be free of such karmic bondage and suffering.

This distinction is in itself of immense significance in the debate with Samkhya. Van Buitenen finds it 'remarkable that the conception of the body as a defect of the soul has hardly any significance for Ramanuja'.[32] But at this juncture we should note its importance in helping him to establish further his fundamental thesis: 'The supreme Self which is essentially free from all evil, thus has the entire world in its gross and subtle form for its body; but being in no way connected with *karma* it is all the less connected with evil of any kind.'[33] This takes Ramanuja one step further in ensuring the moral and personal transcendence of Brahman in relation to the universe. In passing he claims that any texts declaring Brahman to be without a body must intend to deny of the supreme Self 'a body due to *karma*', or the kind of body with which a soul is normally associated.

Ramanuja's initial definition of a body is this: 'The body of a being is that which has its nature, subsistence and activity dependent on the will of that being.'[34] This differs a little from the definition quoted earlier. Samkhya responds with a few objections to such a definition. Injured and dead bodies no longer function in dependence on a will; puppets are controlled by another person's will; even actions can result directly from the exercise of will; and how can an eternal intelligent soul, itself exercising its will, be directly dependent on the will of the Lord? Ramanuja does not appear to take these objections to his definition very seriously, apart from saying that the term 'body' has a very inclusive significance, and that he uses this definition primarily in its application to non-karmic, ideal bodies, such as that of the Lord or his Avatars. Thus he takes what he regards as the perfect body-self relationship as definitive. So he reiterates, with some modification, his definition: 'Any entity that a sentient being is able completely to control and support for its own purposes, and the essential nature of which is entirely subservient to that self, is its body. . . . In this sense then, all sentient and non-sentient beings together constitute the body of the supreme Person.'[35]

In debate with theistic Samkhya, Ramanuja makes the point that unless Brahman is understood as both substantial and operative cause of all, and unless this is explained in terms of souls and Nature as the *body* of Brahman, there is no way in which he can be the inner Self (*antaryāmin*) of all, as scripture declares him to be. If Nature is a substantially independent entity, then Brahman cannot have this immanentally causal relationship with it. If Brahman is to be Self, Nature must be his body. All the texts teach that 'the world, whether in its causal or affected condition, has Brahman for its Self'. The only possible conclusion from this, claims Ramanuja, is that 'the supreme Brahman [has] the whole aggregate of non-sentient and sentient beings for its body'.[36]

A corollary to this is the claim that this supreme Person's 'embodiment' does not refer only to the form of the universe after the emanatory process has begun. For even in the 'unmanifest' state of 'total dissolution, non-sentient matter has Brahman for its Self and continues to exist in a highly subtle condition in the relation of an ectype'.[37] Such a relationship means existing in a body-self relationship. In other words, there is no condition in which the universe of Nature, even when in its purely potential causal state, can be thought of as independent of Brahman. It is still his 'body', though in highly subtle form.

Then there is the question of the soul's role as an agent—an important issue in Ramanuja's debate with both Samkhya and Sankara, who denied that the pure Self can really engage in action. Ramanuja answers this contention in a way commensurate with his body-self analogy. As the 'body' of the supreme Person, souls are entirely dependent upon that Person's will. There is, therefore, a sense in which 'the activity of the individual soul derives from the supreme Self as its cause'.[38] At the same time the individual self is a responsible agent; otherwise scripture, which commands certain actions and prohibits others, with the declaration that the fruit of action is to be 'enjoyed', would be meaningless. Those strands of Nature which are said (especially by the Gita) to determine and even be the agent of actions are only so in an 'occasional' sense, or (to translate Ramanuja's phrase literally) in consideration of what is gained and what is not gained, that is, by *karma*. And *karma* is precisely that which the soul has done.

But how can the soul act as a real agent when Brahman is said to be the one and only Cause? As the inwardly ruling supreme Self, he first gives room for the individual to exercise all possible volitional effort. He then aids that effort by granting his favour or permission (*anumati*); action is not possible without permission on the part of the supreme Self. Nor do texts suggesting that all actions, good and evil, are directly caused by the Lord rule out this partial dependence. It merely means that in these cases, 'wishing to do a favour to those who are resolved on acting so as fully to please his supreme Person, the Lord engenders in their minds a tendency towards highly virtuous actions, such as are a means to attaining him'.[39] The reverse is the case when a soul is 'resolved to displease him'. Thus both the transcendent sovereignty of the supreme Person and the responsible but dependent role of the individual self is safeguarded to Ramanuja's satisfaction.

This section on Ramanuja's understanding of causality in relation to the transcendence of Brahman can aptly be closed with a reminder of the reality that he ascribed to the effected universe. Completely reversing Sankara's maxim that anything dependent must be impermanent, and anything impermanent must be unreal, Ramanuja declared that the universe is real precisely because it is dependent upon its inner Self, Brahman. It is when he first introduces the body-self analogy in Śrī-Bhāṣya that there is also his first declaration of the reality of the whole universe. Because the universe is in a body-relationship with the supreme Self, contended Ramanuja, it partakes of the same real nature, it has real and eternal being. 'The entire complex of souls and matter in all their different estates is real, and constitutes the form, that is the body of the supreme Brahman. . . . The outcome of all this is that we understand Brahman to carry these distinctions within himself, and the world, which is the manifestation of his glory [*vibhūti*] to be something real.'[40]

Even when it is said that 'the world is he', it is by virtue of his 'pervading the world as its Self in the form of its Inner Ruler' that there is an identity of being. It is 'not founded on the unity of substance of the pervading principle and the world pervaded. . . . The meaning is that Brahman prevails in the world in so far as the entire world constitutes his body. . . . The world is the body of Brahman, and Brahman is the Self of the world.'[41] Ramanuja saw the supreme Brahman as not only ultimate Cause of all lesser finite causes; it is the Lord himself who is the intimate Self and immediate Cause in all causal relationships. At every stage in the creative process Ramanuja understands him to be active in producing further effects—for he is the embodied Self in all mediate causes. Thus 'everything originates from Brahman directly'.

MADHVA

The distinctiveness of Madhva's position stands out very clearly in his views on causality. He is not, of course, at variance with the other Vedantins on every point. His causal theory includes such commonly held doctrines as the role of *karma* as a beginningless causal influence; Nature's eternal pulsation from unmanifest to manifest state; the 'enumeration' (following Samkhya) of the chain of cosmic evolution; Brahman's creative activity explained in terms of playful sport; and the conviction that only Brahman is all-powerful and all-knowing enough to be efficient Cause of the whole creative process.

Then on other doctrinal issues, for example, the reality of the effected created state of the universe, Madhva stands squarely alongside Ramanuja over against the sheer monism of Sankara. Nevertheless, when we examine how Madhva sees the relation of the supreme Being to the universe, and by the same token how he sees the nature and structure of that universe, it is clear that Ramanuja's position at this point is, for Madhva, just as untenable as that of Sankara. There seems little doubt, again, that it was his concern for a more radical expression of the transcendent nature of the supreme Person that led him, as presumably Sankara also, to this distinctive position.

Madhva's emphasis on Brahman's role as supreme Cause is impressive. His distinctive interpretation of the second Brahma-Sutra gives an example of this, where he broadens the 'origination, etc' which the Sutra claims to derive from Brahman, to include not only the origination, preservation and dissolution of the universe (which is how the other Vedantins expound it), but another five causal activities which determine the character of finite existence. He calls it the 'eight-fold causal activity, beginning with creation', and adds controlling, enlightening, obscuring (*ajñāna*), binding, and releasing (*mokṣa*). It becomes immediately clear that Madva intends broadening the scope of Brahman's causal activity to bring out more clearly his direct control of the *soul's* destiny, rather than merely the origination of the universe's effected state, and its psycho-physical evolution.

Madhva himself suggests further explanation of this widening of the supreme Being's causal role. He claims that the Sutra on Brahman's causality is no mere secondary definition, touching only on the accidental and non-essential properties of Brahman. For even that text often put forward as an example of an essential definition—'Reality, knowledge and infinite is Brahman'—refers by implication, contends Madhva, to just those eight causal activities he lists under the Sutra's 'origination, etc'. As 'the Real', Brahman confers reality on the universe, being the Controller of its existence. But the root meaning of this word *Sat* also suggests to Madhva the ideas of goal and dissolution. Being the one who liberates souls, he is their goal; though dissolution refers to material nature alone. As 'Knowledge' he provides the means of this liberation, and by implication is also the one who withholds knowledge and is thus the cause of their bondage. As the 'Infinite', Brahman is the source of the infinite bliss of the soul's liberation. In this way, argues Madhva, even within the terms of this Upanishadic 'essential' definition, all the eight-fold causal functions of the Lord are implied.

Madhva further amplifies in four significant ways this view that Brahman's causal activity should give most prominence to his relations with souls.

The power of *karma* is subordinated, perhaps even more emphatically than in Ramanuja's system, to the controlling will of the Lord. Naturally he agrees with this most unanimously held Indian religious theory that *karma* is a potent determinative cause in universal life. And with the other Vedantins he finds it to be an adequate explanation for the inequalities of birth—an explanation which can defend the Lord against accusations of partiality or unkindness. But, says Madhva, there is no question of the Lord himself being determined by *karma* in his actions: 'Just because the Lord's dispensation follows the law of *karma*, it need not be supposed that the Lord is dependent. From such texts as "He is the supreme Lord by whose grace exist matter, action (*karma*), time, nature and souls, and by whose displeasure all these cease to exist", it is clearly understood that even the very existence of *karma* and suchlike entities depends on the Lord.' '*Karma* is quite incapable of independent activity. . . . Although both the supreme Being and *karma* are causes of the fruit of action [effects], it is not *karma* that guides the supreme Being, but the supreme Being that guides and rules *karma*.'[42]

In another work, along with *karma* Madhva lists other causal factors such as ignorance, time, and the constituent qualities of Nature, claiming that it is because these are all insentient and incapable of willing that they cannot ultimately control things. 'It is the Lord Hari alone who controls all these sentient and insentient beings.'[43]

It is clear that the theory of *karma* does not in itself account for the disparity of actions done by souls, and Madhva would seem to have been well aware of this. Why are the actions of some souls good and of others bad? Madhva's answer was that there are eternal and essential differences between souls, a position claimed by one interpreter of Madhva as an important contribution to Indian religious thought on 'the problems of Evil, Freedom and Freewill. . . . It points out that if the inequalities of life are to be explained satisfactorily, the theory of *Karma*, which is supposed to explain such inequalities, must in the last analysis take its stand on the basic differences in the *svabhāva* (nature) of the souls themselves.'[44]

This means, too, that souls are destined for differing degrees of bliss, or possibly of suffering, for they are from eternity differently constituted. Three main types of soul are described—higher, middle, and lower. In one sense these distinctions seem to be due to the inevitable nature of things. But Madhva frequently emphasises that all such differences are determined by the will of the Lord, in the same way as it is the Lord who ultimately controls the causal law of *karma*.

Madhva is conscious, however, that the soul should not be made to feel devoid of moral responsibility. Theoretically at least, putting complete causal power in *karma*'s hands (the work of the individual) should afford a greater sense of responsibility than putting it all into the Lord's hands—unless, of course, this more personal control by the Lord includes some degree of limited freedom on the soul's part; or unless what the Lord determines is in some way held to be perfectly suited to the soul's inner potentiality. This latter idea is the position Madhva tries to maintain: 'The guiding of the Lord is according to the soul's previous works and also efforts that result from its natural aptitude.'[45]

Even the inner potentialities, however, are God-determined. We noted just now that Madhva's idea of soul-differences derives from the more basic theory of the innate particularities of everything in the universe, as determined by the Lord. This accounts both for the essential difference characterising all beings and for their coherent functioning as a universe—all are under the Lord's omnipotent control, determined by his will. Indeed, the term 'creation', in the sense of absolute origination by the Lord, can be used properly in Madhva system only of those innate particularities that comprise the essential character of all beings, selves included. The raw materials out of which they are thus formed—time, space, nature, action, souls—exist, according to Madhva, eternally in separation from the Lord's being, though not independently of his will. Only the distinctive characteristics determining the form of their existence is brought into being directly and *de novo* by the Lord's causal action. This means that the potent essence of everything is the Lord's creation, and being a direct manifestation of his power can even be called the Lord himself, pervading and empowering creatures under his control.

We have already seen some examples of the Lord's all-pervasiveness, according to Madhva. His comments on the Gita's description of the Lord as 'essence' and 'seed' can serve to illustrate here how he feels he is able to establish an intimate and inner relationship between the Lord and the universe by means of his 'innate determining characteristics' theory. 'To say that he is the "essence" in the waters and other elements means that he himself is the determining Cause of the distinctive nature, inner potency and the very quintessence of a thing's essential nature and principal character. It is not to be thought that these . . . are determined by the intrinsic natures of the substances themselves.'[46] In the same way, says Madhva, it is the Lord who causes the 'radiance' intrinsic to the fire—and thus is said to be the fire's essence. Then again: 'Know me to be like the seed; for I am the cause of the manifestation of the world, as a seed is. But I am not the substantial cause which is subject to changes and manifests itself as a more gross effect. Indeed I am the Controller of such cause and effect.'[47]

Madhva goes on to stress the difference between any normal artisan or manufacturer and the Lord in the manner of their causal actions. Normally no one can do more than change a thing from one gross state to another, such artistry also being subject to the given properties of whatever material is used. 'But this is not the case with the glorious Lord. It is not just that he is the cause of the elements such as water and fire (i.e. which comprise any material), but by his supreme Will he determines even their distinctive properties and essences.'[48]

It is clear that in this way Madhva recognised the need for, and was intent on establishing, an intimate and direct causal relationship between the Lord and the universe with its variety of distinct beings, even though he could not bring himself to accept the more traditional Vedantic theory that all existence, all essences, and even all potency for the changes seen in the creative process—all derive from the substantial being of Brahman in some sense. Despite this reluctance, it is clear that Madhva understood Brahman to be the 'Cause of all causes', the One who 'abides in all things awakening their various powers'.[49]

In particular Madhva had to try to establish that the most prominent of the eternal entities found in his cosmic scheme—that is, the soul—was both fully subject to the Lord's control, and also capable of acting freely. Unless the soul is a real agent of action, as Ramanuja had said, there would be no meaning in scripture and its good counsels. Insentient being could not be the object of scripture's counsels and commands, for it is unable to respond. Nor could it be the Lord, for he has no need to be so directed by scripture. If it is the soul that is the object of scriptural injunction, then that soul must also be capable of real action. But, Madhva then argued, far from the soul possessing creative and causal power in its own right (as was argued by the logical atomists and others), the limited powers it does possess are dependent upon the Lord's overall control, and its necessary agency puts no kind of limitation upon that controlling Will. 'The power to be an agent of action is derived from the Other.'[50] Or again: 'Without reference to his will nothing happens far or near.'[51] On this question of effective causality Madhva is more emphatic even than Ramanuja.

In a Brahma-Sutra section dealing with this issue Madhva begins by arguing how ludicrous it is to think of the soul as a primary causal agent. It seems quite incapable even of doing good for itself, and would naturally not work to its own detriment in the way it does, were it an absolute and independent agent. In fact, its constituent nature points to its dependency: 'It is of meagre capability [in comparison to what is required to be an effective agent] and has no sense of accomplishment.'[52] In comparison with the causal powers of the supreme Being, in so far as it is a dependent entity the soul is on a par with insentient stones, or puppets manipulated by another's hand: 'Just as a man . . . makes a puppet dance, or even as he sets his own limbs in motion [by a purposeful act of will], so does the almighty Lord cause these creatures to act.'[53]

No doubt Ramanuja's self-body analogy could lend itself to an interpretation similarly emphasising the impotence and passivity of the soul—but this was not quite Ramanuja's intention. He would of course agree with Madhva when he goes on to compare the Lord 'ruling the self from within' to the 'Breath [an inner presiding deity] which causes a cow's milk to flow'. He would certainly accept Madhva's observation that merely because we cannot establish the Lord's controlling Will by empirical perception this is no argument against the existence of that Will.

Madhva concludes[54] that it is a most sensible thing to assume that 'the Lord is the real doer and the cause of the soul's activity', for there are instances of invisible powers acting as causes, 'even in this world's experience'. This being so, it is only to be expected that the supreme Lord will possess such a power of acting in imperceivable ways. In fact his causal power is both imperceivable and absolute: 'Only this supreme Lord and no other has such extraordinary and inconceivable powers. . . . He is the One who keeps everything under his control.' So then, such capacity for action as is the soul's derives from this supreme Lord, though 'it is the soul's previous works and its efforts and natural aptitude that determine how the Lord is to guide the soul'.

An example of the more directly causal role of Brahman is seen in Madhva's explanation of dream-occurrence. He agrees with Ramanuja that dreams are the direct creation of the Lord, revealing that reality which characterises all creations of the Lord. They are, however, special forms of the Lord's creative action, their material cause being 'impressions' embedded in the mind of the dreamer, which is what is meant by calling dreams 'mere *māyā*'. But their efficient cause is the will of the Lord himself, creating this dream-experience directly and specially for the dreamer. The falseness of dreams is not due to the constitution of the dream-objects, but merely because the dreamer mistakes them for normal waking experience. In so far as both dream-experience and world-experience are 'transitory, mutable and of dependent nature', then there is a sense in which dreams reveal an essential feature of life in the world.[55] But this is very different from saying, as Sankara would, that the illusory nature of experience at the phenomenal level is writ large and clear in the illusory world of dreams.

Madhva, then, never tires of reiterating and reformulating in a variety of ways this theme that every effected state and every causal relation lying behind it is ultimately dependent upon the supreme Lord's all-knowing and all-powerful will. A passage from his metric commentary on the Brahma-Sutras effectively sums up this theme: 'There is no independent causal power anywhere. Only the Lord's power sets things directly in motion, for everything is always under his control. The various potencies of nature and souls for producing various effects are eternally dependent on him. Just as non-eternal things are ordained to be non-eternal by the eternal power of the Lord of all, so eternal substances too are under his control.'[56] In this way, Madhva, with Ramanuja, not only rejects the Samkhya idea that Nature has an inherent potency for changing itself and producing this universe of such varied effects, he also makes clear his conviction about that causality which remains an enigma in Sankara's system; it is the will and power of the supreme Being that effects all changes and all actions.

Another feature of Madhva's world-view, again in agreement with Ramanuja as against Sankara, is his consistent realism. This is not a mere epistemic ploy, but an integral part of his view of the universe and the very being of things. He gives a number of cogent reasons for asserting that the world of becoming and change is real, arguments that are worth following through in some detail.

Scripture teaches its reality: 'Nowhere [in scripture] is it said that the world is unreal.' On the contrary many texts declare, or at least implicitly allude to, the world's reality. For example: 'The supreme Lord . . . created the universe, and a universe created by him will be real, not illusory.'[57]

This undoubtedly then is the reason Madhva himself found most cogent: the world is the Lord's creation and therefore must be real. Only 'those ignorant of the Lord's great power will say that the world is unreal'.[58] These 'godless enemies of the world' fail to realise that it was 'the great Self who created this world in its present real form, for which reason he is known as one who does real deeds', and that his real creation cannot merely disappear on acquiring the knowledge of its maker. Madhva also sees its reality as established by the Lord's 'knowing' and 'protecting' it. As he writes: 'The view of the enlightened is that this world is known and protected by Viṣṇu. Therefore it is proclaimed to be real.'[59]

Among the various logical and epistemological points put forward by Madhva to contradict the view that 'the world is the product of illusion', we may take just one[60] by way of illustration. Any attempt to avoid the supposed problem of having a world in distinction from Brahman by calling it an illusion makes the situation even worse. For such an argument ends up with two worlds having to be presupposed. No one can experience an illusion, such as the traditional one of seeing a shell as a piece of silver, unless there has previously been real experience of a silver-piece; at the same time the existence of the shell too is rightly taken to be real, as is the similarity between the two. In the same way, to assert that the world is an illusion means that you have to presuppose two existents, that is two worlds, and both must necessarily be real if such an assertion is to be taken seriously.

The question of the world being produced by means of *māyā* was one which theists as much as monists had to try to explain, for does not the Gita itself assert this as well as Vedantic tradition? Clearly it was necessary for the theists to interpret the *māyā* of creation in a way that would retain a legitimate meaning of the term, and yet which would contradict the sheer illusionism suggested by some monists.

Madhva uses the term in a number of ways, generally indicating the mysterious or uncanny power of the Lord in creation. Because the knowledge by which the Lord 'comprehends and protects' this universe of 'five kinds of difference' is such a mystery to mere mortals, we may take scripture's description of such differences as 'mere *māyā*' to mean 'the Lord's understanding'.[61] The same is said in the case of the Lord's embodiment by means of his *māyā*. When the Lord's will is called, among other things, 'great-*māyā*', Madhva takes it to mean simply 'greatness' (deriving *māyā* from a root which can mean great). Just as Ramanuja had done, Madhva also quite often refers this term to the inconceivably wonderful power of the Lord, his ability to create wonderful things being similar to that of the magician (*māyin*). At the same time Madhva notes a difference between the magician's act and that of the Lord. The magician never actually *sees* the products of his magic, for they are not really there, whereas scripture often speaks of the Lord 'seeing the world'. Therefore, says Madhva, 'we conclude that the world is not a magically-produced illusion'.[62]

In other passages Madhva brings out the more negative aspect of *māyā*. On the one hand he accepts an epistemological use of the term—it is an obscuring veil. 'The world is kept in ignorance by me . . . being restricted by *māyā*, even those . . . having vast powers of understanding do not fully comprehend me. They possess but a glimpse of my glory.'[63]

Elsewhere Madhva categorically rejects the monist view that 'by his *māyā* the essentially unchanging, undifferentiated Brahman himself comes to be falsely perceived as the world, that is, the so-called *vivarta* or appearance-theory'.[64] Creation by *māyā* cannot mean the production of an illusion.

Sometimes Madhva expressed the more mythological idea that *māyā* refers to the female creative (and destructive) principle frequently called Durgā, meaning 'difficult of access'. In Madhva's hierarchy of 'presiding deities', the three forms of matter corresponding to Nature's three constitutent strand—the pure, the vigorous and the dark—are controlled by Śrī, Bhū, and Durgā respectively. So Durgā's role is normally that of concealing. Here then, Madhva seems to intend to personify the uncanny and miraculous power of the Lord working through his 'concealing deity'.

This great mystery of the Lord's supreme control over every subordinate agency, the coherence of seemingly disparate powers and infinitely varied innate particularities, is generally ascribed by Madhva to the Lord's all-determining will. It is through this sheer will, transcendent in its character, immanent in its operation, that Madhva feels best able to account for the coordination of the various sub-causes in his system, and to avoid making the Lord directly connected with the innumerable changes incurred in the creative process. Despite the proliferation of such secondary causes in his world-view, Madhva contends that because each is dependent on the one, self-determining, independent Cause which is the Lord's will, there is no loss of integrity in universal being. Thus the perfect oneness of the Lord and his will is sufficient to explain scriptural passages speaking of 'non-duality' (*advaita*) at the supreme level (*paramārtha*): 'He alone is one, the Highest above all else.'[65]

He expresses this idea somewhat differently by equating Nature with the Lord's will, significant in view of the fact that Nature is the field in which all causal relations are seen most obviously to operate. Referring to the Rigveda, 'The Lord's will is Nature and the supreme Lord is master of that will. . . . He is will, he is the guiding thought, he is wisdom, he is bliss', Madhva comments that 'the Lord's will is essentially the Lord Himself',[66] even when referring to its determining role within the universal womb, Nature. It is, of course, partly because he also identifies Nature with Śrī, the beloved consort of the Lord, that Madhva is able to equate Nature with the Lord's will, despite his fundamental thesis that Nature cannot participate in the substantial being of the Supreme.

On the few occasions that Madhva, somewhat reluctantly, adopts the Upanishadic body-analogy (so favoured by Ramanuja) to express the supreme Being's relationship with the universe, it is generally used to convey this idea of the Lord Viṣṇu's will operating throughout. 'It is the will of the Lord that causes such a real world to change and decay every day, and being present everywhere in the universe, the perfect Lord is most blessed. Hence this world is called his body.'[67] Again in his commentary on the Bṛhadāraṇyaka-Upanishad: 'Because he alone existed then and nothing else he determined [to become embodied]. He willed: "Let me become self-possessed, that is, let me possess a body". . . . All this universe is the body of the bodiless Viṣṇu, because it is under his control.'[68]

So far we have discussed Madhva's causal theory in terms of an almost unlimited number of subordinate causes which are ultimately determined by the one supreme Cause, the will of the Lord. There is, however, good reason to think of this supreme will as controlling three main causes in his system, in a way that bears a notable resemblance to the three causes of theistic Samkhya, or even of Śaiva theology.

In the first place Madhva agrees with Samkhya, that it is eternal Nature in unevolved form that provides the material cause, the womb as it were, of the universe. Unlike Ramanuja, Madhva finds it necessary to make an absolute distinction between this primordial Nature and the supreme Being. The idea that the supreme Person himself can provide the substantial being of everything was irrevocably to compromise his independence as far as Madhva was concerned.

This means, naturally that the traditional Vedantic theory of Brahman-modification had to be rejected. But then, so too is the Samkhya theory of the autonomous self-modification of Nature. While he derided the idea that this universe, which in itself is devoid of intelligence and is subject to all kinds of changes, could possibly issue from the Lord's being, he also acknowledges that something more than mere insentient Nature must be responsible for its modifications. Creation does manifest something of the majesty and power of the supreme Will that lies behind it. And there is a sense in which creation is a self-manifesting act (*ātma-kṛteḥ*) of Brahman.[69]

But Madhva takes this to be quite different from a self-modification. For how dare we say that it is really the perfect Lord who experiences, in finite disguise, the pain and suffering of the universe? It cannot be said that Brahman does not 'know' the world's imperfections and pain in the way the individual soul does, because Brahman is essentially all-knowing. But why, asks Madhva, should the all-knowing, all-powerful Brahman willingly undergo such a process of painful self-modification? If you say that Brahman, being almighty, is able to will for himself whatever he pleases, it is quite incongruous to make Brahman's self-modification, which is a change from a state of eternal perfection and bliss to a state of suffering and limitation, the token of his omnipotent independence of will. And if there is a change in any part of Brahman there must be a change in the whole. But to say that the whole of Brahman's essential nature is changed means that as long as the universe exists no soul can acquire knowledge of the essential Brahman, and no soul would then be able to attain liberation. In fact, Brahman himself would be the one needing liberation.

Just as Madhva's idea of the substantial cause (or causes) bears some resemblance to the Samkhyan scheme, so too, despite his insistence that Brahman is the Cause of all, Madhva's idea of efficient causality bears some resemblance to Samkhya's 'superintending Lord'. His 'Cause of all causes' is in fact an efficient cause only; there is no essential internal relationship other than that of the 'sheer will' of the Lord. The immanence of the Creator is established by his having 'entered into' each part of the universe and thus caused it to evolve from its primordial state to its fully manifest state.

Madhva certainly goes well beyond Samkhya's account of the 'superintending Lord'. For even the innate particularities of each distinct thing are said to be caused by the Lord's will. And every eternal substance is said to be entirely dependent upon that will. Indeed, creation has to be understood in Madhva's system as a matter of dependence, control, and the inner awakening of the eternal substances by the 'inner Ruler'. One Madhva exponent contends that Madhva alone among the religious philosophers of India has in this theory attempted to reconcile the traditional view that unoriginated substances, like Nature, Time and Space, exist eternally and the equally strong Vedantic view that everything derives from the one supreme Source. Sharma goes on to argue that this solution of Madhva's, while it acknowledges that the raw materials of creation are not originated by the Lord, yet makes them sufficiently dependent on his will in every aspect of their existence for them to be called his 'creation'. The theory is, claims Sharma, 'the same as "Eternal Creation" in the sense of positing an eternal and *constant dependence* of all finite reality in each and every one of its states of being and becoming and the eight-fold cosmic determinations upon the One Infinite and Independent Principle'.[70]

Another recent interpretation goes so far as to claim that because Madhva acknowledged the possibility of the Lord creating, if he so willed, without the use of any eternal substance, his thought is close to the doctrine of *creatio ex nihilo*, though such absolute origination was impossible to Vedanta. Madhva compared the Lord's 'relying on Nature to a man perfectly capable of walking without a stick, yet who, out of playfulness, decides to take one and lean on it; he is quite free not to take it if he so wishes'.[71] Madhva's intention, no doubt, is that 'each cause God uses draws from him its nature as a cause, being effective only because of the efficacy of his power. There is, therefore, only one true cause, the self-determining (*svatantra*) Cause. . . . [Other causes] do not constitute a limitation of his divine power, but on the contrary, help to make known his absolute power in its full light.'[72] Does his theory, however, really convey the impression that all these causes possess an essential being wholly derived from the will of the Lord?

Theistic Samkhya also distinguished a third cause, the instrument, for this is normally found in the production of any effect. In the creative process it is the inexplicable 'concomitant power' that Samkhya regards as fulfilling this instrumental role. It has to be confessed that Madhva does not always express his position very precisely on this question. Often it appears that it is the Lord himself who directly 'enters into' and 'pervades' every being, animating and empowering it so that all function in proper coordination. Elsewhere, however, Madhva describes this animation of the various elements within Nature as due to the Lord's power (*śakti*), a principle of instrumental agency which is expressly said to be dependent on the Lord's will, but yet which seems to function as an entity separate from the essential being of the Lord.

This notion of a separately functioning though dependent instrument is further confirmed by Madhva when he attributes instrumental agencies to the various 'presiding deities'—Śrī, Vāyu, Brahmā, Prāṇa, etc. Each of these deities is thought to be responsible for one or other of the eternal substances. No doubt this was part of the cosmological thought widely accepted in the Vedanta-related religious milieu. The question is why Madhva's system delegated 'all material transformations and psycho-physical functions' to these deities. At least in part the answer can be seen in the need Madhva felt to preserve the pure transcendence of the Lord's essential being. Any direct impulsion of the Lord's own presence in material elements to cause their modification must to some extent threaten his perfection. It is the Lord's work rather to awaken, by his sheer will, those potencies determined by his will that lie latent within all the eternal substances. It is the single, all-determining Will that integrates the many into a single universe. All other causes, whether more directly active or not, are subordinate to the one supreme Cause.

8 Brahman as Supreme Person

More than in any other topic, it is concerning the personal character of the supreme Being that we find the theists closing their ranks in opposition to the monist's supra-personal Absolute. They declare with relatively united voice that Brahman's transcendent nature is most properly described by means of his being as the highest Person (*puruṣa-uttama*). Naturally some of these attributes consist of peculiarly Vaiṣṇava theistic terms. Their distinct theological outlooks precluded any complete unanimity. Nevertheless, as serious theists they are at one in opposing the monistic view which only by way of concession ascribed a variety of personal qualities to Brahman: personal Brahman is a lower-order being. Thus the monist contends that the radical transcendence of Brahman's real and essential nature demands a theological descriptive method that can reach beyond all such attributes. Brahman-with-qualities (*saguṇa*) must be replaced by Brahman-without-qualities (*nirguṇa*). And only in this way can the perfect identity of the inner self and the supreme Self be maintained.

To the theist, on the other hand, this whole method appeared blasphemous, not only because it 'robbed' the supreme Person of qualities essential to his being, but more specifically because it reduced his transcendent supremacy in relation to the individual self. It was just this divine supremacy that the theist experienced as the basis of worship, the highest end of man, and it was the knowledge of the self's dependence on this supremacy that he declared as the only means to ultimate liberation. On this issue the divergence between monism and theism is at its most striking.

SANKARA

Passages ascribing a wide range of qualities to Brahman are not wanting in Sankara's writings. But such descriptions can never be the last word on the supreme Being, for Sankara intends to draw the seeker away from all attachment to a Brahman that can be qualified by attributes, and guide him to a Brahman that is unqualifiably Being-itself. The question is, does Sankara intend us to think of two distinct Brahmans? Or are these two types merely two aspects of the one Brahman? The lively debate engendered by this issue usually fails to come to a decisive conclusion, often because it is not realised that the question of the two-Brahmans is just another way of asking how empirical reality relates to ultimate reality.

Many modern exponents seem unable to accept the ambiguity and inexplicability of the relationship of these two realities. Thus for example: 'The ultimate reality, Brahman, it is true is unqualified, unconditioned, without attributes, without qualification. But it is *the same reality* that is called God, when viewed in relation to the empirical world and empirical souls. *Brahman is the same as nirguṇa* [attributeless] *and as saguṇa* [with attributes]. There are not two Brahmans, as wrongly alleged by some critics.'[1] It is true that the answer to this two-Brahmans question does depend, literally, on the point of view from which one looks at the 'reality' concerned. From the point of view of transcendent Brahman there can only be one reality, and no qualifiable Brahman can exist in the ultimate sense in which this Transcendent has its being. Speaking from the level of the qualifiable Brahman, of course, his reality has to be accepted, and on this basis there will be worship offered to him.

In so far, therefore, as these two levels of reality exist, two Brahmans also exist. In so far as there is only one ultimate Reality, then only the one, unqualifiable Brahman exists; Brahman-with-qualities is but a distorted version of the unqualifiably One—a distortion which is inevitable as a result of the finitising process and its limiting conditions. But the fact that this 'distorted' Brahman is not merely a creation of the mind, with its need for distinguishing attributes, means that it is more than a mere perspective of the ultimate Brahman. The creative process resulting from Brahman's will and power does have reality as a created entity. It is only from the absolute standpoint of the realisation of a Brahman devoid of any such qualifying attributes that this 'other' Brahman does not really exist. Whether described as 'lower-Brahman' or as 'Lord' (and in Sankara's thought there is little difference between these two terms), a personal Being endowed with glorious attributes is, even to Sankara, an unavoidable necessity. A personal Brahman is required to account for the relative reality both of created existence and of the devotional relationship the soul experiences with its object of worship prior to the ultimate enlightenment. Anything less than this leads to the ultimate Void of later Buddhism. Despite his intention to avoid this, Sankara's persistent effort to wean the seeker away from a Creator and Lord of whom personal attributes can be predicated, away from all dependence upon existence distinguished by qualities, earned him the title 'crypto-Buddhist' from his theistic critics.

Sankara, then, finds that all manner of qualities can be attributed to the less-than-transcendent (*apara*) Brahman. These refer principally to his role as Creator, as the Object of devotion and as the incarnate Lord manifesting his grace to his devotees. We have noted briefly the rather surprising fact that Sankara allows far more room for various inferential arguments attempting to prove the existence of a supreme causal Being than does the theist, Ramanuja. This is more easily understood when we recognise that in general it does not refer to the transcendent Brahman. Some of his arguments are based on the principle that a universe characterised by certain qualities must derive from a Cause endowed with attributes capable of bringing such qualities into being. There must in fact be a correlation of the qualities of Creator and creation: 'The origin, etc, of a world possessing the attributes stated above cannot possibly proceed from anything else but a Lord possessing the stated qualities.'[2]

Clearly the concept of creation will also require some explanation of its innate purpose, even if the Creator does not act with an end in view which will benefit himself. Thus Sankara, to some extent following the Logicians, also uses an argument very much like a teleological 'proof'. In opposition to the idea than an unintelligent principle of Nature can account for the creative process, he says that just as those things which provide pleasure in the world are invariably 'made by workmen endowed with intelligence', or just as 'clay and similar substances are seen to be fashioned into various forms, if worked upon by potters', *intelligence* must be assumed to rule the creative process as a whole.[3] In this case the 'correlation' of Creator and creation is essentially one of contrast; matter which exhibits an innate purpose in its created forms cannot in itself account for such an intelligent end. Similarly, the Creator of a world in which there is movement, while himself not being a mover, 'may nevertheless move things. The magnet is itself devoid of motion and yet it moves iron. . . . So the Lord also who is all-present, the Self of all, all-knowing and all-powerful, may, though himself unmoving, move the universe.'[4] Thus even at the level of inferential argument, Sankara is able to introduce the concept of a Cause endowed with powers quite transcendent to the universe it originates.

Again, in accounting for the production of 'the manifold world' by a Cause supposedly devoid of the usual 'instruments of action' seen in the case of most makers of things, Sankara resorts to the 'absolutely complete power of Brahman [which] does not require to be supplemented by any extraneous help', though the case of the milk turning to curds and water to ice does provide a comparable instance.[5] Sankara then goes on to claim that 'the scriptural doctrine of creation [and its accompanying description of the wonderful powers and attributes of the Creator] does not refer to the highest reality; it refers to the apparent world only . . . it moreover aims at intimating that Brahman is the Self of everything'.

Along with the quality of intelligence that must be presupposed in Brahman as the world-Creator, Sankara also attributes to his mere desire the ability to bring all things into effect. Scriptural declarations that he 'desired' and therefore created indicate that Brahman is an intelligent Being; indeed such reflective creativity is another aspect of his omniscience. As an entirely independent causal Being, however, Brahman is not subject to any possible kind of compulsion from such desire: '[These desires] are by nature truth and knowledge, and they are pure by virtue of their identity with Brahman. Brahman is not impelled to action by them, but he ordains them in accordance with the results of the actions of the creatures. Therefore Brahman is independent in his volitions. He has no want.' The Creator is one whose 'wishes are always fulfilled'.[6]

Sankara, however, can allow very little significance to the notion of will, and the creative power of the divine will. Even the idea in such passages as that quoted earlier about the 'absolutely complete power of Brahman', enabling him to create this manifold world without the aid of any instrumental means, does not lead Sankara to develop the idea of the Lord's 'sheer will' (*icchā-mātra*) in the way the theists favoured. The same is true of the next sutra, where Sankara describes Brahman as creating all things 'just like gods and suchlike beings; who without availing themselves of any external means are able to produce palaces, and so on, by their mere intention' (*cetana*).[7] Admittedly the exercise of purpose was suspect to all Vedantins. But it seems especially characteristic of Sankara to regard the exercise of will with any specific determination as a denial of the essential nature of Brahman as pure consciousness (*cit*). Whatever other attributes of a provisional nature may be used in the description of Brahman as Creator, the notion of willing must have seemed over-anthropomorphic for general use. But while to Sankara such acts of will appeared to bind the agent of action inseparably to his action, to the theists, Madhva in particular, action resulting from 'sheer will' showed the highest degree of independence and transcendence of being.

Another reason Sankara offers for ascribing powers of creating, ruling, forgiving and so forth, to the supreme Being is to provide a suitable object of worship, which in turn should help to prepare the mind for the ultimate realisation of transcendent oneness. For at most such a devotional relationship, and the ascription of personal qualities to the supreme Being that accompanies it, can only provide a provisional stage for the seeker, prior to the realisation of absolute oneness.

Even if there are passages in which Sankara lists the glorious qualities (*kalyāṇa-guṇa*) of Bhagavan, the adorable Lord—sovereignty, knowledge, strength, heroism, creative power, and splendour—in general he tries to avoid such personal features. So we find in his writings which are not dependent upon any traditional text such as the Gita, that his lists of Brahman's qualities will be comprised either of negative terms or terms emphasising his sheer otherness. Thus in Vivekā-Cūḍāmaṇi:

> [Brahman is] the real, the one without a second, pure, the essence of knowledge, taintless, serene, without beginning or end, beyond activity, the essence of absolute bliss, transcending all the diversities created by *māyā*, eternal, ever beyond the reach of pain, indivisible, immeasurable, formless, undifferentiated, nameless, immutable, self-luminous, . . . infinite, transcendent, . . . beyond the reach of mind and speech, immeasurable, without beginning or end, the perfect, one's very Self, of surpassing glory.[8]

Then later:

> The wise man realises in his heart, through deep contemplation the infinite Brahman, which is in essence something like eternal knowledge and absolute bliss, which is incomparable, transcending all limitations, ever free and without activity, and which is like the limitless sky, indivisible and indeterminate . . . which is devoid of the notion of cause and effect, the Reality behind all imagining, homogenous, matchless, beyond the range of proofs . . . which is undecaying and immortal, the positive Being which precludes all negations, resembling the placid ocean, unnameable, without merit or demerit, which is eternal, peaceful and the One.[9]

Should there be doubt whether or not this is an authentic work of Sankara's we might refer to such descriptive phrases as 'Brahman who is essentially eternal, immaculate, enlightened, free from limitations', frequently repeated in his major commentaries.[10] This is sometimes slightly extended: 'Brahman is eternal, all-knowing, absolutely self-sufficient, ever pure, intelligent and free, pure-knowledge, absolute bliss.'[11] None of these positive qualities can be applied, of course, without their being stripped of any possible connotation of the plurality their use in the finite realm implies.

Sankara, then, much preferred to use those descriptive terms which best express the unlimited and immutable character of Brahman. Personal categories in general appeared so inadequate to him just because of the finite changes and limitations to which personality is subject. The term 'being' (*sat*) though helping to bridge the gap between finite being and infinite Being, carried none of this notion of mutability. *Sat* is Being in itself, unlimited by any change, or dependence on any other beings. This means it is transcendently free from every kind of bondage. Being in itself, Sankara contends, is without any kind of parts; it is Being pure and simple, which guarantees its unchanging and indestructible nature. Only those things with some principle of inner division are liable to change and destruction. It is the simplicity of Brahman's inner nature that ensures his perfection and fulness of pure Being. This concept of Being has very commonly been linked with two other characteristics of Brahman—consciousness and bliss (*cit, ānanda*). Sankara uses all three terms in his major writings, but it is only in some lesser, perhaps unauthentic works that they are found together as *sat-cit-ānanda*, the compound descriptive term that after Sankara became the most comprehensively definitive term for Brahman.

'Consciousness' in Indian thought is not far in meaning from 'Person' (*puruṣa*) which is used synonymously with Brahman and *Ātman* in the Upanishads. But *puruṣa* cannot be taken as 'person' in the modern sense. The monist in particular felt the need, before attributing personhood to Brahman, to strip personality of all those characteristics normally thought to belong to it, like being a distinctive, willing, feeling, acting individual, and probe beyond these features that bind a person to the outer world, so as to discover the unchanging stream of consciousness that comprises the essence of the self. Only this can provide the analogical basis for the transcendent, immutable Being the monist saw as necessary to self-liberation.

Deussen describes the process in this way:

> Here within our self we gain an infallible guide to the absolute being which we are seeking; that which cannot be laid aside must be imperishable, a conviction which is most clearly expressed by calling the principle of all living beings the Ātman, i.e. the Self . . . we gradually separate from our "I" whatever is not-I . . . consciousness therefore was left as the terminus.[12]

Sankara describes as 'slow-witted' those who complain that this method can lead only to 'non-being'. Such minds are unable to make the leap into transcendence. For this is a method which allows that an initial place must be given to personal, experienced, distinguishable being; but instead of then gradually moving on to immutable Being, at some point all those features characteristic of human personality must be radically transcended. It is a notion of selfhood that does not include and then transcend, but after progressively excluding all that belongs to personal categories, at the moment of ultimate reality utterly trans-personal Being has to be realised.

'Bliss' is the third important descriptive term used of Brahman, though not as frequently in Sankara's writings as we might expect. A notable exception is his commentary on Taittirīya-Upanishad. He uses this term in two ways. In some cases it means that Brahman is free of all qualities and conditions that would cause misery. Being unlimited and unconditioned Reality, Brahman cannot be subject to any of the characteristics of world-existence that cause bondage, fear and misery. Infinitude thus is equivalent to bliss.

Similarly, as we saw in the transcendent qualities listed above, Brahman's purity or freedom from all evil and from all possible imperfection is often stressed by Sankara. But there is no reason to think that Sankara understood the transcendent Brahman's blissful being *only* in negative terms—as absence of what makes for misery. For the role of Bliss in creating the universe and the happiness possible within it is certainly part of Sankara's teaching. Without Brahman's Being, Consciousness and Bliss, Sankara recognises that there is no creaturely being, consciousness and bliss; but in that all such creaturely, effected qualities cannot be real as their transcendent Source is real, some anomaly is inevitable in the transition from pure Bliss to the limited joy of finite beings.

Sankara begins his 'Bliss-creeper' exposition[13] by identifying the 'blissful one' mentioned in the text with the individual, conditioned self. Its joy derives from the proper fulfilment of ritual and meditative acts, which are undertaken precisely in order to obtain enjoyment. At the same time, the most desirable Bliss, relating to all other pleasures as head to tail, is the supremely blissful One, Brahman. It is his Bliss that 'permeates them all'—pleasure in being a father or friend, in having that peace that comes from some mental enlightenment and so on; but all these are merely momentary joys. For it is in direct proportion to the practice of self-discipline that 'particular joys will attain excellence and increase in serenity and freedom of mind'. It is not such efforts in themselves, however, which cause the increase of joy. Only Brahman 'is truly the source of bliss; one becomes joyful by coming into contact with that Source'.[14] Indeed, as scripture says, 'on a particle of this very Bliss other beings live'. And as the self becomes detached from desires, it is able to increase its joy a hundred-fold at each stage of its progress towards that ultimate Bliss. In this sense Brahman is the 'Highest as compared to the blissful self that attains [this Bliss] gradually'. Blissful Brahman 'is the support of the blissful self'; for the essential end of the self is to realise its oneness with this plenitude of joy.

Sankara concludes this passage by claiming that the self's passage to ultimate Bliss is evidence of the existence of Brahman as the source of all such Bliss. He offers similar arguments in the passages which follow. He claims, for example, that 'by virtue of being the cause of everything, Brahman is clearly recognised in the world as the self-creator'. Such a 'universal recognition is only possible if there is an eternal consciousness acting as its Cause'.[15]

Then Sankara finds another more specific reason for the existence of Brahman. He is also recognised (in scripture and generally) as the essence of joy (*rasaḥ*). In that joys do exist there must be such an Essence of all joys. And as such an Essence must also be the source of all joy, then Brahman must exist, for 'a non-entity is not seen in this world to be a cause of happiness'. Moreover, in the case of those who have realised this Brahman, their bliss does not depend in any way upon their own effort or desire. 'It follows as a matter of course that Brahman is the source of their joy', and that such a blissful one must exist.[16]

Again, Sankara argues that every human activity, exemplified in the act of breathing in and out, is done with the expectation of achieving some form of happiness. Now if all the varied bodily functions act towards this single end, there must be some coordinating intelligence which itself is transcendent to the joy-seeking process. 'If this Bliss should not be there in the space lodged in the cavity of the heart, then in this world who indeed would perform the function of breathing? Therefore Brahman exists. People's happiness is caused by that very [blissful] being for whose purpose there are such activities.'[17]

A similar argument regarding the achievement of fearlessness follows: 'Fearlessness can only come as a result of taking refuge in something that exists.' And what are the qualities of this fear-remover? He is immutable, uncognisable, unembodied, imperceptible, incorporeal, inexpressible, not even an abode of refuge. Once the aspirant recognises that it is the notion of diversity that is the cause of all fear, and once he realises his oneness with this unqualifiable transcendent Being, 'he becomes established in his true nature, then he does not see, hear, or know anything else. A person is made afraid by someone else. But it is not reasonable for the self to be afraid of the Self. Hence the Self is the source of fearlessness for the self. . . . Even if he sees the slightest otherness . . . fear is found. . . . Even Brahman, when perceived as an Other and called Lord, becomes a terror.'[18] Sankara then goes on to apply the argument as in the previous cases: 'The whole world is, in fact, seen to be stricken with fear. Therefore, from the perceived fact of fear in the world, it follows that there does exist a terrifying being which is an indestructible agency of destruction.' Brahman is, then, the cause both of fear and of the removal of fear.

To conclude his comment on the Bliss-creeper passage, Sankara returns to his main theme that it is Brahman the blissful who is the ultimate source of all joy. Then comes the contrast between the two types of bliss. He acknowledges that 'even wordly bliss is a particle of the Bliss that is Brahman, which becomes transmuted into impermanent worldly bliss, resulting from knowledge [of the Self's oneness] being covered up by Ignorance.' At this lower level there is the need for a distinct subject and object to be brought into contact with each other. The degree of satisfaction attained at this worldly level will depend on the degree of 'concurrence of external and internal means'. Even so, 'this familiar bliss can be a way of approaching that Bliss which is comprehended by an intellect quite free of objective thought'.[19]

The transposition required, however, means the multiplication of the very highest human bliss many hundreds of times—as bliss occurs in successively higher stages of realisation. Finally we come to the god Brahmā, who 'pervades the whole universe as cosmic and individual persons . . . in him all these varieties of bliss become unified. . . . This bliss of his is directly perceived everywhere by one who is well-versed in the Vedas, free from sin, and untouched by desire. . . . That supreme Bliss, a mere particle of which forms the bliss of the god Brahmā . . . is that very Bliss from which all this bliss has separated like spray from the sea and into which it gets united again. It is the immediate Bliss, in which there is no distinction of joy and enjoyer, for it is without duality.'[20]

In the process of moving from temporal joy to this unqualifiable state of supreme Bliss, Sankara finds that the words taken from the familiar to describe the unconditioned 'without reaching, without expressing [that Bliss], turn back, become deprived of their power. . . . Therefore, that Brahman which is beyond all concepts and all words, and which has such attributes as invisibility [and other negative 'qualities'], from which words, though used by their utterers in all possible ways for expressing Brahman, return together with the mind and its conceptual knowledge, that is able to encompass everything else.'[21] For the Bliss of Brahman is the essential Brahman; and Brahman is the Self, pure Consciousness. Hence the impossibility of describing that supreme Being in terms of personal attributes. Many of these can take us a little way along the path towards such a description. But at the point of the realisation of the ultimate identity of seeker and sought every word 'loses its power', the attributes become devoid of meaning in relation to such absolute, immutable Being.

No doubt this section could have included more of Sankara's descriptions of the qualifiable Brahman. Sankara's attitude, however, is shown by his quite frequent interpretation of scriptural passages that are explicitly theistic, in line with his absolutist position. It is his absolutism that is by far the most crucial aspect of his writings; descriptions of a being-with-personal-attributes are merely by way of a provisional concession. To Sankara's way of thinking such a being must necessarily be inferior, finite, dependent, characterised by objective and separate existence, and hence devoid of that transcendent nature that can provide ultimate liberation to the seeker.

RAMANUJA

Ramanuja's method of attempting to arrive at a proper understanding of Brahman's supremacy is almost exactly the reverse of what we have found in Sankara. Instead of moving away from distinctive personal attributes and turning towards a Brahman-without-qualities as a method of arriving at transcendent Being, Ramanuja preferred to move from impersonal categories towards more clearly personal qualities exalting Brahman. Sankara's stripping down the character of Brahman to such categories as pure-Being, sheer-Consciousness, absolute-Bliss, was anathema to Ramanuja. The various and glorious attributes ascribed to Brahman were, for Ramanuja, not only the most effective means of expressing the transcendence of his being; they were also essential to that being.

A number of modern studies in Vedanta tend to find this predilection for the glorious attributes of the supreme Person something of an intrusion from what is claimed as a strictly Vedantic viewpoint, for they are said to derive from a Vaiṣṇava sectarian background. The assumption is that if Ramanuja were a Vaiṣṇava in theology, he could not be an authentic Vedantin. And in so far as he does allow 'anthropomorphic ideas'[22] to creep into his system, he is failing in his Vedantic duty.

The question of the direct source of Ramanuja's terms, or even of such a determining concept as the self-body analogy, is very complex. Suffice it to say that given the eminently vedantic idea that Brahman's supremacy is to be safeguarded, and that a variety of perfections can be attributed to Brahman, there seems no valid reason to exclude terms taken from 'sectarian' sources, especially when it is perhaps from these that the most striking expression of such supreme qualities can be derived.

Quite naturally, it was while commenting on the Gita's text, with its more devotional and less formal character than the Brahma-Sutras, that Ramanuja found more scope for ascribing to Brahman the intensely personal qualities he thought most apt to his supremacy. It is interesting to find that the content of his largest systematic work that is not a commentary, the Vedārtha-Samgraha, lies somewhere between that of Śrī-Bhāṣya and Gītā-Bhāṣya in this respect. In the case of a commentary the important question is to what extent he has been loyal to the text he comments on. In the case of a more systematic work the criterion should be to what extent he has established a convincing system which is at the same time in line with basic Vedantic principles. The important thing is not whether his terminology is 'narrowly sectarian' but whether the distinctive terms for the supreme Being properly cohere with his position as a whole. Generally speaking, of course, any would-be Vedantin was well-advised to avoid the excessive use of more esoteric sectarian terms, if he intended to receive the widest possible Vedantic recognition.

It is possible to identify at least fifty descriptive attributes that Ramanuja ascribes to the supreme Being. They are mostly found grouped in the definitive passages scattered throughout his major writings. Carman,[23] taking his cue from the introductory ascription in the Gita-commentary, distinguishes two principal topics in the divine attributes. They refer either to the 'supremacy' or to the 'accessibility' of the divine nature, these two poles being held in 'creative tension' throughout Ramanuja's writings.

Fundamental though these dimensions clearly are, I would suggest a somewhat more complex theological scheme. Ramanuja's divine attributes cover four dimensions of Brahman's character: there is an *initial ontological supremacy* described. Ramanuja begins from the Upanishadic description of Brahman as the one *Being* (*Sat*). The 'knowledge-of-being' (*sadvidyā*) passage from the Chāndogya-Upanishad is the basis of his initial statements in Vedārtha-Samgraha. Van Buitenen, in an illuminating study of the meaning of *Sat* in the Chāndogya-Upanishad, argued convincingly that *Sat* is 'the irreducible stuff of which everything is made ... the atomic minimum that remains after all successive products have inversely been dissolved in their causes'.[24] So the translation 'being' in the sense of pure *esse*, may be misleading. For it is the immanent causal power 'somehow present and accessible.... *Sat* preserves its ancient meaning throughout the fluctuations between an eminently transcendent, disembodied and unqualified Brahman and an eminently immanent, embodied and qualified Deity: the *Sat* is the one that is *present*, the transcendent that is immanent.' It is Ramanuja, asserts Van Buitenen, who gives most prominence to this aspect of the Upanishadic seer's teaching.

Ramanuja first describes *Sat* as distinguished by innumerable attributes not characteristic of effected being. His initial intention, therefore, was to refute the monist interpretation of *Sat* as unqualifiable pure-being. *Sat* has 'all the perfect attributes which according to other contexts belong to Brahman—those myriads of immeasurable, glorious and innumerable perfections like omniscience, omnipotence, universal sovereignty, his being unequalled and unsurpassed, having all desires materialised and his will always realised, and being all-illuminating, as well as his absolute freedom from evil....'[25]

He goes on to argue the common theistic case that only on the basis of the reality of the 'all' can the promise made in this Upanishadic passage be realised; that is, by knowing the One, all things can be known. Again the argument is clearly from the reality of the one causal Being, *Sat*, to the reality of the many caused beings, which all form the body of Brahman. Ramanuja goes on:

> All is known when the One is known: the One whose proper form is solely knowledge, bliss and perfection, whose greatness is immeasurable, who possesses boundless, unequalled and countless perfections, such as the power of having his will always realised, and who is essentially not subject to mutability: that is, the supreme Brahman himself, whose body ...[26]

It is sufficiently clear from these initial accounts of the character of the 'irreducible' Soul of all existence, that its ontic supremacy is to be established precisely by its distinctiveness from all other beings, and thus by listing its glorious attributes. For Ramanuja, to speak of this one *Sat*, Brahman, as pure, undifferentiated Being, is to miss its very nature as *Sat*, the essential Being of all beings. Brahman, is, by definition as far as Ramanuja is concerned, the 'Distinguished', the supreme *Person*, and hence supremely personal in the perfection of his being. Even if Ramanuja does remain faithful to the Upanishadic concept of *Sat* as the 'irreducible stuff', the infinitely subtle element of all material beings, it is also true that this 'substance' is inseparably related to its innumerable attributes of infinite perfection.

Ramanuja does maintain a formal distinction between the definitive attributes of the Upanishads and the innumerable other attributes further defining the perfections of the supreme Being. These are the definitive attributes: reality (*satya*, the real being that relates to *Sat*), knowledge, bliss, infinity and purity. The distinction is made, significantly enough, in the context of his questioning which of the many attributes of Brahman are absolutely essential in any proper meditation on his being.[27] Thus it is the needs of devotional meditation—for Ramanuja essential to the proper knowledge of Brahman—that make the distinctive perfections of Brahman so necessary to descriptions of his being. Ramanuja is, however, prepared to recognise that there are primary and secondary qualities. Thus, 'lordship, profundity, generosity and compassion' are mentioned as examples of attributes which although 'they cannot exist apart from the subject to which they belong', nevertheless are not absolutely essential in the object of meditation unless specifically mentioned.[28]

No doubt one reason for this formal recognition of the prominent Upanishadic definitions is the need for Vedantic orthodoxy. Another practical reason is the point Ramanuja himself makes—it is not possible to include all the attributes in each act of meditation, so at least include those that find most prominence in the primary Vedantic texts, and which may be taken as representative of other innumerable glorious qualities.

Ramanuja has two terms for 'essential nature', *svarūpa* and *svabhāva*. And on the basis that in some places he uses these terms with distinct meanings, Carman suggests that Ramanuja holds, at least theoretically, a distinction between Brahman-in-himself (his *svarūpa*) and Brahman-in-relation-to-others (his *svabhāva*). 'His first thought about *svarūpa* was as a distinct essence or substance, not as a definition of a relation to other entities . . . [the supreme Self's] essential nature can be defined without reference to his relation to any other entity.'[29]

In one sense, the individual self's essential character is similar to that of Brahman. So the attributes used of Brahman in the five Upanishadic defining terms are also used of the soul. But the soul's dependence on the supreme Self for this character is just what makes Brahman so distinct as the supreme Self. And whatever Ramanuja's formal recognition of an unrelated Brahman-in-himself in fact, he finds it both necessary and appropriate to write mostly about Brahman's relations with the soul and with the world. For him, the reality of *Sat* is not pure and infinite Being, but infinite Being in inseparable relation to finite beings. To this extent it could be said that it is precisely his related-attributes of compassion, lordship and so on, that distinguish the supreme Being most clearly from all other beings, and thereby establish his supremacy.

That Ramanuja was principally interested in those distinctive qualities of Brahman most conducive to the devotional spirit of love, adoration, and commitment is further confirmed by noting the qualities to which he applies the term 'distinctive' (*vilakṣaṇa*). Ramanuja first lists the Upanishadic definitive terms and the supreme acts of Brahman as 'sole cause of creation, and so on'. Then he points to what is 'distinct in the essential nature': 'He is opposed to all evil and is of wholly infinite perfection (*kalyāṇata*). He has a host of such glorious qualities (*kalyāṇa-guṇa*) which are countless and incomparable in excellence.'[30] These are the qualities (more so than either the somewhat abstract Upanishadic terms like knowledge, reality, infinitude, or the somewhat remote powers of creation, sustaining and so on) that are most suitable in the relation of devotee to the supreme Object of devotion, and hence are most 'distinctive'; they most directly and effectively distinguish his Person from all other entities. It is these supremely adorable qualities that make him the 'highest Person' (*puruṣa-uttama*), the 'supreme Self' (*parama-ātma*), or the 'worshipful Lord' (*bhagavan*). While these terms may also be used of finite beings in a derived sense, they are only to be used in their fullest, most perfect sense of the great Being, Brahman, the abode of the 'six glorious attributes'.

Ramanuja does frequently stress the immutability of Brahman's essential nature in his lists of the glorious attributes. But it is not immutability of being as such that Ramanuja is primarily concerned about. What he wished to establish was that none of the changes taking place in the creative process in any way marred the perfection of Brahman's essential attributes. At the microscopic level the soul too has an unchanging essence, though its attributes are subject to 'decrease and increase'. But at the supreme level the highest Person retains his every perfection, whatever changes there might be in its universal 'body'.

Brahman's immutability is therefore expressed mainly in terms of the perfections of his impregnable personal being. But there are two aspects (*ubhaya-linga*) to such perfection, the negative and the positive. Brahman is also untouched by imperfections (*amalatva*). This in fact is one of the five Upanishadic definitive attributes. Those Upanishadic texts seeming to declare a Brahman devoid of qualities (*nirguṇa*) are also usually interpreted by Ramanuja in this sense: Brahman is not characterised by any conceivable evil quality. He is entirely free from 'every trace of defilement' as Ramanuja frequently expresses it.[31] In some passages imperfection is closely related to freedom from change. Brahman is 'devoid of imperfection or change'.[32]

Change in itself is not said to be evil. It is, however, invariably related to the influence of *karma*, and so to pain and misery. The supremacy of Brahman is seen in his being entirely unaffected by this process. Being of 'incomparable and countless perfections [the supreme Person] has the power of always realising his will, and is essentially not subject to mutability'.[33] As the unchanging Self subsisting throughout all the mutations of the creative process, there is not the slightest diminishing of his selfhood or his person.

The foremost six glorious qualities listed in Ramanuja's supreme Person are 'knowledge, strength, sovereignty, heroism, creative power and splendour; qualities which are essential to him (*svābhāvika*) and of incomparable excellence'.[34] It is just because these qualities remain intact and perfect that the supreme Person can be called immutable.

In defining Brahman as *Satya*, the Real, he calls him the 'unconditioned' which 'distinguishes him from non-intelligent matter, which is subject to change, and from intelligent beings, which are linked with such matter in the created world; for since both souls and matter are capable of entering into various states called by different names, they are excluded from the possibility of unconditioned being'.[35] But in the passage following, which defines Brahman as 'infinite' (*ananta*), Ramanuja reverts to his more characteristic view that immutability can best be expressed in terms of the impregnable persistence of the distinctive personal qualities of Brahman. However frequently, then, we may find Ramanuja referring to the absence of imperfection in the supreme Being, it is clear that he sees far more significance in his positive 'opposition to everything defiling', an expression that usually occurs just before mentioning the five Upanishadic attributes.

That the concept of bliss (*ānanda*) comprises one of the definitive attributes of Brahman has already been noted. On the one hand we find Ramanuja linking it closely with Brahman's knowledge. Following the lead of the Upanishads he sometimes describes Brahman as one whose 'essential nature is solely knowledge and bliss' (*jñāna-ānanda-eka-svarūpa*).[36] By this he means that because there is no kind of limitation to Brahman's consciousness (or even to his omniscience, as later Vaiṣṇavas often interpret *jñāna*), it is comprised essentially of bliss. This is the 'single essence' of Brahman in which there is no inner contradiction of character. But just like his consciousness, his bliss is still one of his attributes. He is 'a subject enjoying bliss'. He enjoys this blissfulness 'infinitely' and 'unqualifiedly'. He is 'an ocean of bliss'.[37]

The infinite and immeasurable nature of his bliss is brought out in his comment of the Sutra[38] referring to the Bliss-creeper Upanishadic passage we noted when discussing Sankara. This passage 'arrives at bliss supreme and unsurpassed'. Its 'measureless abundance' cannot be fully defined: 'If one undertakes to state the definite amount of the bliss of Brahman—the superabundance of which is illustrated by the successive multiplications [of inferior bliss] by a hundred—mind and speech have to turn back powerless, no such definite amount can be assigned.' However, it does not mean that Brahman 'transcends all thought and speech' entirely. And although the bliss of the soul and the supreme Self are in such contrasting degree, any permanent happiness that the soul is able to enjoy derives from the infinitely blissful One. Quoting the texts 'Brahman is bliss', and 'He is essential delight' (*rasaḥ*), Ramanuja goes on to say: 'Since Brahman is essential delight, one is happy when Brahman is attained. The supreme Person, who is bliss of a boundless, incomparable nature by himself and in himself, also becomes bliss to others, since this is his nature in an unqualified way.' It should be noted, though, that the context in which Ramanuja writes of this participation in the supreme Person's bliss is that of loving, devotional attachment to him. For, he says, in the end it is this devotion that is the knowledge we require—the knowledge with bliss as its essence.

This ontic dimension, interpreted in terms of personal qualities, moves quite naturally into a cosmic dimension in Ramanuja's theological scheme. It is his use of the self-body analogy that effects such a smooth transition, as we have seen earlier. His exposition of the Upanishadic *Sat*-knowledge and its culminating 'That thou art' text contains a number of expressions of Brahman being the Self of all as the basis for all things being his body. For example: '. . . Brahman is the Self of all as he is the Self of the entire universe, [and] this entire universe constitutes his body.'[39] It is, then, Ramanuja's understanding of the supreme Person's selfhood as inseparably related to the finite universe that leads him so frequently to stress the cosmic, immanental dimension of that selfhood. His being includes all beings: it is the self-existent Being from which all originates and on which all depends. As his body, type, accessory and so on, it is an expressive *attribute* of the supreme Person's being. While it is theoretically possible to define the supreme Person without reference to his creation, there is no possibility of the latter's existence without its relationship to the supreme Person upon whom it depends for its being.

Creation is also the self-manifestation or self-emanation of Brahman. So in a Śrī-Bhāṣya passage commenting on the knowledge-of-*Sat* passage: 'That which is called "Being" . . . who is the Cause of everything, willed thus: "May I be many". After he had created the entire universe. . . .'[40] This picture of a single, perfect Self 'throwing out' the universe as an extension of himself includes substantial and effective causal ideas in almost equal proportion. 'The magnificent variety of material bodies' comprising the stuff of the universe all derive from the substantial being of the one primal Self. Equally, such self-manifestation only takes place as the result of a deliberate act of that Self's willing.

Ramanuja contends that only in Brahman's case it is not a contradiction for 'one Being to have an infinite and wonderful variety of forms and still to retain his oneness of being in this infinite and immeasurable diversity'.[41] Herein is his distinctiveness, and herein is the basis of his activity as Creator.

A number of the supreme Person's attributes, sometimes included early in the definitive passages, refer to his saving qualities and activities. As in all theological systems in which the supreme Being is held to be both Creator and Saviour there is an apparent incongruity that has to be resolved. In Vedanta it is primarily a question of how *karma* relates to creation: creation is according to the souls' deserts, but in that Brahman transcends this karmic chain he is able to provide a way of liberation for the beginningless bondage of souls. And many of the qualities ascribed to him refer directly or indirectly to this liberating potential. This is certainly part of the reason for Ramanuja's emphasis that the supreme Person is devoid of any defilement by the universe that is his creation, and for his creative activity being without any specific 'purpose', or benefit to himself. Along with such indirect references, there are frequent direct descriptions of Brahman as 'the sole cause of the cessation of the cycle of rebirth'.[42] There seems little doubt, too, that of the six great attributes so dear to the Vaiṣṇava community, the qualities of 'untiring strength' and 'heroism' originally expressed (in mythological form?) aspects of the saving power of the Lord.

Ramanuja's writings also contain explicit descriptions of both the saving power and the saving mercy of the supreme Person. In Śrī-Bhāṣya, for example, there is the following comment on the final Sutra: 'Just as it is known from scripture that there is a supreme Person . . . who is an ocean full of forgiving love for those who take refuge in him, who is supremely merciful . . . even so it is known from scripture that this supreme Lord, when pleased by the faithful worship of his devotees . . . liberates them from the influence of Ignorance which consists of *karma* . . . leads them to attain that supreme Bliss which is the direct intuition of his own true nature, and after that certainly does not turn them back into the cycle.'

In other places Ramanuja stresses that feature of Vaiṣṇava theology which teaches that Viṣṇu is the all-powerful preserver of all existence and in particular the merciful protector of his devotees. As the Vaiṣṇava Purāṇas also teach, Ramanuja cannot allow that Viṣṇu, or Nārāyaṇa, as he prefers to call him, is only a preserver. As he quotes from Viṣṇu-Purāṇa: 'The world originated from Viṣṇu and in him it subsists. He is the one who sustains and annihilates the world.'[43] Nevertheless, as the tradition maintains, Viṣṇu does have special concern for preserving the world's being: both as the all-pervader holding things together for their good, and as the one who intervenes in order to ensure the welfare of the world when this is threatened. The latter function will be dealt with in the next chapter. The role of general preserver is illustrated by another quotation Ramanuja makes from the Viṣṇu-Purāṇa: 'All beautiful qualities are inherent in his nature and he supports the whole of creation with a fraction of his omnipotence. The vast body he has assumed is in harmony with his pleasure and taken on by his own volition, and in that body he fulfils what makes for the welfare of the entire universe.'[44]

Finally, Ramanuja in a number of passages describes the supreme Being in terms that intensify his distinctive identity and consequently serve to intensify the devotion of those worshipping this supremely personal Being. In particular, drawing on the Vaiṣṇava devotional, mythological and ritual tradition, Ramanuja focuses attention on the majestic beauty of the Lord's supernatural body. This constitutes a kind of third dimension of his self-manifestation, along with his cosmic and *avatāra*-bodies. In the Vedārtha-Samgraha much more prominence is given to this supernatural body with its glorious attributes than to the Lord's activities in his incarnation-body. This need not be over-stressed, as Ramanuja may well be thinking both of the glorious incarnations and of his image-manifestations when he is eulogising in such explicitly physical terms the majestic beauty of the Lord's body:

> His splendour is like that of a gigantic mountain of molten gold and his brilliance like the rays of a myriad suns. His long eyes are spotless like the petals of a lotus. . . . His eyes, his forehead and his nose are beautiful, his coral lips smile graciously, and his soft cheeks are radiant. His neck is delicately shaped. . . .[45]

This rapturous description continues at length, concluding thus: 'His profound majesty eternally encompasses the entire universe. He looks upon the hosts of his devotees with loving eyes, full of compassion and affection. . . . All evil is foreign to him, for he is a treasury of all glorious qualities and he is essentially different from all other beings. He is the supreme Self, the supreme Brahman, Nārāyaṇa.' Only this quality of being beautiful and thus attractive to the whole world is common to passages (especially the Gita's introduction) defining both the Lord's majesty and his compassion.

Ramanuja did not regard this supernatural form of the Lord as being real only from a devotional point of view, or as a temporary phenomenon granted to the devotee merely as a stimulus to his faith at a particular time, later to be superseded. 'His bodily form belongs to [the supreme Brahman's] essential nature' just as surely and as permanently as does his knowledge or bliss. The main reason for claiming this is that 'the scriptures declare that his essential nature is such' (i.e. qualified by such a supernatural form).[46]

In answer to those who would reject such a concept of the supreme Being as hopelessly compromising the perfection of his simplicity, Ramanuja would reply[47] that it is an entirely *supernatural* form; its attributes are 'infinite' and 'inconceivable', except to the eye of the devotee, and it can comprise part of the 'essential nature' of Brahman only by reason of his supreme power, just as he can remain untouched by the defects of the changing universe even while that universe comprises his manifest body. This is how Ramanuja describes the divine form in his introduction to the Gita: 'His one permanent celestial form is a treasury of infinite qualities such as radiance, beauty, fragrance, tenderness, charm, and youthfulness, which are inconceivable, wonderful, eternal, unblemished and supremely excellent'—a remarkable example of aesthetic, almost erotic, attributes exalted by metaphysical categories of transcendence.

To those with a monistic bias this will look like crude anthropomorphism. Ramanuja himself, however, insisted on the unique and transcendent character of the divine bodily form. Just as in the case of the supreme Person's essential nature, of which it is part, the 'supra-natural body' is not without some degree of comparison with human bodies. But in that all its attributes are exalted to an infinite degree, resulting in a body that is perfectly suited to his essentially pure, infinite, blissful, all-powerful and all-knowing Being, then it is an incomparable and inconceivable body, a transcendent instrument of the supreme Person's character.

Ramanuja uses more than one name to identify the supreme Person, the distinguishable Brahman of his system. Occasionally the name

Viṣṇu is used, being taken to mean the 'all-pervader', or perhaps the 'highest abode'. Sometimes the name Vāsudeva is used, explained with a quotation from the Viṣṇu-Purāṇa as 'he who is everywhere and in whom everything abides'.[48] Then there is the name commonly used to address Krishna in the Bhagavad-Gita, 'Bhagavat'. An esoteric interpretation of this name too is taken from Viṣṇu-Purāṇa: 'To that pure one of mighty power, the highest Brahman to which no term is applicable, the Cause of all causes, the name "Bhagavat" is suitable. The syllable *bha* means that he is the cherisher and supporter; *ga* means that he is leader, animator and creator. The two syllables, *bha-ga*, indicate the six attributes [see above]. . . . The syllable *va* indicates that in him—universal Self and Self of all things—every being dwells and he dwells in every being.'[49]

Nārāyaṇa is the name Ramanuja favours as most appropriate to denote the supreme Being in all his distinctive character. Having begun (in Vedārtha-Samgraha) with *Sat*, the most featureless of terms for the supreme Being, he moves by stages through to the most particularised form of that supreme Being known to him, that is, Nārāyaṇa. His own religious experience and its tradition leads him to regard this name as signifying most precisely all those distinguishing qualities he has found essential to Brahman. In some passages Ramanuja uses the apologetic technique of applying all texts declaring some aspect of divine supremacy to the great Nārāyaṇa, principally on the basis that he can see no other divine being of whom such attributes can properly be asserted. Then the fact that Nārāyaṇa is denoted by the first letter of the alphabet (the short *a*), which is also the root letter of the sacred syllable *aum*, which in turn is the basis of all scriptures, means that Nārāyaṇa must be the supreme Being.[50] All language and every existent entity derives from this primary letter, hence it is proper to declare Nārāyaṇa, denoted by the same letter, as the supreme Person.

Vedanta's acceptance of the many deities of the Hindu pantheon could be taken as contradicting the claim for the one Brahman's supremacy. Ramanuja finds no such problem; they are all merely part of the Lord's body. Just as other beings in the universe, they are subordinate to the one Self. But does not the Lord's consort, Śrī, constitute a possible threat to the supremacy, especially the essential oneness of the transcendent divine will? Here we find that the explicit role Ramanuja gives her differs somewhat from the place she has in later Vaiṣṇava thought. This difference cannot be fully explained by Ramanuja's natural reticence to include all his Vaiṣṇava beliefs while endeavouring to present a universally viable Vedantic theology. For even in his devotional work, Śaraṇāgati-Gadya, clearly intended for Vaiṣṇava devotees, although Śrī is given more prominence than in his 'Vedantic' writings, there is still not the kind of contrast in function and character between the Lord and the Mother that we find being made later. In all his references to her his principal intention is to show not only the eternal reality of Śrī along with the Lord, but more important the sovereignty of the Lord in relation even to her. She is omnipresent with him, but assumes whatever form he himself first wills. She has 'incomparable glory in her essential nature, beautiful form, qualities, and manifestations, she possesses sovereignty, gracious conduct, and suchlike qualities that are pleasing and appropriate to him'.[51] She is called 'Mother of the universe'; but so too is Nārāyaṇa, along with terms like Friend and Father. Thus the 'Mother' merely reflects his character which is 'an ocean of motherly affection towards devotees . . . distinct from all other beings [including Śrī, he] is a desire-granting tree, a Friend to the distressed, Śrīman ['one accompanied by Śrī'], Nārāyaṇa, the Refuge of the helpless'.[52] Neither Ramanuja nor his Śrī-Vaiṣṇava successors accepted the idea that it is the female principle that is the essential creative power (*śakti*), an idea so dominant in the Tāntric system.

The use of a variety of distinct personal attributes to describe the supreme Being is eminently suitable to Ramanuja's system, for that Being is primarily to be regarded as the 'distinctive' supreme Person. He begins where Upanishadic speculation begins, with the search for the essential, substantial Being within all things. And because he is led to think of this essential Being in terms of a fully related Self—a Self or Person that is corroborated by his experience of theistic religion both in its devotion and in its scriptures—he concludes that a variety of eminent qualities are ultimately real in such a Being. Supremacy, causal power, saving action, inner control—these are the most outstanding qualities of this distinctive One. Or to use Ramanuja's own analogical approach, while the Self's supremacy may not require a relationship to anything outside its own being, in fact it is continually manifest in varied forms of embodied existence. Thus at every point great and glorious qualities are to be found as evidences of this Person's immanental transcendence over all.

MADHVA

Madhva is, if possible, even more emphatic than Ramanuja that Brahman's transcendence must be expressed in terms of the supreme excellence found in his personal qualities. Only Madhva takes the whole of the first section of the Brahma-Sutras as indicating the Lord's 'fullness of qualities'. He also frequently insists that only when the soul acknowledges the supreme Person's excellence of personal being, his lordship over all other beings in particular, can the soul attain the liberation it desires. 'He who knows Viṣṇu as perfect in all good qualities is able to throw off his bondage (*samsāra*) and for ever enjoy bliss without any misery.'[53]

Nor can the soul properly desire these perfections for itself. With the exception of such attributes as reality, consciousness and bliss (*sat, cit, ānanda*), which are essential in some measure to the soul's proper being, and await the knowledge of the Lord for their realisation, the supreme Person's excellences are quite beyond the soul's attainment. It may be said that these soul-qualities are characteristic of all selfhood. But in the supreme Lord they are of infinite excellence, and in him they are accompanied by so many other attributes ensuring that his Selfhood is infinitely realised. Madhva's favourite analogy, in which the soul is a reflection (*pratibimba*) of the Lord, obviously can be applied in a limited sense as a way of showing their resemblance. He is generally more concerned to point out the contrast between Lord and soul. While many of the passages in which he makes this sharp contrast may be polemical in intent, there is no doubt that they do introduce us to the heart of his thought.

So, then, the first characteristic of Madhva's description of Brahman we need to note is that this supreme Being is essentially qualifiable and 'distinguished' (*sa-viśeṣa*) by a variety of attributes. Every statement made about Brahman, he claims, even negative statements, in some sense distinguish him from all other beings. Certainly a doctrine such as that of Brahman as the Cause of all requires a number of other supporting qualities and cannot be claimed of any attributeless Being. 'The Creator must be omniscient, omnipotent, and capable of fulfilling whatever he wills. This is what being a "Brahman-with-qualities" (*saguṇa*) means.'[54]

While we cannot say that Madhva is only interested in such 'functional' qualities in Brahman, it is true that he is less concerned than Ramanuja to ascribe to Brahman the more abstract descriptive terms of Upanishads, or even the six glorious attributes traditionally ascribed to Viṣṇu. Possibly he felt that special mention of such a limited number of attributes does less than justice to the 'fulness' of attributes that he wished to stress. With meditational needs in mind, however, just occasionally he does refer to 'the four-fold features summarising all the qualities—being, consciousness, bliss and selfhood. Generally, though, his preference is for the manifestly more personal qualities of the later Upanishads and the Purāṇas. And while he quite frequently makes quotations from earlier texts, as well as writing commentaries on them, his interpretation of the more monistic-sounding terms like being, consciousness, infinity and bliss shows very clearly his concern for an eminently personal supreme Being. In fact, the major portion of his writings is comprised of selections from more clearly theistic texts, especially when describing the divine nature and its attributes. Such a wide-ranging collection of theistic texts serves to provide us with a most valuable introduction to an important aspect of traditional Indian theology, in addition to expressing so effectively Madhva's own theological attitude.

'The perfect one with fulness of good qualities' (*guṇa-pūrṇa*) is Madhva's favourite term for the supreme Being's distinctive nature. He uses this or some equivalent term in virtually every important passage referring to the divine nature. When he outlines the essentials of his theology in thirty-two brief verses,[55] the first part of the work, which deals with the divine nature, refers to this 'fulness' in every verse but one.

Madhva intends to convey a number of inter-related ideas by this term *pūrṇa*. The Lord possesses 'fulness-of-qualities' in that they are innumerable and each is found in perfection. There is no possible excellence that he lacks, nor is any quality lacking excellence. It is just for this reason that he is called 'Brahman', says Madhva: 'Viṣṇu's qualities cannot be separately described, for they are immeasurable. Being called Brahman means he is completely perfect. . . . No one other than the Lord has unlimited qualities (*amita-guṇa*).'[56] He even explains the text 'All this is Brahman' [57] by saying that all qualities predicated of the world can be found, though in exalted form, in Brahman. Then there are also qualities which may seem to be defects in others, but which prove to be excellences when found in the One 'perfect-in-all-good-qualities'—an argument to which most theistic apologists have to resort in one form or another in order to reconcile the doctrines of divine omnipotence with divine goodness.

Though Madhva uses a variety of sectarian names for the supreme Person, his principal theme is that one Person's supremacy by virtue of his infinite perfections. As he opens his commentary on the Brahma-Sutras: 'Nārāyaṇa is exalted by all his excellences.' Similar declarations are found a number of times in his more systematic theological treatise, Viṣṇu-Tattva-Nirṇaya: '[He is] the Supreme . . . perfect by reason of his unique qualities, by his distinctiveness, being in every way the Other'; 'Hari is above all these [deities] because he is infinite in his full complement of qualities like independence, power, knowledge and bliss'; 'Viṣṇu, having the full complement of attributes, perfectly and constantly, in all his divinity, is the independent and supreme One'; and by way of conclusion—'Nārāyaṇa has the fulness of unlimited attributes'.[58]

In order to meditate properly on these various attributes the Lord's infinitude or vastness should be taken as chief attribute. Not that Madhva gives great significance to it on its own; but in conjunction with the other attributes it must be taken to lead to an understanding of each excellence as infinitely realised in the Lord.

This term 'fulness' is also invariably linked with the negative description, 'devoid of imperfection'; Madhva thus shows the typical Vaiṣṇava predilection for the 'two forms of ascription' that we found in Ramanuja. The supreme Person's perfection is comprised as much by his freedom from any possible defect as by his infinitude of good qualities. On aggregate there is a greater use of such negative ascription in Madhva than in Ramanuja. In one brief but important statement of the supreme Person's transcendence (from his exposition of Mahā-Bhārata 1.10–12) there are some thirteen negatives.

From the many other instances of this mutuality of freedom from defect and fulness of attribute we may take the first verse of Viṣṇu-Tattva-Nirṇaya: 'Nārāyaṇa is transcendent over (*samātīta*) perishable souls and imperishable Lakṣmī, is flawless and has the full complement of good qualities.' The same concern for Brahman's freedom from imperfection is seen in his interpretation of the word 'I' (*aham*), in the great saying 'I am Brahman'. It means, he says, 'free from evil'. Thus he takes it as a play on *aham*, reading it as *aheyam*, literally 'not that which is to be avoided'.[59] Rather similar in intent are those passages describing Brahman as the 'unchangeable' (*avikāra*), or as 'untouched by changing beings', an emphasis to be expected from Madhva in view of his rejection of the long-standing Vedantic doctrine of Brahman as the substantial Cause of creation. He felt unable to accept this doctrine precisely because it seemed to threaten his conception of the perfect flawlessness of the supreme Person.

In the next chapter we shall see that Madhva's doctrine of the descent (*avatāra*) of the supreme Person also gives importance to this conviction that his being is in no way diminished by his contact with the temporal, material world.

In enumerating the perfections of Brahman as understood by Madhva we should include his 'wonderful powers' by which he manifests his supremacy in bringing into being all natures and all activities in the universe, though in all dependent beings no nature and no action will have the full perfection of their Cause. In other words, it is the Lord's 'fulness' of causal power, though not from his substantial 'fulness' of being, that all created beings derive. When he is described as 'all-powerful', it is primarily of his power to pervade and activate all creatures, while remaining unchanged in his perfection of character and being, that Madhva is thinking.

On the few occasions that Madhva does refer to Brahman as *Sat*, the real Being, he sometimes takes it to mean, 'the Good', or even as 'Being of the purest quality'.[60] But more often *Sat* is taken to point to the Lord's self-existent *causal being*. For example, souls are said to continue in bondage only because they do not realise that they derive from this being. Such a being can be called 'One only', 'One without any second in the beginning', because he is so distinct from all other beings; for he is the One on whom they all entirely depend, their being and reality deriving from him alone.[61] When the world is called 'un-real' (*a-satya*), it simply means that its reality derives from the Lord. For the negative prefix 'a' as the first letter in the alphabet, signifies the Lord. Hence, 'the all-pervading Lord is the Reality of realities (*satyasya-satya*)'.[62]

'All-pervading' is the meaning which Madhva normally gives to the term *Ātman*. There is also an even more esoteric interpretation suggested: 'The supreme Hari is *ātmā* because he is pervasive (or "extensive", *ātatatvāt*) and because he is a knower (*mātṛtvāt*)'—thus explaining the two syllables *āt-mā*.[63]

More importantly, Madhva also interprets one of his usual names for the Lord, Viṣṇu, primarily in terms of his all-pervasiveness. This is particularly frequent in his Brahma-Sutra commentary. The Gita commentary also has many references to Viṣṇu's all-pervasive, omnipresent being, though there are few attempts to trace such a quality to the inner meaning of his name. This emphasis of Madhva's on the supreme Person's 'fulness', or extended immanental power was, at least in part, made necessary because he rejected the earlier Vedantic doctrine that all being arises out of the substantial being of Brahman. At the same time it does serve to give a special dimension to Madhva's basic idea that Brahman is that 'fulness' accounting for the existence of all things in their particular form and character, even if their existence as such would seem to be given in Nature.

The description of Brahman as 'blissful' is clearly related by Madhva to his concept of the divine 'fulness'. He defines the indivisibility of Brahman's nature, for example, primarily as the basis of his 'supreme bliss': 'The one indivisible Being, the supreme Person . . . is the immutable and supreme Hari. Having no divisible parts, he consists of supreme bliss (*parānandaḥ*), is eternal and possesses eternal attributes.'[64] Thus Madhva can quite happily use the Upanishadic definitions of Brahman as 'sheer bliss', or as 'being, consciousness, bliss', or even the extended definition 'the essence of perfection as immutable Self comprised of strength, consciousness, bliss and heroism',[65] which echoes both Upanishadic and more typically Vaiṣṇava attributes.

However he may use the term, Madhva intends it to describe the bliss that belongs to the supreme Person as a supremely excellent quality; he is not aiming for the ultimately unqualifiable bliss-ness of Sankara's system. Thus the term 'bliss' usually occurs along with other distinguishable qualities. And consciousness is sometimes interpreted in terms of such bliss. For example, 'Lord Hari is of the nature of consciousness and [so?] has the quality of self-delight'.[66] Elsewhere the Lord's 'consciousness' is taken to mean 'knowledge', or preferably 'omniscience'. Thus Madhva's equivalent of *sat*, *cit* and *ānanda* is this: 'The supreme Self is supremely blissful—the supreme (*paramaḥ*).'[67]

Though the soul too has its essential blissfulness, Madhva is primarily concerned to point the contrast between the supreme and original blissfulness of the Lord, and the limited and reflected bliss of finite beings. This Brahma-bliss, says Madhva, as do other Vedantins, is quite distinct in character from that of the world.[68] In general the contrast between the two is greater than in Ramanuja's system. There is not the continuity that Ramanuja finds between the world's limited joy and that fulness of bliss realised in the supreme Person. In part this is a result of Madhva's stress on the otherness of the supreme Being in his 'perfect fulness'.

As 'perfect Being' the Lord is also the proper goal and ultimate end of the soul. In some places Madhva takes up the Purāṇic play on the name of the Lord and this End of the soul: 'Nārāyaṇa is the *parāyaṇa*.' Related to this is the notion, found in different forms in various Vedantins, that all words refer to the supreme Person. As the highest *pada*, meaning footstep, standpoint, or even word, the Lord is that final destiny to which all steps must move and to which all words point. In one passage he expresses the idea thus: 'Viṣṇu, whom all names enter, is said to be supreme (*parama*). All names refer to him who is different from all. . . . As all other names signify him alone, the texts point out that no other being can be the Lord of all.'[69] Clearly Madhva's main intention in finding the meaning of all names and all words in the supreme Lord is to stress his exclusively distinct nature as the 'perfect One'.

The most important of the supreme Person's attributes, which make up his 'fulness', is his self-determining, self-existent nature. In Madhva's theology he is primarily the Independent (*svatantra*). This is intended to point most decisively to the way in which he contrasts with all other beings. All others are dependent on his will and power and so are *para-tantra*, 'determined by another'. As we saw, it is from this fundamental division of reality that the term Dualism (*dvaita*) is used of Madhva's system. Although Madhva often lists independence as but one of a number of attributes belonging to the supreme Person, it is this special quality which distinguishes him most clearly, focusing attention as it does on his essential sovereignty, his omnipotent will, his all-pervading control, his eternally realised desires, his self-existence—in a word, his unconditioned being as the supreme Person.

A number of distinctive features can be brought out under this term *svatantra*. We have already noted that as the 'self-determining' Lord, he stands contrasted with all other beings. 'All the Vedas teach the difference of Lord Hari from all else. The difference lies in his independence, omniscience and sovereignty over all.'[70] The following are the more important features of this distinctive 'independence'.

Madhva is convinced that texts which speak of oneness of being, and indeed the whole notion of creation and universal existence from a single source, can be accounted for by reference to this concept of dependency, based on the one, all-determining and independent will of the Lord. It has to be extended, of course, to include the concept of his all-pervading power, and a number of subordinate causes, which are the means by which the independent will accomplishes its creative intention. Nothing can be done by dependent beings unless the Lord who is free from every kind of dependence on others himself determines that they shall so act. That the Lord is not 'supported by' anything other than himself, that he is 'nowhere dependent on the world, the world being dependent on him',[71] is because of his perfectly self-determining being.

Madhva, then, uses this term *svatantra* as a way of describing the supreme Lordship of Brahman. For this reason it is frequently found along with a number of other titles describing his 'supremacy over all', claimed as the most important theme propounded by the scriptures. They teach him to be 'independent, omniscient, Lord over all', 'the support of liberated souls, the exalted, the Ruler, the only controller of all, supremely divine, he is the Lord'. So, he concludes: 'Praise to Nārāyaṇa, the independent and sovereign Lord of all.'[72]

Another activity in which the Lord manifests his independence, perhaps the most conclusive evidence of this lordly quality, is his ability to grant liberation from *karma*'s bondage. 'The giver of freedom must himself be independent, for anything dependent is still bound itself. How can that which is conditioned grant freedom that is wholly transcendent?'[73] Such liberation, however, is only granted to those who know the Lord as the one independent and supreme Being, controller of all and endowed with all excellences—and who are lovingly devoted to him because of this supremacy. Given in response to the soul's devotion, for the soul to attain its eternal release is nevertheless an act of grace on the Lord's part. In other words, the Lord's grace is, for Madhva as well as for Ramanuja, the ultimate expression of the supremacy and independent will of the highest Person.

Madhva puts this succinctly in his Gita commentary: 'As the absolutely imperishable, he alone is the self-determining ruler of the universe. [Therefore] release is wholly his gift.' 'In that the Lord alone is absolutely independent of all he is the giver of release from all miseries and giver of the highest good to the soul.'[74]

Madhva also describes the Lord's independence in terms of his perfect freedom from any attachment to or limitation by his various activities and their consequences. Action is normally the cause of the soul's bondage, indeed of all the misery it can experience. But this is in no way the case with the Lord, claims Madhva: 'At all times and in every respect the Lord alone acts independently. . . . In that he is independent he does not accept the evil arising from any action, nor its merit.'[75] Madhva explains this independence of action in various ways, but these were discussed in the previous chapter. His basic theme is that everything, whether the Lord's creative or saving action, results directly from the exercise of his free will, as befits the supreme Person who is essentially self-determining. He echoes the Upanishadic statement: 'Creation is entirely the Lord's freely-willed act.'[76]

Another way in which Madhva expresses the Lord's independent character is by stressing his immutability, using many of the well-established Vedantic terms for this. He is called the 'immutable', the 'imperishable', the 'minutely subtle essence', the 'unmanifest' by whom all is controlled. In his Gita-exposition (*Tātparya*), Madhva gives an extended note on the meaning of being the 'imperishable'. 'The Lord is the imperishable by whom all this is pervaded.' To this extent he is 'connected with all time, space, etc. . . . Destruction or perishableness may be of four kinds—to be non-eternal, to be subject to loss of bodily life, to be subject to misery, and to be imperfect. The Lord is *the* imperishable in every sense. . . . Being absolutely imperishable he is the only independent Ruler of the universe.'[77] Thus he is unchangeably constant in his perfection, he is vulnerable to no possible change, even though his power really pervades all, and his perfect being is fully manifest in all his descents.

Another important feature of Madhva's description of the Person of the Lord is his contention that there is a perfect oneness of attribute and essential being. 'The attributes and actions of Viṣṇu are one with his essential nature.'[78] Far from intending thereby that the attributes do not make any real distinctions within the essential nature of the supreme Person, Madhva goes on to say quite explicitly that 'the principle of distinction (*viśeṣa*) is there in the essential nature just as much as the essential nature itself'.[79] The personality of the Lord, therefore, constitutes no kind of limitation to his inner being. Not only is each attribute a perfect expression of the Lord's essential being, and therefore one with it; each attribute is also inseparable from and perfectly in harmony with the Lord's other attributes.

On this issue Madhva has obviously made a useful contribution to the theistic description of the supreme Being. It is appropriately included here in the section elaborating the Lord's self-determining independence because it expresses in a novel way the Vedantic understanding of the inner freedom of the supreme Person. 'The supreme Self is in every way free from all inner contradiction.'[80]

It is this perfection and independence of being that belong to the Lord which distinguish him from all other deities. Thus he alone can be called 'supreme Person', the title favoured by most Vaiṣṇavas. In Madhva's case, however, it seems that the rather complex hierarchy of deities comprising his religious scheme is not merely a part of his inherited tradition and its mythology, but is theologically necessary to his Vedantic system. He is quite consistent in maintaining that all these meditating agents—Vāyu, Brahmā, Prāṇa, Vaiśvānara, and so on, and even the highly important Śrī, who is almost indispensable as the Lord's consort and instrument of a number of his activities—all these deities are ontologically dependent upon the supreme Lord. While Śrī and Vāyu are his immediate agents, according to Madhva, they were only able to act in this capacity because the Lord had willed and empowered them so to act. Śrī, as the highest of all this hierarchy, even partakes of the infinite and imperishable nature of the Lord, being eternally free from all karmic influence, unlike other deities. She is, nevertheless, quite dependent upon her Lord Śrīpati for her imperishable being. She is in eternal communion with him but her blissfulness derives from him alone. 'Hence Viṣṇu who is blissful in himself is called the Supreme.'[81]

The question arises: is it just because Madhva so stressed the character of the Lord as the Other, the transcendently Independent, that this hierarchical structure of his system became theologically necessary? Does the style of transcendence he attributes to the Lord make him so ontologically removed from the level of an imperfect creation that he can operate there only by means of these intermediaries? Madhva's insistence that all means which the Lord adopts are his own free choice reflects this same view of the Lord's ontological independence, and in one sense further accentuates the distance between Madhva's Brahman and the finite creation. Is the Lord's supremacy so stressed that finally the relationship between himself and his creation becomes theologically tenuous? It is significant that Madhva makes much more use of the *via negativa* to describe the supreme Being than does Ramanuja. It is necessary to say 'Not this, not this' of every attempted description; his powers are quite 'incomprehensible', his qualities 'immeasurable', his being 'inconceivable', his form 'incomparable'. He can quite properly be called the 'unqualifiable', and his essential being is ultimately known only by means of 'immediate realisation'. No doubt all these negative descriptive terms are derived from Vedantic sources and should be capable of use even by a theistic Vedantin. And Madhva is adamant that the Lord's attributes are not intended in a merely provisional sense. His interpretation of various aspects of the Lord's fulness and freedom of being has made a substantial contribution to Vedantic theological understanding.

9 The Lord's Grace

The sharp theist-monist divergence concerning Brahman's personal qualities becomes most serious on the question of divine grace. For while the theistic Vedantin tended to see the very highest form of transcendence, again immanentally expressed, in the supreme Person's freely bestowed grace, the monist is bound to regard such ideas as little more than anthropomorphic projections, to be interpreted in line with his dominant theme—the limited reality of all relational existence.

In terms of the Vedantic sources, of course, the interpretation of the Gita is a crucial issue. Are the numerous passages in the Gita that describe the Lord's gracious accessibility to his devotees, and the background of his incarnate existence against which this is set, intended merely to lead the seeker on to a level of self-realisation that supersedes all such personalised categories of divine activity? The reverse seems to be the more convincing interpretation, in which two stages of self-realisation precede an ultimate or climactic recognition of the Lord's transcendentally personal and gracious character. The later Upanishads, whose thought the Gita quite clearly reflects, tend to confirm this, though by itself exegesis certainly does not settle the issue of what is authentic Vedanta. Each system has to be examined on its own merits, and in terms of a more broadly-based Vedantic authenticity.

The universally held Vedantic belief that every person's life-experiences are given by the Lord as recompense for the good and evil *karma* accumulated by that person need not be taken as a contradiction of the doctrine of divine grace. In fact this law of *karma* that the Lord normally operates is precisely what makes necessary some form of intervention into the cause-effect chain of experience. So we find that the Gita, which declares the ability and willingness of the Lord to break this causal chain, also accepts that at the normal level of activity, even at the level of lower devotion, each person gets precisely what he is looking for in life, and in the afterlife too. Thus in commenting on the Sutra which states that the Lord cannot be charged with partiality or cruelty, all three Vedantins quote the Upanishadic passage asserting that 'a man becomes good by a good deed and bad by a bad deed'.[1] Sankara goes on to quote the Gita's assertion that 'I [the Lord] treat men according to the way in which they approach me'.[2] He likens it to the Rain-giver (Parjanya) who is the common cause of all crops. There is no discrimination in the rain he showers on the earth. The difference determining what sort of crop will result lies in the potentialities inherent in the various seeds. 'Hence the Lord is bound by regard [for the various types of *karma* associated with each soul]'. And with this no Vedantin would disagree, that is, as far as it concerns the general ordering of universal life. It is the level of experience transcending this general order about which they do not agree.

SANKARA

It is not entirely surprising that a system in which the ultimate Reality is taken to be absolutely transcendent should concede the existence, even if impermanent, of some agent of initiation into the path of knowledge leading to the transcendent experience. There is nothing built into the causal chain operating at the lower level that can account for the initial point of transition from an unenlightened state to that state of ultimate realisation. Such an initiating agent must necessarily be 'gracious' in some sense. To what extent does Sankara accept this idea?

It is true that in one or two places Sankara does refer to a 'gradual liberation' (*krama-mukti*), where devotion and meditation are expected to lead to the Brahma-world, in which there will be the gradual attainment of perfect knowledge. But essentially Sankara's system is based on a 'leap theory', which ultimately abandons all possible 'means' of release; it is a realisation in which the self becomes what it essentially is. This still leaves the process with the need for an initiating agent. And in just a few passages Sankara acknowledges that 'the grace of the Lord' is responsible for this initial turning of the soul towards such a proper knowledge of its essential being. On Gita 2.39, for example, he comments: 'You have to sever the bond of *karma* only by attaining that knowledge which is caused by the grace of the Lord' (*iśvara-prasāda*). Similarly, attainment of the final goal is said to be by the Lord's grace: 'Then, by his grace you will obtain supreme peace and attain my supreme eternal abode.'[3] Elsewhere, however, he asserts that such a description is merely for the purpose of devout meditation. In this Sutra-commentary he bases such a theology of grace on the fact that 'scripture teaches it'. Just as 'the Superintendent of all actions, the Witness residing in all beings and the Cause of all intelligence' permits apparent bondage to occur, 'so we must assume that final release also is brought about through knowledge caused by the grace of the Lord'.[4]

More usually in Sankara's writings it is 'the grace of the spiritual preceptor', the Guru, that is said to be immediately responsible for guiding the soul into the way of ultimate enlightenment. Even in the above passage, Sankara seems to speak of the Lord's grace more by way of concession to the explicit teaching of the Sutra, and its reference to scripture, rather than intending to state an ultimate truth.

Such a suspicion is confirmed both by his attitude to the human side of the divine grace, that is devotion, which he takes in an entirely provisional sense, and by his strained interpretation of texts which should more naturally be taken as declarations of divine grace. One such is found in Kaṭha-Upanishad: 'Through the grace of the Creator (*dhātuḥ-prasādāt*) he beholds the greatness of the Self.'[5] Sankara interprets this as 'through the tranquillity of the senses . . .'.

He consistently maintains this absolutist interpretation when he comes to the following statement three verses later: 'This Self is not to be obtained by instruction, nor by intelligence, nor by much hearing [of scripture]. Whom he choses, by him he is obtained. To him the Self reveals his own nature.' All this choosing, obtaining, and revealing is explained by Sankara in terms of the one Self: 'That [the seeker's Self], which he [the seeker] chooses [or prays to], by that very Self (which is the seeker himself) his own Self is obtained and known. . . . The meaning is that to a person without desire who seeks for the Self alone, that Self becomes known of its own accord. . . . It reveals its own nature.' On the same verse in Muṇḍaka-Upanishad[6] he suggests that the attainment of this Self, which is 'by its very nature always attained', is due to the seeker's 'praying for this realisation to the exclusion of everything else'.

That Sankara has generally been consistent throughout these commentaries cannot be denied; and much of the material preceding these verses in the Upanishads concerned is about the search into the inner self. But in these texts it would surely be more faithful to the actual wording to take the self which 'chooses', which is 'obtained and reveals itself', as the supreme Self, distinct from the seeking self. This then makes it possible to give a more natural interpretation of the words three verses earlier, taking them as a direct reference tô 'the grace of the Creator', which is the appropriate basis for seeing 'the greatness of the Self'. But such a concept of personal grace can never play more than a concessional role in Sankara's scheme, any more than the idea of Brahman's personal attributes. Presumably this explains his almost cursory treatment of passages in the Gita in which such a concept is expounded.

When we turn to his treatment of the *avatāra*-doctrine in the Gita the situation is very similar. Parrinder has rightly pointed out that 'the Avatār doctrine, . . . as illustrated in the Epic [including the Gita] and later works, seems to demand some degree of [theistic] transcendence. The Avatār is a heavenly being, who comes to earth to manifest grace, to restore right and destroy wrong. Such transcendence, though found in Vedic and popular religion, is not harmonious with Vedantic monism.'[7] This seems to be the reason for Sankara's general reluctance to take very seriously the Gita's texts which refer to the Lord's *avatāras.*

On the other hand, in his introduction to the Gita and during his commentary on the Sutras,[8] Sankara has expressed some ideas on this doctrine. The following are his more important points:

1. An incarnate appearance of the Lord encourages emulation in his followers. Loyal devotion will result in the sincere attempt to follow the Lord's example, as the Lord himself urged Arjuna to do when he thought of giving up his duty as a protector of his society. In this way each person will engage in the social action required of him by his birth, but carrying out his duties in a spirit of worship, with his mind centred on his Lord. This, however, will only apply as long as a person remains unenlightened by that ultimate knowledge of his identity with the supreme Self.

2. The 'original Creator', Viṣṇu-Nārāyaṇa, also assumed an embodied state in order to maintain the established social order. He came 'to preserve the earthly Brāhman and the earth's spiritual life'. This is usually taken to mean the Vedic cult and scriptures. But Sankara also says that the intention was 'to help the world at large', and 'to prevent it from becoming a void (*śūnya*)'.[9] There may well be a veiled reference to the Buddhist movement here, for there is no doubt that Sankara felt the need to preserve orthodox Hinduism against the threat of Buddhism, even though he himself clearly incorporated some features of that movement.

3. The 'descent' is also intended 'to gratify his devout worshippers, whenever he pleases'. Whenever the highest Lord is spoken of as though possessing qualities that are found in the effects of which he is really the Cause, such descriptions may be taken as merely 'for the purposes of devout meditation'. In reality, any such manifestation of the Lord will have been created out of his illusory *māyā.* To speak of the Lord's 'special place of residence' will likewise be true from the point of view of devotion only. In reality the supreme Being 'abides in his own glory only'.[10]

4. The descent is not really a form of new revelation according to Sankara for it can do no more than summarise the essence of Vedic, or Vedantic revelation.[11] When Sankara insists that nothing novel must be

ascribed to the Krishna-revelation, he is implying also that definite limits should be set to any ideas of special divine grace being made available in this manifestation.

5. When Sankara describes the descent of Krishna as intended to enlighten souls concerning their oneness with the supreme Self, he comes nearest to acknowledging the ultimate reality of the descent itself. It is because Krishna was able to realise his absolute identity with the Transcendent, because he was not subject to the defect of an obscuring intellect (*āvaraṇa-doṣa*), because he had his *māyā*-power fully under his control, because he was endowed with absolute omniscience, a perfect knowledge of his own supreme Being, that he was able to lead others from the stage of lower devotion up to the highest state of enlightenment. 'The spirit of complete devotion [though in itself only useful for leading men to the world of the gods, also] leads to purity of mind. Then the man whose mind is pure is competent to set out on the path of knowledge.'[12] Sankara admits that it is far more difficult to reach this higher path of 'identity with the Imperishable and contemplation of the supreme Reality'. But the realisation of supreme Bliss, as well as the encouragement of the Lord (Krishna), always accompanies such knowledge, making the more difficult path infinitely worthwhile.

6. Then there are various qualifications that Sankara makes concerning the incarnations. (a) Krishna is to be understood only 'as if embodied' (*dehavan-iva*).[13] It should not be thought that he is incarnate 'as the world' (*lokavat*) imagines an embodiment to be. (b) In fact he only 'appears to be born', while in reality it is by means of his illusory *māyā*-power that he so appears. His body is 'formed of this *māyā*', for in reality he is the 'unborn Lord of all beings'.[14] (c) It is only the ignorant who imagine that previous to this *avatāra* embodiment he has been 'unmanifest'. In reality he is 'the ever-luminous Lord', the 'indestructible', 'eternal, intelligent, free'. (d) To incarnate himself in this way the supreme Being 'brought Krishna into being with a part of himself' (*amśena-sambabhuva*).[15] In that the Avatār has been held even by Sankara's followers to be a full manifestation of the highest Lord, some commentators have had to paraphrase this wording rather inaccurately. (e) Then Sankara also comments—following the Gita itself fairly closely— that the transcendent being hidden behind the incarnation 'is not manifest to all people; that is to say, I am manifest only to the few who are my devotees. I am veiled [to all others] by my illusory activity.'[16] It should not be difficult for all Vedantins to go along with this idea. Ramanuja, however, interprets this to mean simply that people without insight see only a great prince, only the embodied form with which

Krishna has been temporarily associated. Thus, even in this verse apparently so easy of interpretation, their variant understanding of *māyā* leads to divergence.

Although we began by suggesting that the radical monist position seems to call for the notion of some kind of agent to lead the soul initially into the path of enlightenment, it is clear that the concept of the 'Lord's grace' takes a negligible role in Sankara's scheme. Taken seriously, such a Lord introduces an intolerable anomaly to the absolutist system. Sankara's references to 'the grace of the Lord' are, therefore, largely a matter of concession to the teaching of scripture, wherever the text cannot possibly be interpreted in a monistic sense. Perhaps there is also a recognition that the soul's first step on the road to enlightenment does require some such explanation.

The doctrine of the gracious Lord's coming in embodied form poses a similar dilemma for Sankara's absolutism. But he is able to interpret it in just the same way as he does the other provisional elements in his system, in particular the concept of creation and causal relationships. In fact, we shall see just how precisely the doctrines of creation and incarnation are made to complement each other by the three Vedantins, each in a different way. Sankara had no intention of denying these doctrines altogether; yet the 'realities' they indicate must be based on illusory *māyā* having no ultimate existence.

RAMANUJA

While Ramanuja's attitude to the supreme Person's grace is strikingly at variance with that of Sankara—in that he not only recognises man's need of divine grace, but also ascribes the most ultimately real status to it—the role of that grace in his system is not without its complications. As with other Vedantins, Ramanuja's teaching is generally based on the assumption that human experience is the result of the causal chain of *karma*. Even in the religious life, different forms of devotion result in different degrees of benefit. There is a sense, suggests Ramanuja, in which this principle of attaining only what is deserved extends even into the higher devotional sphere: 'For it is to the one who constantly remembers me and whose thought never wanders to any other object that I am easily attainable.'[17] Similarly, in his Sutra commentary, it is possible to say that 'the meditating devotee receives the reward of meditation, that is, ultimate release—which means attaining the supreme Person'.[18] There are however, sufficient grounds in Ramanuja's writings for denying that he sees no divine grace outside of the working of karmic law. The 'reward of release' is 'a gift received from the supreme Person himself'. Then, basing his interpretation on the Sutra's words, 'because only that is possible' Ramanuja expounds this gracious gift as follows: 'For it is only he, the omnipotent, omniscient and greatly generous one, who having been worshipped . . . is pleased to grant different kinds of enjoyment and final liberation; and this means attaining his own essential nature.'[19]

Effort within the operation of *karma* can never be quite commensurate with so great a gift. What should be noted here is Ramanuja's emphasis that just as the ultimate means to release must be the gracious Lord himself, so the attaining of his being is the ultimate End. Clearly something other than the just-desert principle must be involved in the attaining of such an End. Ramanuja is well aware that this is not a state of being that the soul can earn for itself, however intense its devotion, or exalted its worship.

Thus he can write (continuing the Gita-commentary quotation above) in a remarkable passage stressing the supreme Person's own concern for an inseparable union with his devotees: 'I am easily attained, for I am unable to bear separation from my devotee [who also feels unable to live without me]. This means that I myself choose him, and I myself grant him that fruition of his worship that can result in his attaining me; I destroy all obstacles to this end and I make myself very dear to him.' Ramanuja himself does not use the term 'uncaused grace' (though some of his followers do); divine grace is, nevertheless, the sole means of the soul's release. Significantly, Ramanuja confirms this thought by quoting the Upanishadic text that Sankara brought unnaturally into line with his monistic outlook: 'He whom this [Self] chooses, by him can he be attained.' Ramanuja had clearly stated just prior to this what it is that is to be attained: 'It is I myself who am to be attained, not merely some aspect of my nature, such as my sovereignty.'[20] Such an exalted objective makes necessary the grace of that same supreme Goal.

If the supreme Being himself is made the only ultimately valid means and the only ultimately worthy End, why does he not ensure that everyone is saved? Ramanuja was well aware of this dilemma posed by a theology of the Lord's supreme grace, and the related issue of the soul's freedom of action. But no commentator could take the Bhagavad-Gita seriously as an authoritative source and avoid the conclusion that whatever may be the role of the just-desert principle, in the end the supreme Person is responsible for the soul's action, generally through the subordinate agency of *karma* and Nature. He is even more responsible as both the means and the End of the soul's liberation. Ramanuja's exposition of the Lord's grace in relation to man's effort gives great weight to human action and devotion, but in the last analysis he attributes the attaining of the highest Goal to the divine grace alone.

This echoes correctly the final message of the Gita itself as expressed in 18.54–70. In this final passage the Lord's 'most exalted saying' (*paramam-vacaḥ*), 'of all the most mysterious', is said to be, 'I love you well'. In response to this the devotee is to bear the Lord in mind, love and worship him, by means of which he will come to the Lord, for he is dear to the devotee. In fact the devotee is to 'give up all his duties' and take the Lord as his 'only refuge'; he alone can set the soul free from all sin.

Now the question which has been a matter of such fierce contention among the followers of Ramanuja, and still generates no little emotion, is—did the Master himself teach that there is a path distinct from and superior to that of even the most intense devotion? Is the devotee to give up all hope of any ultimate benefit other than through the Lord's unmerited grace, and so to cast himself (*prapatti*) in utter abandon on the Lord's grace, taking refuge (*śaraṇāgati*) in his mercy alone? It is to this question that we now turn, though it does overlap with some of the issues raised in the next chapter.

The Gita's verse most relevant to this question is that usually called the 'final great text' (*carama-śloka*): 'Give up all duties (*dharmas*), turn to me as sole refuge: I will set you free from all your sins.'[21] Ramanuja suggests two ways of interpretation:

First he interprets the *dharmas* that are to be given up as the three methods (*yogas*)—works, knowledge and devotion. What is to be renounced is not action as such, but the improper attitude of mind possible when engaged in religious methods. No action should be done hoping to gain some benefit for oneself, or in the belief that such actions, even devotional acts, are one's own, or with the arrogant idea that we ourselves are the principal agents in such actions. He also goes on to say that the three wrong attitudes of mind mentioned above should be replaced by 'continuously thinking of [the Lord as] the agent, as the object of worship [and of all other action], as the Goal to be attained, and as the means to this'. In any case it is not works as such, but attachment to works which are to be given up. 'It is not possible for one who is embodied to give up works altogether. He who has renounced the benefits of works is said to have renounced works.'

Then Ramanuja suggests an alternative explanation of this 'final verse'. Arjuna may have been depressed by the thought that he was not fit to make a start on the path of devotion, and there would be insufficient time to perform all the expiatory ceremonies necessary to remove those many sins that were an obstacle to such devotion. It is these expiatory rites that are here classed as duties (*dharmas*) and which may be given up: 'In order to make a successful start to your way of devotion, surrender yourself and find refuge in me alone; for I am supremely merciful, the refuge of all without any consideration of their differences of birth, etc, and I am an ocean of parental affection for those who become dependent on me. I shall set you free from all your sins . . . which are an obstacle to your setting out on the way of devotion.'

This latter interpretation certainly gives *some* basis for the later Vaiṣṇava doctrine that sheer surrender (*prapatti*) transcends all the three traditional 'methods'—works, knowledge and devotion—as a means of attaining the Lord. But can it be taken as a fourth method quite independent of and superior to the other three, even superseding them because only this 'surrender' method makes divine grace open to everyone?

The issue is further complicated by the rather marked difference of style found in his formal works from that in his devotional works, one of which is the prose-poem, *Taking-Refuge* (*Śaraṇāgati-Gadya*). Some recent scholars find the discrepancy so great as to make the authorship of the devotional works questionable, which seems a rather unnecessary conclusion. However more devotionally intense the style of *Taking-Refuge* may be, there is nothing in its teaching that cannot be taken as a consistent elaboration of what Ramanuja has written in his commentary on the Gita and in some passages of his Vedārtha-Samgraha. His use of terms like 'highest devotion' and 'supreme devotion' (*para-bhakti, parama-bhakti*) need not be taken with the technical sense they later acquired.

The point which seems to be missed in much of this Vaiṣṇava debate is Ramanuja's conviction that the Object of worship and meditation being the supreme Person he is, every devotee should also recognise (whether at the outset or in the last resort) that just as his own being is utterly dependent upon that supreme Being, so the basis of his life of devotion, his acts of sacrifice and meditation, is the grace of that all-determining Lord. It is his will to be accessible to men, and that by a variety of means. But such 'methods' are all to be 'renounced' in the sense that none can be effective of itself, apart from the Lord's grace active in it, and apart from conscious recognition of the soul's dependence on that divine grace. Thus, even though Ramanuja never explicitly wrote of a surrender-method as a separate cultic act in which a person is absolved of the need to perform any other duties, the surrender-doctrine is quite fundamental to his theological scheme. And just as we find a continuity in Ramanuja's thought (with devotion to the supreme Person and his grace as the determining feature) leading from Vedic sacrifice, through Vedantic knowledge and meditation, up to Vaiṣṇava devotional practices, so we can see a valid continuity between Ramanuja's most formal writings, his Gita-commentary, his more devotional works, and in a certain sense even the extreme surrender-method of his later followers.

In general, then, Ramanuja finds no problem in allowing that life is determined by the law of *karma*. It is initiated by the Lord himself and thus good works are duly rewarded by the Lord, who is always pleased by any such service done to him. This normal pattern of the religious life is reflected in most of Ramanuja's writings. At various places in his writings, however, there are clear intimations of the soul's need to cast everything on the efficacy of divine grace, to recognise that his whole being is grounded in this grace.

Thus in Ramanuja's thought the Lord's supremacy includes the orderly functioning of the universe. But it is equally clear that the Lord himself transcends this normal order of things, so that his grace makes it possible even for those who should by right be excluded from his presence to become acceptable. In the last resort the Lord's grace is transcendent to any of the appointed means by which men may approach him.

The Lord's descents (*avatāras*) and embodiments can be taken as special evidences of his gracious attitude. Ramanuja took such incarnate existence not only with his usual realism, but also as a necessity for finite souls in view of the transcendent Goal that is their objective. He suggests the following reasons for the divine descents:

1. They were prompted by the Lord's compassionate concern. Thus he writes: 'Being a vast ocean of boundless compassion, condescension, affection and generosity . . . he assumed bodily forms'; 'overwhelmed by his affection for those seeking refuge in him', 'the most compassionate Lord' thus embodies himself.[22] The act of 'descending' and becoming embodied is for Ramanuja a concrete expression of that graciousness he attributes to the Lord.

2. There is the practical desire 'to help the world'. This Viṣṇu-Purāṇa idea is reflected in one of the two references to the saving action of the Lord found in Ramanuja's Vedartha-Samgraha: 'The supreme Person, while remaining the supreme Brahman, descended to the earth in order to rescue the entire universe.'[23] Or as he puts it in the Gita-commentary:[24] 'These descents have been in order to relieve the earth of

its burden [of evil] . . .', here picking up the Gita's phrase 'for the world's welfare'.

3. Elaborating this idea of an intervention for the general benefit of mankind, Ramanuja takes up the Gita's claim that it is especially for 'the protection of the virtuous', and interprets this to mean both those who are 'devoted to *dharma*' (social and religious duty), and those who are 'devoted to me', that is, 'those who turn to the Lord as their only refuge, who feel that without him they cannot live or support their own existence'.[25] The other side of this action is the destruction of those who are against *dharma*. But as this can also be accomplished by the Lord merely willing it, it is only of secondary import. According to Ramanuja the salvation of his dear ones is by far the more important motive.

4. His descent is not only for their protection, however, but that he may become accessible to them. 'The supreme Brahman, this Nārāyaṇa, the supreme Person, when he created the entire universe from motionless stones up to the god Brahmā, remained in his essential nature and is thus inaccessible even by means of meditation, worship and suchlike acts. . . . But being a vast ocean of mercy . . . still without loss of his essential nature, he has assumed embodied forms . . . and in these different forms he has descended repeatedly to the various worlds these creatures inhabit, where he has been [accessible to] worship.'[26]

5. As a result of such worship and prayer to him, 'he has granted the desires of these various creatures—merit, wealth, pleasure and ultimate release, according to each one's wish'. Again following the lead of the Gita, Ramanuja broadens this 'wish-fulfilling' aspect of the Lord's work to include anyone at all who approaches him for help. 'The distinctions between people do not even enter into consideration.'[27]

6. Another result of his embodied existence is that the Lord, 'by making himself visible to all mankind', has been able to accomplish 'such divine acts as captivate the minds and eyes of all'.[28] In other passages it is the Lord's beauty and glory that are said to have been especially manifest in the incarnations: '[I] have made myself visible to the eyes of all . . . and have made the entire world shine with my unbounded and incomparable glory, and have gratified the entire universe with my own loveliness.'[29]

7. Another important aspect of Ramanuja's Avatār-doctrine is his emphasis, found also in Madhva, that the Lord embodies himself by an act of sheer will, not because such a body is a necessary effect of *karma*, as is the case with ordinary mortals. The supreme Being is quite free of any such compulsion.

8. Elsewhere the reality of his embodiment is stressed, by saying that it

is as real and physical as the embodiment of Arjuna himself. When, however, the Gita says that just like Arjuna, Krishna has also known many births, which Ramanuja takes as the basis of the reality of his embodiment, is it not implied that Krishna has experienced a succession of births due to the bondage of *karma*? Ramanuja would no doubt reply to this by asserting again that such a series of births is, in the Lord's case, not caused by the effects of *karma*. That such embodiments are not thought of as mere appearances either, is illustrated by the following description: 'He has assumed various bodily forms, which on each occasion conforms to the generic structure of one of the various species of creatures. . . .'[30]

9. The reality that Ramanuja attributes to these embodiments is further confirmed by his interpretation of the Gita's statement that it is 'by my own *māyā* that I consort with Nature . . . and come into existence'.[31] Ramanuja takes this in one of its less common meanings as 'knowledge'. Thus, 'it is by my [controlling?] knowledge that I am able to embody myself'. This means, goes on Ramanuja, 'by my will' or 'according to my own purpose' (*ātma-samkalpa*).

10. This is further elaborated by saying that the Lord's embodiment did not entail the slightest loss of his essential nature, it was 'without giving up all those characteristic qualities that belong to the Lord of all'.[32] But he makes no attempt to explain the mystery of how such a sovereign Being can be embodied in all reality without suffering any loss of his essential nature. It is assumed that the Lord's incomparable power is sufficient to accomplish this.

The tension involved in such a doctrine is not so severe in Ramanuja's teaching, however, because it merely brings into sharper focus what he has been asserting throughout his writings in a less particular form. The whole universe is an embodiment of the supreme Being, a manifestation of his glory, the instrument of his will. And as he never tires of asserting, the 'modification' that takes place in his universal body does not affect his essential perfection of being in the slightest. Is it not possible that this cosmic dimension of the supreme Being's embodiment derives, in Ramanuja's thought, from its individualised form in the Avatār-doctrine, so central to the experience of the Vaiṣṇava community?

Krishna's Descent was not the only form of embodiment in that tradition, of course. As well as a number of other Avatārs, there were also the special Vaiṣṇava 'emanations' (*vyūha*), and the divine embodiments thought to take place in the images around which worship revolved. No doubt all these too played their part in formulating the conviction of a cosmic embodiment. It is a remarkable fact, however, that neither the special Vaiṣṇava emanations, nor the image-embodiments feature in Ramanuja's writings as more than passing or indirect references. Perhaps his vivid descriptions of the glorious and beautiful form of the Lord reflect the reverence he felt for those images upon which the Lord's devotees focused their meditation. But the more compelling 'image' for Ramanuja is that of the gracious descents, such as the embodiment witnessed to by the Gita. Taking this embodiment with such seriousness, it was impossible that the utter dependence of the devotee upon that Lord's grace could fail to be taken with equal conviction.

MADHVA

Madhva alone makes his theistic attitude towards divine grace quite clear at the outset of his Sutra-commentary. Having opened with a brief but impressive eulogy of the exalted Nārāyaṇa, he goes on immediately to an interpretation of the 'therefore' of the first Sutra. This enquiry into the being of Brahman is possible, he says, because it is 'through the grace of the all-pervading Lord'. He concludes that it is 'only by means of his perfect grace that the soul attains release'.

In some respects we find that Madhva brings out more explicitly even than Ramanuja why it is that such dependence upon the Lord's grace is a necessary element in his theological scheme. As the supremely self-determining Lord, in relation to whom all beings are other-determined, his grace is essential to the realisation of their destinies. In particular, the soul's release is the gift of this independent Lord, just as he is the ultimate Cause of the soul being 'obscured' and in a state of bondage. This means that the 'knowledge' leading to release is also the gift of the Lord, for his essential being is quite outside the reach of the soul, no matter how intensely devout. 'The light revealing him comes only through his grace . . . "The glorious Lord is eternally unmanifest to perception; but for the grace of this supreme Lord, who could see him, the immeasurable and almighty Being."'[33]

To Madhva, however, any system that defines the soul's condition essentially in terms of ignorance, and denies the reality of its bondage, immediately precludes any authentic role for divine grace; an inner enlightenment becomes quite sufficient. In his system, therefore, knowledge means at least initially the recognition of the supremacy of the Lord, and the soul's experience of dependence upon that independent Being. But Madhva's liberating knowledge cannot be limited to such a simple view, nor is its relationship with the Lord's grace without a certain ambiguity, as we now see by outlining some of the ideas associated with his doctrine of the Lord's grace.

Madhva finds no difficulty in accepting the concept of 'just-deserts', which we have already noted as of some importance in the Gita. Commenting, for example, on the verse that says, 'In whatever way people approach me, so do I return their love', Madhva writes: 'According as they seek my grace hoping for release or with a desire to attain the heavenly region . . . so do I give to them, I bestow on them only such things as they wish to receive, or whatever their worship and knowledge merits; never differently from what they deserve or pray for.'[34] Obviously this could set very stringent limits to the operation of divine grace, unless some further concept of the transcendent character of that grace is introduced.

It is possible to interpret Madhva's distinctive doctrine of inherent characteristics determining each soul's nature, actions and thus karmic associations as confirmation of the need for the operation of grace. For this means that what is both the inherent qualities and the *karma* resulting from them is the Lord's gift determined by his gracious will. Systems of divine determinism will usually have a corresponding doctrine of divine grace. And by making it an *inner* determinism, a determined nature which may become later a recipient of divine grace, Madhva went some way towards resolving the conflict between karmic law (in which the soul determines its own condition) and merely external determinism. It was at least an attempt to cater for both the supremacy of the Lord and the freedom of the soul.

That Madhva intended to include both the soul's responsible action and the Lord's supreme grace is further confirmed by various aspects of Madhva's teaching on the operation of divine grace. In the first place he frequently describes it as given in response to the soul's prior devotion, though we have seen that this is also a part of the Gita's thought. Madhva, however, sometimes puts the idea that 'the Lord has to be moved to graciousness' quite starkly. He says, for example: 'Devotion alone leads to the supreme Being, devotion alone shows him.'[35] He does go on to qualify this as the Lord's independent response, though given 'in consideration of the soul's devotion'. Similarly he bases his explanation of the Lord accepting the worship of people 'even of sinful birth' not on the Lord's freely offered compassion, but on the 'very great virtue of devotion'.[36]

In this Viṣṇu-Tattva-Nirṇaya he uses an analogy that confirms his grace-by-way-of-response idea. The context is the repudiation of the monist doctrine of identity: 'Those in high places respond with the opposite of love towards their inferiors if the latter assert identity with them. Kings put down a subject who claims "I am the king". . . . There is no love equal to that of Viṣṇu, the adorable One, towards a devotee who recognises his surpassing excellence. By thus pleasing him all devotees attain liberation.'[37]

Then Madhva also speaks of the experience of the Lord's grace as needing to be preceded by the soul's knowledge of the Lord. Thus in the same opening passage in his Sutra-commentary that asserts the soul's need of the Lord's grace in order to gain that knowledge which leads to release, he also says: 'Without knowing him his supreme grace cannot be obtained . . . by knowledge only is the full measure of the Lord's grace obtainable . . . only by his perfect grace is the soul liberated.'[38] This, however, should probably not be taken as a contradiction of the divine initiative, but rather as reflecting the interplay of knowledge and grace at the various stages of the soul's progress towards perfect liberation. The soul's initial knowledge, also given by the Lord, leads to a recognition of the greatness of the Lord and of its own dependent state. This in turn results in a deeper experience of the Lord's grace, and so on.

What Madhva frequently asserts is that the Lord himself is responsible both for the soul's initial glimpse of the Lord's greatness, as well as for its progress in understanding and thus for a fuller sense of dependence at each stage. But does the ontological relationship underlying Madhva's account of such spiritual progress provide the kind of grounding for the soul in the Lord's being that makes this gracious devotional relationship an appropriate culminating stage?

There is another aspect of this spiritual process in Madhva's system that differs from Ramanuja's. The ultimate knowledge of the Lord is often described as having the character of 'direct realisation' (*aparokṣa-jñāna*), which transcends the devotional relationship as such. Invariably when this immediate experience is mentioned there is reference to both the greatness and the grace of the Lord along with it. In other words, his greatness is an otherness that requires a kind of direct, unmediated vision; and such 'knowledge' seems extrinsic to the soul at least to the extent that it requires the Lord's 'supreme grace', the 'full measure of his grace'. Thus: 'Direct knowledge of the supreme Lord can be gained only through his grace.'[39]

It is such declarations of the need for the transcendent vision that more truly fit into the ontological relationship between soul and Lord that Madhva presumes as the grounding for the spiritual life and the experience of divine grace. They are related as original to reflection. So Madhva's followers describe the kind of knowledge the reflection can gain as having 'the immediacy of the Original' (*bimba-aparokṣa*). 'This vivid flash-like intuitive perception of one's own Bimba marks the journey's end.... Its intensity and vividness vary according to the innate capacity of the selves.... The supreme Being is pleased to reveal himself to his devotees through sheer grace.'[40]

The extent to which the soul-Lord ontological remoteness in Madhva's system makes necessary an act of special grace and transcendent vision is seen in another aspect of his tradition—the converse side of the same idea. The Lord's grace, says Madhva, is quite inoperative without the mediating grace of the Lord's consort, Lakṣmī. 'Unless her grace is secured, there is no grace of the Lord. In the absence of her grace there is no way of attaining him.'[41] Here again we see the extent to which the intermediary is essential to Madhva's system.

Finally, we may note the way in which Madhva deals with the 'final great saying' of the Gita[42] and the question of giving up everything in favour of the Lord's grace. In agreement with Ramanuja, he cannot allow that the Gita intends all duties to be given up literally. This cannot be the meaning here, Madhva contends, for elsewhere there is the explicit command to continue with action, just as the Lord himself does. It does intend that all evil deeds, and 'every undertaking which may not be pleasing to the supreme Lord', or that is 'not meant for the delight of the Lord' should be given up. The Lord's devotee also renounces everything in the sense that he 'offers every undertaking for the acceptance of the Lord' and recognises that 'even the possibility of renouncing other things wholly depends upon the grace of the Lord'. So that 'by the grace of the supreme Self he is content with him alone and has given up all longing for other things'. He 'rests upon the Lord', realising that 'not even a single act ought to be done without feeling the grace of the Lord'.[43]

But the most important kind of renunciation that Madhva sees in this 'final verse' (as does Ramanuja) is the abandoning of 'the fruits of all duties performed', and the 'sense of being an independent agent'. Thus basing his very existence on the Lord's grace, the devotee has a 'clear perception of the supremacy of the Lord, sets his mind on him, loves him above all other things, and offers everything to him. Such devotees worship from spontaneous delight in him, having the faith that he will protect them, with the constant remembrance, "I belong to him". This is the way of surrender (*śaraṇa-āgati*) to Viṣṇu, and leads to liberation.'[44] Whether or not Madhva sets up for himself an ontological ground to this spiritual experience that makes for a less easily integrated scheme, at the experimental level there is a quite unambiguous sense of dependence upon the Lord's grace, at every stage.

Turning to Madhva's teaching on the supreme Person's descent and incarnate existence, we find Ramanuja's ideas or those that are common to Vaiṣṇava tradition, being echoed in more than one aspect of this doctrine. The principal difference between the Lord's embodiment and that of the soul in its cycle of rebirths is the Lord's freedom from all determination by the power of *karma.* This is but one aspect of Madhva's Avatār-doctrine that fits in very neatly with other supreme qualities that we noted he ascribed to the Lord. A *karma*-body will have the three essential constituents of Nature—heavy darkness, vigorous light, pure goodness—in varying degrees. Even though the Lord makes use of Nature in his incarnations, his body cannot be so constituted. For this would mean his body being subject to all manner of limitations, whereas even in his Avatār-form the Lord retains his essential character as the supreme Being.

Perhaps this implies that Madhva 'refuses to invest the Avatārs of popular theology with any material vesture', on the grounds that this would make 'the unlimited limited'.[45] Although Madhva certainly qualifies the Lord's embodiments in every possible way, he did not think of them as being less than real, in the manner of Sankara's *māyā*-body. In fact, he interprets the Gita's statement that embodiment is caused by *māyā* to mean 'out of Nature (*prakṛti*) [of which the Lord's consort is the personified form], under his control'.[46]

What he does stress is that the Lord did not become embodied because of any kind of necessity. We have already noted that there was no karmic necessity. Neither was there the need to secure some kind of benefit to himself. Because of this freedom from desire for any personal benefit, the self-determining Lord was able to create for himself whichever kind of body he wished, a body perfectly suited to his purposes.

Naturally Madhva follows the Gita's lead in seeing the well-being of the world-order, in particular the protection of virtuous devotees and destruction of the unrighteous, as the intention lying behind all the Lord's embodiments, though he does not seem to feel the need to explain this intention in quite the detail that we found in Ramanuja. What he does assert even in this case is the Lord's freedom from necessity: 'His birth was not a necessary act [even] for protecting his virtuous ones; being one who acts according to his own will, even this [protecting act] is from his own playfulness, prompted by his inner nature.'[47]

In a similar way Madhva teaches that the motive prompting the Lord's embodiments is precisely that prompting the creation and eventual dissolution of the world—the sporting playfulness of his inner nature.

He also expresses the difference of Avatār to other living beings by reference to their different relationships to the supreme Being. Both Avatār and soul can be called 'parts' of the supreme Being. But while each Avatār is an 'essential part' (*svarūpa-amśa*), sharing the essential being of the highest Lord, the soul is merely a 'distinct part'. The difference between these two is like the difference between the tiny fire-fly and 'the great Fire at the end of the world'.[48]

Madhva emphasises too that every recognised Avatār, even such great beings as Vyāsa, compiler of the Vedas, is comprised of this 'essential' nature of the Lord to an equal degree. No distinctions should be maintained between the great Avatārs and those whose praises are sung to a lesser extent, calling some 'perfect' and some 'partial'.[49] On the other hand Madhva did not acknowledge image-embodiments to be of the same essential character, as Ramanuja is said to have done.

Then he described the Avatārs in terms suggesting that their reality is of a rather different material nature from other beings. The Descents are, claimed Madhva, 'merely manifestations'; or as he puts it: 'In the case of Vāsudeva [the embodied Viṣṇu] origination (*utpatti*) means merely manifestation.... The body of Lord Hari is unoriginated and eternal. Beings like the deity Brahmā, have bodies that are not eternal. Other beings are all the product of birth in a primary sense.'[50]

Similarly, when such descended-bodies of the Lord are removed from the earth it should not be thought that there is dissolution (*laya*) in the manner of the dissolution of creation at the end of the age. The 'fulness' or 'perfection' of the Lord's essential being that we noted in the previous chapter is attributed by Madhva to his Avatār-forms too. They also are 'all-perfect, all-unlimited, all-incomparable, all-immeasurable'.[51] Even in his embodiments the Lord's nature differs radically from that possessed by other beings. His transcendent being remains intact.

The tension that Madhva seems to find in reconciling such transcendent features with the materiality of the embodiments reflects his more fundamental dichotomy between the transcendence of the Lord's independent being and the determined, limited being of the universe. In Madhva's case also, therefore, incarnation-doctrine runs parallel with creation-doctrine; in both, the problem of reconciling transcendent Lord and finite existence is rather acute; in both the 'sheer will' of the Lord is thought to be sufficient explanation. Unlike Sankara, however, in Madhva there is virtually no loss of the experimental quality in the relation of the divine grace to the soul, and especially in the grace felt to be manifest in the incarnations of the transcendent Lord.

10 Means of Approach to The Transcendent End

The Vedantic enquiry is pursued within a very definite religious context. As the 'later exegesis' (*uttara-mīmāmsā*) it takes for granted the 'previous exegesis' (*pūrva-mīmāmsā*), even using much of its exegetical method. But these Ritualists attributed ultimate value to the Vedic duties. Every Vedantin, therefore, had to make quite clear how he felt Brahma-knowledge related to ritual duty. In what sense was the Vedic ritual system a preparation for knowing the transcendent Being? Or put differently—how does doing relate to being? And how does the body of Vedic scripture, including the Upanishads, mediate this Brahma-knowledge that leads in some sense to Brahma-being?

There was also the system of meditative discipline evolved for weaning the self away from its attachment to material existence and focusing its attention on the supreme Self. Was this discipline a necessary part of the process of acquiring Brahma-knowledge? The question was further complicated by a variety of sectarian practices, of both ritual and meditative types, and reinforced by distinctive doctrines. Do these also comprise part of the means of approaching the supreme Being? In particular, how does devotion to the supreme Person relate to transcendent Brahma-knowledge?

SANKARA

Sankara asserted that Brahma-knowledge follows immediately on grasping the proper meaning of the absolute identity of self and Brahman as revealed in scripture. As we saw, however, there is a moment of transcendent, intuitive realisation when even 'knowledge' no longer seems the proper descriptive term. It too is transcended as fire burns itself out, not only the fuel that feeds it. The ultimate identity is all that is left. Then as soon as this oneness is realised, 'all further expectation comes to an end, and no further effort is necessary'.[1]

It should not be forgotten, though, that the process of enquiry and effort preceding this is lengthy and elaborate. In a sense it is the culmination of this period of intense preparation in the course of which a radical renunciation is required. But being a transcendent experience, it is in reality attained 'without the help of any direct means'.[2] In fact part of this renunciation is 'the giving up of all such means' (*sarva-sādhana-sannyāsa*). So, then, renunciation of the world and acceptance of the meditative discipline may be a necessary element in the approach to the knowledge of Brahman, but it can never properly be called a 'means' to such knowledge. All such means are quite incommensurate with the transcendent End.

Sankara begins his Brahma-Sutra commentary with a radical interpretation of its opening statement, 'Then therefore the Brahma-enquiry'. The introductory 'then', he asserts, 'does not indicate order of succession'. An antecedent of some kind is clearly intended, but there can be no essential continuity from action to realisation. Knowledge of the Self, of its transcendent oneness, is the only valid means to such realisation.

> The result as well as the object of the enquiry differs in the two cases. The knowledge of active religious duty results in a transitory benefit. . . . The enquiry into Brahman, on the other hand, results in eternal bliss. . . . Acts of religious duty do not yet exist at the time of enquiry into them; they are something still to be accomplished, for they depend on human activity. The object of the enquiry into Brahman, on the other hand, is something already accomplished; for Brahman is eternal, and does not depend on human endeavour.

It is against the theory of the Ritualists principally that Sankara is arguing here. Their assertion that all texts merely indicating the being of Brahman are quite ancillary to the 'imperative' texts—those enjoining ritual action in particular—was based in part on their theory of language. They held that the potency of words, their effective signification, is inherent in them from eternity, not merely by usage. But when constructed in a sentence, words can only bear significantly on a fact yet to be established or a deed to be done. Children, they argued, learn things when elders by their actions indicate the meaning of words, so enabling the children to act also. Sentences are inherently functional. Thus even sentences about Brahman are either injunctive in themselves, or are connected with other texts which clearly make some action imperative.

Sankara not only found no reason why scriptural sentences should not indicate the 'established being' of Brahman, though merely indirectly. He also asserted that such 'indication' is the only proper role of language which purports to reveal Brahman's eternal being and lead to eternal bliss.

The 'antecedent conditions' (implied by 'then' in the Sutra) expected before the Brahman-inquiry can be undertaken, are not, therefore, ritual action, social duty, or any other kind of human endeavour. They are rather: 'Discrimination of what is eternal and what non-eternal; the renunciation of all desire to enjoy the fruit of one's actions, either in this world or the next; the acquiring of tranquillity, self-restraint and the other means [usually listed as discontinuance of religious ceremonies, patience in suffering, the controlling and concentrating of the mind, faith], and the desire for final release.'[3] Sankara acknowledges that up to the moment that a person becomes fully intent on release and so becomes a world-renouncing Sannyāsin, he should continue to carry out all the social duties required of him. And at the moment of liberating insight, he will certainly see that there is no *essential* connection between his life's actions and the condition of ultimate enlightenment. All action will then be renounced, absolutely, except in the case of the few who continue their social roles for the sake of unenlightened society.

In another way also Sankara did not give an entirely negative role to human action. In commenting on the first four Sutras, he is adamant that Brahman cannot be the object of action, or the object of an injunction to perform an action—not even when we are urged to meditate on, or to know this supreme Self. In the Sutra-section[4] on social duties (the so-called āśramas), however, Sankara concedes a more positive role to action. The duties required of a person up to the moment of enlightenment can help in the origination of that knowledge, even though the goals of these two are so different. The Sutra itself declares that there are scriptural texts advocating the quest of Brahman by means of 'study of the Vedas, sacrifice, gifts, penance and fasting'. Thus religious and social duties can be a 'means to the *origination* of knowledge'. For one thing, he suggests, such works help to purify the performer. And 'when impurity has been removed, knowledge begins to act'.

Taking the simile suggested by the Sutra, he says that just as horses are suitable only for pulling fast chariots, not for dragging ploughs, so social duties can help in the initial arousal of knowledge, but are entirely useless in helping to bring about the result intended by knowing the supreme Being. In particular, the person following the Gita's (*niṣ-kāma-*

karma) method of acting-without-desire-for-benefit will find such disinterested works helpful in the origination of knowledge. But even the most important sacrificial duties, 'which scripture connects with the search for knowledge', can never be other than 'remote, indirect means'. Only the spiritual states of mind that duty helps to produce, such as tranquillity and renunciation, can be of direct help in knowing that Being which transcends all empirical life.

Similarly, devotion seems to have direct usefulness as a means of approach to Brahman. The prominence of *bhakti* in the Gita meant that it had to take some positive role. But in a number of cases in his commentary Sankara changes the clear meaning of the dependent bond of trust and love intended by the Gita and interprets it as steadfast knowledge (*niṣṭha-jñāna*).[5] Elsewhere he allows the devotional bond to stand, and even describes it with attractive literary elegance, as for example in his comment on Gita 10.11 with its 'shining lamp of knowledge' metaphor. Sankara describes this by combining ideas of devotional dependence and 'knowledge of the Self', with the latter being the higher path. The usefulness of the devotional relationship is merely provisional.

> In mercy . . . I destroy the darkness of ignorance, which is that deluding knowledge caused by lack of discrimination, by the lamp of wisdom and discriminating knowledge, which is fed by the oil of pure devotion, fanned by the wind of intense meditation on myself, furnished with the wick of right intuition, purified by the cultivation of piety, chastity and other virtues, held in the inner organ which is completely detached from all worldly concerns, placed in the wind-sheltered enclosure of the mind which is withdrawn from sense-objects and unpolluted by either attachment or aversion, and shining with the light of right knowledge generated by the constant practice of concentration and meditation.

The context in the Gita where the 'shining lamp' is spoken of is without doubt the gracious initiative of the Lord in drawing the self to the knowledge of his own transcendent character. This emerges clearly in the preceding two verses and the subsequent declaration of the Lord's supremacy throughout every being in the universe, followed by the glorious vision of all beings included within the Lord's transcendent being. Yet Sankara generally finds it extremely difficult to allow any significant place either to the concept of divine grace, or to the devotional relationship thought by the theists to be established by virtue of this grace. But devotion implies a non-identical relationship, so no matter how characterised by mutual love, Sankara can see it as only a preliminary stage, to be superseded in the ultimate experience of the one Self. Dependence on, trust in, love of another being can only be a provisional means to the pure identity of Consciousness.

Sankara was far more impressed by the Upanishadic scheme of spiritual discipline—hearing, mental reflection and inner meditation. This, he believed, comes much nearer to being a direct means of approach to Brahman. But as I have already discussed these means of approach, a few supplementary points here will suffice.

Firstly, we may note some further aspects of his view of scripture (the subject of 'hearing') as a means to knowing Brahman. It is the supreme Being alone who is 'to be regarded as the special topic of all scripture'.[6] Thus, even passages ostensibly giving information about creation and suchlike secondary topics should be seen as 'serving the purpose of [indirectly] teaching Brahman', i.e. his omnipotence and similar characteristics. And it is only from scripture that this knowledge of Brahman is derived. 'The profound Brahman cannot be fathomed but with the help of scripture, for it escapes all reasoning.'[7] For in its *essential* character scriptural knowledge is just like the pure knowledge, or the pure consciousness, of Brahman. One way of putting it is that 'the eternal Vedas . . . are like the breath of the Infinite'; that is, they are not the production of some person's effort.[8]

So just like the transcendent Self, the authority of scripture is quite beyond any external proof. 'It is independent (*nirapekṣa*), just as the light of the sun is the direct means of our knowledge of form and colour.'[9] Precisely because it provides the knowledge of the supreme Being, as no other means of knowledge can do, it possesses supreme authority. Sankara also mentions such signs of its non-human origin as its size, its range of subject and so on. But these are peripheral features. Its ability initially to open the way to attaining the knowledge of the Transcendent is its greatest attribute. When theists argue that scripture is authoritative because it is given or 'spoken' by the Lord, and then justify their faith in the Lord by appeal to the witness of scripture, they use, claims Sankara, an unacceptable circular argument.[10] Its authority is self-validating, just as the Truth it conveys is self-validating.

Holding scripture's authority to be intrinsic is not the only aspect of the Ritualists' doctrine taken over by Sankara. Like most other Vedantins, he also complied with the six principles of exegesis evolved by the Ritualists in their effort to discover the proper meaning of the Vedic injunctions they held to be so imperative. In any given passage initial and final meaning should be given prominence; so should any repeated as well as newly introduced idea; the benefit to be expected has also to be considered; then one should ascertain whether subordinate statements in the passage confirm or contradict; likewise consistency with preceding passages has to be checked.

While, however, the Ritual exegetes regarded all 'merely indicative' texts, those declaring the nature of Brahman for example, as subordinate parts of scripture, quite ancillary to those texts enjoining some action to be done, Sankara held just the reverse position. All action-oriented texts refer to something still to be done, something therefore imperfect. As perfect Being, Brahman is simply to be realised, in a way involving no further activity. It is the declaration of this perfect Being that is the principal intention of scripture, according to Sankara. The appeal to 'context' also becomes arbitrary. The monist will often claim that his understanding of scripture's most important theme, and the select method of interpretation by which he identifies this theme, is authenticated by 'experience', by which is meant the experience of the Self's oneness. But this carries only relative weight in that the theist can make exactly the same claim for his experience of the otherness of the supreme Person from his own self.

In that the spiritual teacher is an essential mediator of the 'revelatory text which is handed down traditionally'—for 'Brahman can become understood only through the traditional teaching of the preceptors and not by reasoned argument [though this plays some part in the reflection-stage], nor by clever exposition, mental ability, learning, austerities, or sacrifices'[11]—the teacher probably is the most important of any outward means available to the aspirant. Intuition into a transcendent form of existence, then, requires an esoteric method directed by an accomplished teacher, its esoteric character making it more appropriate as a 'means' to the desired End.

The meditative discipline is based on a number of theories that developed in the late Vedic period, the most important being the idea that in the world of the sacrifice and the deities there are prototypes corresponding to the inner world of the self. Thus the self should meditate on one or another of these prototypes, on the principle that 'a person becomes just as the one he meditates on'.[12]

Sankara quotes this principle and then elaborates on it: 'Throughout the Vedas it is stated that even in this life a person becomes identical with and attains the god he meditates on.'[13] Even in the Upanishads, however, there was a tendency to isolate meditation on the prototype from the ritual action with which it was associated originally. Sankara not only isolated the meditation from the ritual, he also made much more clear the merely provisional use of the various symbols and prototypes thought to have some inherent correspondence with the essence of the sacrifice. All the other meditations, he claims, are but a preparation for the pure contemplation of the Self, through the highest meditative practice, yoga.

Sankara's commentary on the Gita's sixth chapter also describes the meditative discipline (*dhyāna-yoga*) at some length. It is this 'meditation-method', says Sankara, which among all other ways of approach is the most immediate means to acquire the knowledge of Brahman. The 'action-method' at the most can only lead step by step, and it must be doubtful if by this means a soul ever actually arrives at the realisation-stage. It is merely 'an external aid to the meditation-method'.[14] Only meditation within the Self can arrive at the desired ultimate End—oneness of the Self.

Sankara has with complete consistency maintained his great thesis that no means employed to realise the transcendent End of absolute identity can provide more than provisional validity. Each is given some role in reaching that ultimate Goal, but each can do little more than help the soul along the preliminary path. The only direct means is the Knowledge of Brahman, by which is meant the realisation of oneness with Brahman. To this end all other preliminary means are quite subordinate. Yet it is for the origination of this transcendent Knowledge they are intended, even though indirectly.

RAMANUJA

Ramanuja's attitude to the means by which the supreme Person is attained shows a number of significant points of divergence both from Sankara and, to a lesser extent, from Madhva, his fellow-theist.

We begin with the question of the role of scripture as a means to attaining Brahman. Here also we should take note of the related discussion in Chapter 6 above. Like the other Vedantins, Ramanuja held that scripture is the only infallible source for the knowledge of the supreme Being. He too asserted that scripture is without beginning or end, and is entirely non-human in its origin (*apauruṣeya*).[15] He also taught its intrinsic authority, though the Logicians' idea of God-given authority must have attracted him. When the Ritualists denied the periodic dissolution and renewed evolution of the universe as being a threat to scripture's eternal and wholly infallible status, Ramanuja argued that at the beginning of each new age the supreme Person taught the scriptures afresh to the highest of the deities that are part of his body. This avoids the need for recomposition and possible loss of authenticity. In Ramanuja's case, however, his high doctrine of scripture led him to deny that there is in scripture anything incomplete, inconsistent or provisional.[16]

With Sankara and other Vedantins Ramanuja accepts that merely hearing Vedantic texts, even grasping their meaning, cannot in itself liberate the soul. In fact he and Madhva argued against the monists on this basis. If it were the case that merely to know the identity of the inner and the transcendent Self affords immediate liberation, merely hearing an identity-text should be sufficient, whereas, in fact, scripture makes it imperative that the supreme Self be continuously meditated on. There is a process of enlightenment to be engaged in. An essential part of this is understanding of and obedience to the whole of scripture. Accepting the validity of scriptural injunctions, therefore, injunctions both to ritual action and to devotional meditation, meant that scripture's role does not become obsolete as soon as its intention is grasped. There is a need for continual reference back to this sole source of knowledge about the supreme Person who is the object of various forms of worship and service.

Ramanuja claims too that the declarations of scripture, being the sole basis of the knowledge of Brahman, are in no way subsidiary to that knowledge. So he questions the monists' somewhat relativist view of scripture: if verbalised statements about Brahman function at the level of 'differentiating ignorance', how can they be the means of introducing knowledge of the perfect Being, and so lead to the ultimate freedom that should accompany such knowledge? In that the supreme Person is himself the author of this eternally composed scripture, there is a sense in which he transcends his own composition. But there is no possibility of the self, subsequent to his realisation of that supreme Person, being able to transcend this eternal revelation. To compare scriptural descriptions of creation, the Lord's qualities, the religious life and suchlike, to the 'fables' and 'white-lies' told to small children and sick people is not only insulting to scripture, it is also rather ridiculous. Once people realise the fictional character of such stories or statements, their reaction will certainly not be one of joy and liberation. Rather, they will feel cheated.[17]

Ramanuja's exegetical method is marked by four important principles:

1. The authority of the Revelation lies in its 'power to denote completely established objects . . . [and therefore] can and does bear completely and harmoniously on Brahman . . .'.[18] Thus Ramanuja rejects the Ritualists' claim that because texts merely indicating Brahman's

being have no purpose, they also have no authority in themselves, and are ancillary to the texts of injunction. Sankara was the first of the Vedantins to subject this theory to serious examination and, as we saw, more or less inverted its exegetical implications, taking the realm of action to be entirely subordinate to and superseded by the realm of knowledge.

While Ramanuja accepted Sankara's argument that scripture is not principally injunctive, nor is it unable to bear on an eternally established being, he also added a new dimension. In the first place he observed that children invariably learn by having things named, not by watching the actions of their elders in response to words, or sentences comprised of words. And scripture is even more able to indicate the being of Brahman. However, in that this same Being is the essential subject-matter of all scripture, and in that the worship of this Being is intended by all scripture, both through action required in the ritual-realm and through meditation expected in the knowledge-realm, the attempt to separate these two realms both by ritualists and monists is quite mistaken. Thus Ramanuja sees an unbroken continuity leading from action to knowledge, and from knowledge to action—with the devotional relationship as the integrating factor. 'Systematic enquiry into religious duty', therefore, is just as necessary a preliminary to the enquiry into Brahman as such an enquiry is a necessary culmination to all ritual action. It was the continuity from the one to the other that Sankara denied, even though he allowed that action has its necessary role. Ramanuja's response to the serious tension between knowing and doing found in the extremes of religious thought represented both by the Vedic ritualists and the Vedantic monists is to bring knowledge and action into an interdependent synthesis (*karma-jñāna-samuccaya*). But I return to this issue later.

2. Implicit in this 'synthesis' of Ramanuja's is the notion that *all* scripture is equally authoritative. Although he makes frequent reference to the great sayings which comprised the essence of Vedanta as far as Sankara was concerned, he refers even more extensively to passages making clear the greatness of the supreme Being. His use, too, of the soul-body analogy to determine the meaning of the Self-world relationship meant that considerable weight was given to passages suggesting this kind of relationship. Again, he recognises that it is the ultimate aim of scripture to lead to such knowledge as will ensure the soul's liberation. Therefore, those texts which he believes most clearly impart such knowledge are given a greater intrinsic importance.

In spite of these various criteria for the evaluation of texts, there is a fundamental faith in scripture as a whole. For this reason he criticised the monists' singling out of a few texts supporting their theory and according them alone the privilege of absolute authority. He acknowledges that there appear to be divergent attitudes expressed in scripture. But rather than arbitrarily selecting just one of these attitudes and thereby eliminating the others from a position of authority, Ramanuja claimed that some principle of reconciliation has to be employed. 'We have to interpret all these texts in such a manner as to avoid contradiction between their statements, however diverse, and so that their primary sense is not sacrificed. This we have done.'[19] In the passages following this claim it is clear that Ramanuja believes the soul-body analogy to be just such a principle of reconciliation in interpreting the wide range of material presented in scripture.

That the various kinds of texts are able to be reconciled means also that they should be given equal consideration and exposed side by side. Thus while there may be texts like 'That thou art', which undoubtedly lead to the soul's liberation, it should also be recognised that other texts speak of liberation as resulting from the knowledge of difference. Thus: 'After having acquired the knowledge that the soul and its Mover, i.e. the inner Ruler, are separate from each other, by his favour one attains immortality.'[20]

Sometimes Ramanuja interprets a passage he finds a little difficult as it stands by reference to a comparable passage in which there is explicit mention of the supreme Lord. Thus texts which speak of Being, or Self, as having been 'alone at the beginning', can be referred to the statement, 'Nārāyaṇa was here at the beginning'.[21] In such cases we see his theistic tradition determining the interpretation.

3. Ramanuja also asserted the need to interpret each text by reference to its context (*prakaraṇa*). This was ostensibly part of the exegetical method followed both by Ritualists and Vedantins. The most obvious way of employing reason (*tarka*) in the merely subordinate role allowed for it in relation to revelation, was in the correlating of texts and in ensuring that the exegesis of a text was properly supported by the entire passage in which it stands.

A good example of Ramanuja's contextual exegesis is seen in his denial[22] of the monists' interpretation of the text, 'Not thus, not thus'. Is this intended, as Sankara suggests, to contradict the statement initially made in the passage concerned—'There are two forms of Brahman, the formed and the formless'? What value would there be, asks Ramanuja, in introducing such an idea, only to deny it immediately? (He quotes the proverb, 'Better keep from touching mud than have to wash it off'.) In the subsequent passage also there is declaration of various qualities of

Brahman. Therefore, when initial statement and concluding statement are so clearly in agreement, what basis is there for interpreting 'not thus, not thus' as the absolute denial of all qualities in Brahman's being? Contextual exegesis suggests a denial merely that the supreme Person can be limited to such qualities as were previously mentioned. The author of the Brahma-Sutras is quoted: 'It denies that Brahman is only so much as has been said and asserts that he is more than that.' The 'that thou art' and other important texts are similarly interpreted with reference to their context.

4. That all words, especially scriptural words, refer to the supreme Being in an analogical sense, and yet that all statements about that Being are to be taken in a direct sense, are further important hermeneutical principles of Ramanuja's system. But I have already discussed these aspects of his thought in Chapter 6, so will add nothing more here.

We find then that Ramanuja's understanding of scripture as the source of the great revelation of the supreme Being is faithfully reflected in his exegetical method. What of his attitude to the other means of revelation of, or means of approach to, the supreme Being? Far from being entirely provisional in character, lacking reality when compared to the ultimate enlightenment by which they must be superseded, Ramanuja sees all the appointed means as directly mediating that immediacy of divine being which we have found so typical of his religious realism in other areas also. There are a number of ways in which he expresses his viewpoint.

Ramanuja contends that there is a continual interplay between knowledge and action, as we have already noted. The 'works-section' of the Vedic tradition and its 'Knowledge-section' form two interconnected parts of one great body of teaching. Performing religious and social action helps to qualify a person for knowing Brahman in two general ways. In the first place the discipline of ritual duties purifies the mind and prepares it for that 'steadfast pondering on' the being of Brahman that is required of the Vedantic student. This at least is the beneficial result if such duties are carried out solely with the desire of pleasing that supreme Being. Then there is the more negative result of inducing in the mind of one performing these required duties 'discrimination between the permanent and the transient', that is the ability to 'discern that the benefits of mere works are limited and transient'.[23]

Some of this is reminiscent of Sankara's attitude to works, but the contrast comes when we remember that Ramanuja had no intention of drawing a sharp line between action with its limited benefits, and the knowledge of the supreme Being which brings with it unlimited benefits.

For he goes on to claim that 'sacrifices and suchlike actions are a means to this steady pondering on Brahman . . . and so all works connected with the different conditions and appointed states (*āśrama*) of life are to be performed throughout life with the intention of originating such knowledge of Brahman'.[24] Sankara had argued that no activity can do more than help to prepare the soil, as it were, for knowledge to spring up and bear its own unique fruit—identity with the eternal, unqualifiable Brahman. Once such knowledge is attained all activity is superseded. The Self has realised its proper existence in its own transcendent realm.

By contrast, Ramanuja suggests not only that the practice of calming the mind, restraining the senses and so on, is conducive to the proper knowledge of Brahman, but that continuing with the various duties of the different stages of life helps to perfect such knowledge as a person has already attained. He quotes from the Gita: 'He from whom all beings proceed and by whom all this is pervaded, is to be worshipped with the proper works: thus man attains to perfection.'[25] Then he interprets similarly the Sutra's rather cryptic 'as the horse': 'As the horse, which is a means of carrying man about, requires attendants, grooming, and such like, so knowledge, though by itself the means of release, demands the cooperation of the various works.'[26]

In this same passage Ramanuja insists that meditative worship is 'in no way inferior in intuitive clarity to the clearest form of immediate vision (*pratyakṣa*), [even though] by constant daily practice it has to become ever more perfect'. There are ways in which works can help towards that perfect End. 'It should not be said that between works on the one hand and calmness of mind on the other there is an absolute antagonism.' For instance 'the householder, although engaged in outward activity, must, in so far as he possesses knowledge, also practise calmness of mind, etc. For these qualities are enjoined in scripture as auxiliaries to knowledge,' and also accompany, can even be produced by, works. 'For works enjoined by scripture have the power of pleasing the supreme Person, and thus, through his grace, are able to bring about the destruction of all those mental impressions that obstruct calmness and concentration of mind. Hence calmness of mind and the rest are to be aimed at and practised by householders also.'[27]

It is no wonder, therefore, that Ramanuja did not, like Sankara, insist on formal renunciation (*sannyāsa*) and initiation into one of the ascetic orders as the way to liberation. Ramanuja himself eventually became such a 'renouncer', but always held it to be an optional matter for others.

Thus, far from accepting Sankara's idea that once knowledge has dawned in the soul there is no further obligation to carry out the appointed duties, Ramanuja even appears to take over, though in a seriously modified form, the Ritualists' notion that action is the ultimate End of man. He can do this by interpreting 'knowledge' in terms of an equally prominent Upanishadic feature, 'meditative worship' (*upāsanā*). This latter is clearly an action that can be the subject of authoritative demand, which indeed it is in scripture. So Ramanuja concludes that 'knowing Brahman' is not something which once attained elevates the soul to a state in which no further effort is required. 'Repetition' is essential: 'The meaning of scripture is fulfilled only by repeated acts of knowledge . . . "knowing" (*vedana*) being synonymous with meditation and meditative worship (*dhyāna, upāsanā*).'[28] And this means uninterrupted focusing of the mind on the supreme Object in continual meditative worship.

Elsewhere Ramanuja maintained that this 'repetition' is necessary for knowing Brahman, because while an initial meditation may recall the whole essential character of Brahman, in subsequent meditations particular attributes can be recalled. In general this interpretation of knowledge brings it rather closer to the essentially functional approach of the Ritualists, but in order to stress the exalted character of such meditative and worshipful knowledge, Ramanuja concludes that 'knowledge of that [devotional] kind has not even the trace of a relationship with works' (i.e. with the Ritualists' attitude).[29] So whatever similarity we may find between the Ritualists' dominant idea that the end of man's life is the performance of (primarily ritual) duty, and Ramanuja's interpretation of that end in terms of worshipping and meditating on the supreme Person, essentially the two positions are poles apart.

The basis, therefore, on which Ramanuja was able to construct this synthesis of knowledge and action is his view of Brahman as the supreme Person. To 'know' Brahman means to be devoted to him; and devotion to him is precisely the reason why all the prescribed duties are to be done. Meditative worship of the supreme Person, made possible by his grace, is the point, therefore, at which knowledge and action meet. Thus Ramanuja never forgets the supreme Being's transcendence in relation to all human endeavour. Hence his admission that knowledge transcends works. But when the soul is related to the supreme Being by means of devotional and meditative worship, that Being's grace is able not only to provide the necessary benefits of action (for which the soul will no longer be concerned), it will also establish a link between works and transcendent knowledge. In the passage quoted below concerning the clarity of intuition that devotional meditation brings, Ramanuja goes on: 'Such meditation is originated in the mind through the grace of the supreme Person, who is pleased and conciliated by the different kinds of acts of sacrifice and worship duly performed by the devotee day after day.'[30]

In another passage, replying to the Ritualists' contention that knowledge is inferior to works, for the whole purpose of knowledge is that proper works be performed, Ramanuja immediately points to the 'absolutely faultless and perfect nature of the highest Brahman', as the basis of his elevating knowledge over works. For this supreme Object of knowledge is 'other than the individual soul that acts . . . the highest creative Brahman with all its perfections and exalted qualities, which cannot possibly be attributed to the individual self'.[31] By thus establishing the perfect, distinctive nature of the Object of knowledge as the basis for making knowledge superior to works, Ramanuja has repudiated both ritualism and monism with one thrust.

In the final analysis, of course, this personalising of the process, so that action and knowledge are inter-related in devotion, means that divine grace is its basis. A passage in Vedārtha-Samgraha illustrates his method rather well:

> When a person . . . has become wholly turned towards the supreme Person as a result of taking refuge at his lotus-feet; when he has acquired the qualities of a quiet mind, subdued senses, etc . . . daily cultivating them and applying them to his previous knowledge of the true nature of things gathered from the scripture and corroborated by the teachings of the true teachers; when he devotes himself to performing both regular and occasional acts fitting to his condition and his life-stage, as the forms in which he is to worship the supreme Person; when he avoids what is forbidden; when he throws himself with all that he has at the lotus-feet of the supreme Person; when the darkness veiling his inner self is dispelled by the grace of the supreme Person, who, being supremely compassionate, is pleased with the continual acts of worship such as praising, pondering, glorifying, saluting, striving after, exalting, listening to and declaring his perfections, meditating, worshipping and prostrating before his presence, and so on—then he will be able to attain the supreme Person by means of his devotion, which takes the form of a direct vision of supreme clarity, and which is directed constantly to him alone, who holds it to be pre-eminent and most precious.[32]

Ramanuja goes on to quote the text that Sankara had to struggle with to interpret monistically: 'This Self cannot be grasped by skilful exposition, nor by erudition, nor by listening to many texts; only the one whom [the Self] chooses can attain him; he selects his soul to become his body,'[33] which Ramanuja takes to imply that meditation in the form of devotion is what is needed. So he concludes:

> Devotion is a kind of knowledge that is so excellent, precious and exclusive that it removes a person's thirst for anything else. The one who has this knowledge is 'chosen' by the supreme Person, so that the Supreme can be grasped by him. . . . It is through this method of devotion—furthered at first by the method of action that is intensified daily as described above, and subsequently by the way of knowledge —that knowledge in the form of supreme devotion arises.

It has now been made unquestionably clear that in Ramanuja's system it is the devotional relationship, prompted by the supreme Person's perfections, and made possible by his grace, that determines the synthesis of the various means of approach to him.

Ramanuja also brings out (more clearly than Sankara, I believe) the Vedantic view that Brahman is both the means and the goal of all religious activity. In the later sections of the Brahma-Sutras comment was necessary on a variety of questions concerning meditative practices. Ramanuja's principal argument is that there can be only one basic type of meditation, and that is meditation on the highest Self. In the first place it is only this supreme Being who is able to grant release to the soul as the consequence of its meditation. The same applies to the sacrifices offered seemingly to many deities: 'It is fundamentally the highest Self—as constituting the inner Self of Vāyu and the other deities— which is pleased by offerings.'[34]

Thus only the supreme Person can properly be the object of meditation. He alone is both the means and the ultimate End of all religious practices. Ramanuja makes the same point on the question of the various symbols (*pratīka*) used in meditation, such as mind, name and even visible images. Can they be thought of as carrying the nature of Brahman the supreme Self? In one sense, contends Ramanuja, the identity cannot be made, 'for the symbol is not the self of the mediating devotee'. When the inner self is the object, 'identification' can be made, as we noted in Chapter 5. 'What is to be meditated on is the symbol only, not Brahman: Brahman enters into the meditation only as qualifying the way it is looked at . . . so that something that is [known as] not Brahman is looked at as Brahman.'[35]

Ramanuja goes on to make clear that his position here is different from Sankara's. It is quite legitimate, he says, to superimpose 'a Brahman-view' on to such objects which are clearly less than the essential supreme Self. What is not permissible is to reverse this and take such objects as in reality Brahman, but Brahman on which the objective image has been superimposed. Ramanuja's fundamentally personalistic theology shows through again: 'To view a superior person, a prince for example, as a servant would be degrading to him; on the other hand to view a servant as a prince would be exalting to the servant.'[36] Here also, then, the ultimate object of meditation is the supreme Person; so that in these subordinate symbolic meditations it is his Person which should ultimately dominate the devotee's thought.

It is presumably in order to make his objection to Sankara's interpretation absolutely clear that Ramanuja seems to take these symbols with a little less 'realism' than he shows in other issues. It would have fitted his general scheme to have said, as in fact Madhva said, that the symbols can be taken as direct mediations of the supreme Person's presence, because he is present in them as their inner Self. They are his body in a sense similar to which the inner self of a person is the body of the Lord and therefore can be meditated on as that supreme Self. Polemical considerations could be dominant here. Or it could be that this is the only way he feels justified in interpreting the words of the Sutra: 'The view of Brahman, on account of superiority.'

In any case, it is clear that just as this supreme Person alone is the perfect Object of meditative knowledge and the supreme Goal of all human action, so, according to Ramanuja, the supreme Person himself is the ultimate means of attainment. Vedic ritual and Vaiṣṇava cultic practices are valid methods of approach to the transcendent Being. But they are direct means to such a transcendent End only because that Being makes himself immediately present to the devotee engaged in such practices. Again it is the supreme Being's mediated immediacy, his self-body relationship, that makes these subordinate means effective in attaining their desired end, and also makes possible the unbroken continuity between limited action and transcendent knowledge. For in so immediately relating himself to the devotee as he uses his various means, the Lord himself becomes the ultimate means as well as the supreme End the devotee seeks.

MADHVA

With other Vedantins, Madhva regarded scripture as the vehicle of divine revelation. As well as using Upanishadic texts, there is no lack of emphasis on the Vedas, for Vedanta was defined as 'ascertaining [the meaning of] the Vedas',[37] even Rigveda being frequently quoted. But he had no intention of limiting himself to these usual Vedantic sources, even with the Gita included. He defines 'right-scriptures' (*sad-āgama*) as consisting of 'the four Vedas . . . the Bhārata (which will include the Gita), the whole of the traditional Vaiṣṇava scripture called Pāncarātra, the original Rāmāyaṇa, the Purāṇas corroborating these and all other works following them'.[38] As far as Madhva is concerned there is no question of the Vaiṣṇava tradition contradicting what earlier Vedanta had regarded as the essential scriptures. Given that such 'remembered traditions' always corroborate the truths of the originally 'heard' scriptures, then it was quite logical for Madhva to treat either almost indiscriminately as his authoritative sources. But it does often lead to a somewhat esoteric interpretation of the 'primary scripture'. There is, for example, his discovery of veiled references to Viṣṇu in all manner of texts, especially in the various names of deities. In other cases it is to one or other of these lesser deities, Vāyu in particular, that such veiled references are found.

Yet at these times Madhva's use of scripture is surprisingly sophisticated. While he asserts frequently that the supreme Lord can be known only through scripture, this is qualified by his saying that in cases of doubt reason has to be employed to ascertain the proper meaning, that in cases of apparent contradiction (such as between the monistic and dualistic statements) it may be found that perception is the more basic 'means of knowledge', and that in all cases the final arbiter of the validity of revelation is the inner witness.[39] These qualifications reveal a very candid analysis of the way in which believers actually determine what is established revelation when using scripture. But it does tend to weaken the concept of a given authoritative revelation.

On the other hand Madhva also gives a new dimension to the traditional concept of scripture's infallibility and non-personal or supernatural origin. Like other Vedantins he points to the lack of specific human authorship, and claims that scripture's reliability and authority is self-validating. Its authority does not derive from its authorship, even divine authorship. He allows that to claim such self-validity assumes that there is a tradition to this effect and that there is a reliable evaluator (in Madhva's case, the inner witness) of this authority.

To substantiate this self-validating character of scripture Madhva points to its immediately convincing revelation of *dharma* and *adharma*, or the fundamentally right ordering of things in the world. There is a revelation of what is of ultimate value and what is detrimental to human life in the widest sense, especially in the realm of the moral value inherent in religious and social duty. Thus Madhva starts from the premise that all philosophical systems must at the same time work for the world's welfare. So any who hold *dharma* and related issues to be unreal admit by implication the futility of their own system. They certainly have nothing of value to say to the world. But matters of such importance and requiring such authority cannot be based on the authority of any one author, who will always 'be liable to ignorance and deception'. To postulate an 'omniscient author' would be equally invalid, resulting in 'the flaw of excessive postulation. Omniscience, not a matter of experience, has to be postulated; that the omniscient person is not deceptive and that he is the author of statements about *dharma* and *adharma* also has to be postulated.'[40]

Here Madhva uses a very similar argument to that of Ramanuja in his rejection of the Logicians' attempt to prove the existence of the supreme Being. Just as Ramanuja had argued that the existence of such a Being is sufficiently established by the declaration of scripture, Madhva argues that the authority of scripture has to be accepted solely on the basis of that scripture's authoritative declarations regarding the whole range of human welfare. In any case, no author can be identified as having been responsible for scripture, its supra-personal origin remains established and, more important, nothing in scripture can be taken as of merely provisional significance.

We have already seen that in Madhva's religious system the immediate vision of the supreme Being is held to be greatly superior to the mediateness of all meditative practices. The usual spiritual discipline of hearing, reflecting and meditating was accepted as an essential prerequisite to such direct knowledge of Brahman. In fact, the discipline of meditation appears to have been more systematised into its progressively graded stages than is the case in Ramanuja's writings. But Madhva's more frequent reference to direct intuition as the most impeccable means of the knowledge of the supreme Being makes his devotional discipline in a sense less significant within his system as a whole. The direct vision of the Lord is not so much intrinsic to the devotional relationship as a superior stage *beyond* it, granted by the Lord's grace, though resulting from meditation when accompanied by intense devotion.[41]

The whole meditative discipline has to be preceded by a renunciation (*vairāgya*), but this is not merely a matter of discriminating between body and soul, and denying the importance of the former; it is a recognition of the great difference between the Lord and the soul and the handing over to the Lord of everything previously imagined by the person to have been his own.[42] For in reality it all belongs to him. Only this sense of dependence makes a person eventually eligible for the transcendent knowledge of Brahman.

Distinctions of birth cannot be completely ignored, but the devotion to the Lord which accompanies a sense of dependence on him makes people of all castes elegible for some knowledge of him—as was recognised in all devotional sects. Madhva holds that it is only the devoted even among those of high birth who are eligible for the full knowledge of the sacred texts. But even low-born people, if devoted to the Lord, are eligible for the liberating 'knowledge of the sacred names'.[43] Women and others, again when properly devout, can be initiated into a special esoteric (Tantra) knowledge of the Lord.

This gradation of people into various categories is typical of Madhva, though, with Ramanuja, he does not insist on formal initiation into the ascetic style of renunciation as Sankara does. It is his classification of souls both according to their unique inherent characteristics and (so) according to their devotional capacity which explains the grades of knowledge acquirable, as also the fact that even among those engaging in the meditative discipline their vision of the Supreme will vary. There is perfect vision only to those given the ultimate and immediate knowledge of the Lord.[44]

The intrinsic difference among souls that leads to various levels of meditation and devotion also means that the spiritual Teacher directs the soul at whichever level is proper to its attainment, and innate capacity. 'Devotion to the Guru' (*guru-bhakti*) is essential in Madhva's system (as in Ramanuja's, though less explicitly). The soul is to reflect on the meaning of scriptural texts, as directed by the Teacher. In fact, only Madhva sees such 'practice of scriptural meanings' (*śāstra-artha-abhyāsa*)[45] as a separate stage of meditation. This should continue until all possible doubts concerning scripture have been cleared. The usual stages of systematic yoga, leading up to complete concentration of the mind, also have their preparatory place.

Likewise, many other souls are destined to pursue the path of action rather than that of meditation. Some souls, though fully enlightened like the Kings Janaka and Priyavarta, have been 'commissioned by the divine will to follow the path of works and serve as examples of disinterested action to their fellow men'.[46] In most cases, however, such work-oriented lives will be determined by their inherent capacities. It is these which lie behind the various degrees of *karma* inherited from previous births—*karma* acting as the more direct cause of the soul's present condition.

In an attempt to show the usefulness of the ritual actions of the Vedas as a preparation for the devotional attitude, Madhva interprets them in terms of the disinterested duty of the Gita. All dutiful action can be undertaken in a 'spirit of devotion and dispassion'. In this way, the rewards mentioned in the Vedas as accompanying each ritual act are not intended as the principal aim with which to act. They are rather temporary inducements intended to turn the devoted worker and sacrificer away from worldly affairs to the Lord who enjoins such action. It is like a sweet offered along with medicine, to induce a child to take that which is for his benefit. So it is not the pursuit of rewards as such that is enjoined in the Vedas, only the action itself.[47]

Unlike Ramanuja, however, Madhva sees no real continuity between such action, however properly and disinterestedly performed, and the knowledge of the supreme Lord. Action may help to provide the mental purification required, and to this extent it is a means to attaining transcendent knowledge. But it cannot, claims Madhva, in itself be of the slightest help in achieving the soul's liberation. Indeed, the knowledge of the supreme Person is necessary precisely to offset the effects of the soul's actions. When performed in the Gita-spirit they can provide a preliminary (but non-consequential) basis for acquiring such knowledge. But to set the soul free, such knowledge must be in no way dependent on previous action. Subsequent action done after the soul has 'realised' the Lord's perfections will be suitably rewarded with an 'upwelling of bliss'.[48]

Then, too, an important place is given to various types of representative meditation, a practice concerning which Madhva again is at variance with both Sankara and Ramanuja. He held that such representations, whether visual symbols, images and even parts of Nature, or whether mentally apprehended gods, avatārs, and the self, are not to be taken in Sankara's 'as-though-they-are-Brahman' sense, in which there is to be the gradual realisation that each image is a mere projection on to the supreme Being.

Madhva's claims for the relationship of supreme Being and mental image include both greater realism and greater reserve. He asserts[49] the complete reality of the Brahman who is meditated on in the image, on the grounds of his having entered and being actually present in the concerned representation. At the same time his concern for the otherness and independence of the supreme Being prevents him from identifying any meditated object or mental image with the ultimate object of worship. Both as 'formed' and 'unformed', Brahman is beyond all representations, though he is also in them. It is the supreme Brahman who is to be meditated upon, the infinite Being endowed with all perfect attributes. His 'fulness of being' is the principal among such attributes, for it is the basis of all other perfections.

We noted in Chapter 5 that it is meditation on the self that provides the most effective means of attaining the direct vision of the supreme Being and its perfections, for the soul is a reflection of that Being. As against the partially effected signification of symbols like breath (*prāṇa*), the 'word "Self" alone expresses the fulness of all his attributes ... [being] the receptacle or substratum of all the qualities that we find in different objects in the universe. Therefore the Lord should be worshipped under the name of *ātman* alone. . . . Through this worship one "knows all this", because the Lord alone is the giver of knowledge. For this reason it is proper that his worship should be by such a word as will express the complete fulness of all his qualities.'[50]

Despite a rather complex development of meditative techniques in Madhva, there are a number of passages where he clearly insists that devotional dependence is the principal, even the sole, means of 'knowing' Brahman perfectly and attaining liberation fully.[51] And although we noted earlier that meditation appears to be superseded by the immediate vision, devotion as such is never made redundant. The End attained by devotion and by direct perception is in many respects the same, though Madhva never equates them as does Ramanuja.

Presumably these two types reflect the intrinsic differences of souls. The devotional attitude is required of all; but only in the case of souls with the qualities necessary for the immediate vision will devotion have this result. And only such elegible souls will go on to the most mature form of devotion on the basis of their immediate vision. Attachment is necessary to all; the inner perception only to some, for this is the essential distinction between the two. Taking up the traditional simile of the flow of oil, Madhva sees devotion as a 'steady flow of deep attachment' between the Lord and the soul; the direct vision is a 'steady flow of inner perception'.[52] Another distinction is that while the immediate presentation of the perfection of the supreme Lord is entirely his grace, given in accordance with the soul's inherent capacity, the devotional relationship seems capable of moving the Lord to graciousness. 'Devotion alone leads the soul to the Supreme, devotion alone shows him.'[53] Madhva goes on to stress that this is done by the supreme Being of his own accord, though 'in consideration of the soul's devotion'.

Devotion, then, brings about an interplay of influences between the Lord and the soul. This attachment to him has the effect of arousing the Lord's love by way of response. It also draws the soul further under the

Lord's influence. It is thus 'the bond between the Lord and the soul', 'the chief instrument of the supreme Ruler'.[54] More important perhaps, the devotional attachment 'manifests the likeness which the soul has with the Lord',[55] so that the soul realises its true nature.

So in spite of Madhva's distinction between the meditative relationship and immediate knowledge, the devotional attachment is the essence of the liberation the soul seeks; it is the End itself, not the means to some other end. And this is the point of the theist's assertion that devotion is the supreme path to the Transcendent. The devotional relationship with the supreme Person contains within it all that is needed for the soul to realise both its own essential being and that of the supreme Being with whom it is related. It is therefore questionable whether such a process requires either the hierarchical structure with which Madhva works it out, or the specially granted experience of 'immediate knowledge', which does not seem to be an integral element in the devotion-oriented structure of much of Madhva's spiritual discipline. Again, it would seem to be his sharp distinction between the supreme Lord's independent being and all other beings, linked with an innate ontological pluralism, that makes these aspects of Madhva's devotional scheme necessary.

11 A Summary of Vedantic Viewpoints

To do justice to the wide range of Vedantic material presented in the preceding chapters I would like to have been able to make a much more detailed comparative analysis of the most important concepts. But as my main intention has been simply to give a parallel description, as systematic as possible, of the three principal types of Vedanta, comparisons have had to be limited to a few observations in passing. However, I trust that by now the most important Vedantic doctrines will have been made sufficiently clear for my conclusions to be listed as a series of summary statements, rather in the style of the Vedantic Sutra-tradition.

1. Vedanta's over-riding concern has been to express in appropriate doctrinal forms the perfect being of Brahman, the supreme Person.

2. He is said to be the ultimate Goal of human existence as well as the means of its attainment.

3. His transcendent perfection must in some way include all finite existence, for transcendence has a necessarily immanental dimension.

4. It is in the interpretation of this immanental transcendence of Brahman's being that Vedanta is so seriously divided; thus a common concern for his perfection is the cause of the most radical divergence among Vedantins.

5. The immanental aspect of Brahman's transcendence means that causal categories are of great importance in Vedantic articulation; while all ostensibly accept that Brahman is the supreme Cause, the mystery of his relationship to the created universe has meant that terms like *māyā* and *līlā* have had to be used.

6. Some ambiguity is also assumed in the finite soul's knowledge of Brahman; *avidyā*, literally ignorance, obscures the soul's vision of the ultimate Reality.

7. Selfhood is taken as the primary model for understanding the being of Brahman, thus implying some kind of analogical relationship between finite self and supreme Self.

8. Vedantins drew out the implications of this common model in a rich variety of conceptual systems, each taking some variant feature of selfhood as his determining analogy.

9. Each Vedantin has built his system closely and coherently around the inherent logic of his determining analogy—transcendent consciousness determines Sankara's interpretation, the self-body relationship determines Ramanuja's, self-determining will Madhva's.

10. Although it is claimed that only scripture makes Brahman known, for he is not accessible to sensory perception or logical argumentation, in fact each Vedantin's interpretation of scripture is determined by different presuppositions, especially those underlying their respective analogies. Thus Vedantic method is very complex.

11. The most radical conceptual divergence is that between monistic and theistic positions ontologically, epistemologically, and soteriologically.

12. The monist takes the absolute oneness of selfhood to be the only ultimate reality, empirical existence being unreal from that absolute perspective; this absolutist position made necessary a corresponding selective interpretation of scripture.

13. The theists' principal intention was to establish the distinctively glorious character of Brahman as supreme Person, the Lord of all.

14. A transcendence of such personal greatness, they felt, also implied the distinction of all other beings from Brahman; even souls that have attained their ultimate state of release can realise only such essential qualities as are similar to, but not identical with, Brahman.

15. Thus they felt that the idea of an absolute identity of Selfhood threatens Brahman's perfection and lordly qualities; just as does the equating of Brahman directly with the changing universe.

16. As all things derive from Brahman, are eternally dependent upon him, and are characterised by essential subservience to him, the theists believe that the devotional relationship and the divine grace undergirding it cannot merely be provisional states for the soul; they have an ultimate reality.

17. For rather similar reasons, all created states are claimed to be ultimately real; this position demanded a detailed rejection of the various monistic theories of ontological and epistemological distortion.

18. Theistic theory, however, is not uniform; not only do Ramanuja and Madhva differ on crucial issues, but we even find Madhva's theistic doctrine converging at unexpected points with Sankara's monism, due to their common transcendental emphasis, very differently though this may be expressed.

19. These points of convergence include the belief that Brahman cannot be substantial cause of the universe in any directly related sense; that the finite soul has a substantially tenuous relationship with Brahman, of whom it is a 'reflection'; that there is need for a trans-relational vision of Brahman; that action, even an act of altruistic devotion, is not an integral part of such transcendent knowledge; that the Avatār-existence of the Lord is a manifestation rather than a real embodiment.

20. In most respects, however, Madhva's emphasis on Brahman as the one independent Lord—whose supreme will controls the immense variety of really different entities throughout the universe, each with its distinct innate characteristics—is quite radically opposed to Sankara's monism.

21. Of these three Vedantins, only Ramanuja, basing his system on the self-body relational analogy, was able to speak of an ontological continuity of such inclusiveness that even mediated knowledge and experience has the power to convey the immediacy of Brahman, a Brahman characterised by innumerable great qualities, super-eminently realised in his infinite perfection.

22. Similarly, causal and dependent relationships lose their monistic anomaly. For Ramanuja, creation is real and its effect-states distinct, yet they are authentically present in their Cause; souls too are really distinct, though inseparably related to and eternally dependent on the supreme Person, as a body to the self which controls it.

23. If, then, we assume the distinctiveness of the supreme Being, the reality of individual selfhood and the created world, the reality of divine grace and divine accessibility as a result of special embodiments within creation, of the individual as a real agent of action, especially in his acts of loving devotion—if these are all assumed to be matters of ultimate value within a continuum of being deriving from the one Brahman, then Ramanuja would seem to provide the most convincing system. But only those accepting similar presuppositions are likely to be convinced.

24. On the question too of the inner coherence of each system, a good case can be made out for favouring Ramanuja because of the more intrinsic inclusiveness suggested by his determining analogy—the self-body relationship. The somewhat more exclusive transcendental dimension indicated by Sankara's pure consciousness and by Madhva's sheer will certainly do not preclude Brahman's immanence. But some degree of strain is placed on the coherence aimed for in Vedanta.

Notes

CHAPTER 1

1. S. K. Das, *A Study of the Vedānta*, 2nd ed. (Calcutta, 1937) p. 30.
2. S. N. Dasgupta, *A History of Indian Philosophy*, vol. I (Cambridge, 1922) p. 429.
3. V. S. Ghate, *The Vedānta; A Study of the Brahma-Sūtras with the Bhāṣyas of Śamkara, Rāmānuja, Nimbārka, Madhva and Vallabha*, 2nd ed. (Poona, 1960) p. 184.
4. S. S. Raghavachar, *Introduction to the Vedartha-Samgraha of Sree Ramanujacharya* (Mangalore, 1957) p. 5. He also says that if the word is taken to mean 'a systematic inquiry into *God*', it 'would be a very happy designation' of Ramanuja's intention.
5. Cf. KU 1.2.7.
6. BSB 1.1.4.

CHAPTER 2

1. BSB 1.1.1.
2. BU 2.4.5.
3. BG 6.27-9.
4. R. C. Zaehner, *The Bhagavad-Gītā* (with a commentary based on the original sources) (Oxford, 1969) p. 233.
5. BG 6.30.
6. BG 18.66.
7. CU 6.2.
8. E.g., B. N. K. Sharma, *The Philosophy of Śrī Madhvāchārya* (Bombay, 1962) p. 25.
9. BSB introduction.

CHAPTER 3

1. CU 6.1.3.
2. BG 7.10–12.
3. BU 3.8.
4. BU 3.4; 3.7.
5. SU 3.7.

CHAPTER 4

1. 6.2.
2. Bhāskara probably taught his system of difference-cum-non-difference in the eighth

century, i.e. more or less contemporary with Sankara. Vallabha's similar theory of 'pure non-difference', meaning that Brahman really transforms himself into this 'all', so that his effected state is equally real, dates from the sixteenth century, showing the persistence of this Vedantic type.

3. CU 6.2.3.
4. P. N. Srinivasachari, *The Philosophy of Bhedābheda* (Madras, 1934) pp. 45–6.
5. The traditional date given for Sankara is A.D. 788–820. Of the great number of works attributed to Sankara, I depend largely on the following: Brahma-Sūtra-Bhāṣya, Bhagavad-Gītā-Bhāṣya, Commentaries (Bhāṣyas) on the ten principal Upanishads (especially Bṛhadāraṇyaka, Chāndogya, Taittirīya, and Kaṭha), Upadeśa-Sāhasrī and Vivekā-Chūḍāmaṇi, two smaller works dealing with a variety of monistic themes. Not all scholars accept the authenticity of the last mentioned.
6. The Vaiṣṇava tradition claims that Ramanuja was born in A.D. 1017 and died in A.D. 1137. We may assume the major part of his writing to have been done during the second half of the eleventh century. The works mainly used in this study are Śrī-(Brahma-Sūtra)Bhāṣya, Gītā-Bhāṣya, Vedārtha-Saṃgraha (a systematic work providing a very useful introduction to Ramanuja's thought), and a more devotional work, Śaraṇāgati-Gadya. For some reason he did not write formal commentaries on the Upanishads. Perhaps he thought that sufficient reference is made to them, in a more systematic Vedantic form, in other commentaries and Vedantic writings.
7. Madhva's lifespan is said to be from A.D. 1238 to A.D. 1317. He seems to have been a far more prolific writer than Ramanuja, but wrote in a more condensed and so more enigmatic style. Translations sometimes have to be more in the nature of paraphrases. I am dependent largely on his Brahma-Sūtra-Bhāṣya, Anu-Vyākhyāna, which is a metrical commentary on the same Brahma-Sūtras, his Bhagavad-Gītā-Bhāṣya (and to a lesser extent the Gītā-Tātparya), his commentaries on the Bṛhadāraṇyaka and Chāndogya Upanishads, his Viṣṇu-Tattva-Nirṇaya, which is a very useful introduction to his system, and a very brief summary of the Sūtras' teaching, Aṇu-Bhāṣya.
8. BSB(M) 2.3.28.
9. BUB(M) 1.4.7; cf. VTN 214–17.

CHAPTER 5

1. BSB intro.
2. BSB 1.1.4, quoting CU 6.2.1; 6.8.7; AU 1.1; BU 2.5.19.
3. Ibid.
4. So also US paras. 7–9, 28–9, 32–3, 37–40, etc.
5. BSB 1.1.4.
6. BUB 4.3.7.
7. BSB 4.3.7–14.
8. BSB 3.2.5; 2.3.43; cf. 1.1.11; 2.3.43; 3.2.24, 27; BGB 2.17; MuU 3.1.8.
9. BSB 1.1.1 and intro.
10. US 55–73.
11. E.g. BSB intro.; 1.1.1; 1.1.4; 1.2.21–2; 1.3.1, 19; 1.4.22, etc.
12. Cf. BUB 3.8.12.
13. BSB 1.1.9; 1.3.8–9, 15; 2.1.27, etc; US 49–53.
14. BSB 1.1.4; BU 4.4.7.

15. BSB 2.1.14.
16. BUB 4.4.22.
17. VS paras. 19–20; cf. also SB 1.1.1.
18. Ibid.
19. SB 4.1.3.
20. Cf. E. J. Lott, *God and the Universe in the Vedantic Theology of Rāmānuja: A Study in his use of the Self-Body Analogy* (Madras, 1976).
21. SB 2.1.9.
22. VS para. 143.
23. SB 1.2.2.
24. GB 9.4–5.
25. SB 1.1.1 (Thib. p. 135); *padārtha*, i.e. a distinct, cognisable thing.
26. GB 3.30; 9.27, etc.
27. Ibid. and 11.2.
28. GB 9.4–5, 14.
29. Cf. GB 7.18; 9.29.
30. J. Carman, *The Theology of Rāmānuja: An Essay in Inter-religious Understanding* (New Haven, 1974) p. 136.
31. VS para. 77.
32. SB 2.3.42.
33. VS paras. 10–14; cf. CU 6.1.4–6; 6.2.1ff.
34. VS paras. 17–18; cf. SB 1.1.1 (Thib. p. 138).
35. SB 1.1.1 (Thib. pp. 98–9).
36. SB 1.1.1 (Thib. pp. 70, 99–102). Ramanuja contends that if consciousness as an attribute of the self is lost in *mokṣa* 'final release is the annihilation of the self'.
37. VS para. 142.
38. H. N. Raghavendrachar, 'Madhva's Brahma-Mīmāmsā', in *The Cultural Heritage of India*, vol. III (Calcutta, 1969) p. 331.
39. VTN vv. 330–3.
40. AV 2.3.69.
41. VTN 231.
42. AV 3.2.148.
43. BSB(M) 2.3.49; 3.2.18; Rig-Veda 6.47.18 is quoted.
44. B. N. K. Sharma, *Phil. of Sri Madhva*, p. 219.
45. *Svatantra-asvatantra prameyam dvividham matam*, Tattva-Vivekā 1.
46. BSB(M) 1.2.8, quoting Garuḍa-Purāṇa, repeated in VTN 275.
47. Ibid., 1.4.23 and 1.2.12.
48. Ibid., 2.1.37 and 2.2.5.
49. CUB 6.2.1; VTN 226, 230.
50. VTN 266.
51. BSB(M) 1.3.16.
52. Ibid., 1.2.20 (BU 5.8.22).
53. Ibid., 1.2.1 and 2.2.21.
54. VTN 200.
55. VTN 206.
56. VTN 217.
57. BSB(M) 2.3.27, quoting Kauśika-Śruti.
58. Ibid., 2.3.27.
59. VTN 279, 281; cf. BSB(M) 3.2.19.

60. VTN 301, quoting Parama-Śruti; cf. 294–6.
61. VTN 305–7, quoting Nārāyaṇa-Śruti.
62. VTN 193–4.
63. BSB(M) 3.2.1–8.

CHAPTER 6

1. KeUB 2.1; BSB 2.1.4; 2.2.2.
2. KeUB 2.1.
3. E.g. BSB 1.1.1–4; 2.3.7 (where the self-established nature of the Self is said to do away with the need for any kind of *pramāṇa*-proof); BGB 2.18–19.
4. BGB 2.25, 29, 69.
5. TUB 2.6; also BUB intro.
6. KeUB 2.4.
7. BSB 4.1.3, quoting BU 4.3.22, 'Then a father is not a father . . . then the Vedas are not Vedas'. So 'when knowledge springs up scripture ceases to be valid'.
8. BSB 1.1.8.
9. BGB 13.12–13.
10. BSB 4.1.6; cf. 3.3.9.
11. By R. V. De Smet in his unpublished thesis, The Theological Method of Śaṃkara (thesis Pontifica Universitas Gregoriana, Rome 1953).
12. BU 1.4.2.
13. BSB 1.1.4; also CUB 6.8.7; 6.13.3.
14. BG 13.12, beginning, 'I will tell you that which should be known; once a person knows it he attains immortality'.
15. BSB 4.1.1–2.
16. Later in BSB 4.1.2.
17. TUB 2.6–7.
18. CUB 7.1.3.
19. BSB 1.1.1, the root being *bṛh* which Sankara takes to imply also his eternal, omnipresent nature.
20. TU 2.1.
21. Ibid.
22. TUB 2.9.
23. SB 1.1.1 (Thib. p. 41).
24. Sharma, *op. cit.*, pp. 317–18.
25. SB 1.1.1 (Thib. pp. 15–16); 3.4.26.
26. Cf. Carman, *op. cit.*, pp. 140–6; also SB 1.1.1 (Thib. pp. 88–9); 4.4.19; GB 9.10, 10.42.
27. J. A. B. Van Buitenen, *Rāmānuja's Vedārtha Saṃgraha* (Poona, 1956), pp. 64–5.
28. SB 1.1.1 (Thib. pp. 40–6).
29. SB 1.1.1 (Thib. pp. 47–61).
30. Ibid. (pp. 102–18).
31. Ibid. (pp. 88–101); 1.1.4.
32. SB 1.1.3.
33. Ibid., *Aśarīraḥ samkalpa-mātra-sādhana. . . .*
34. Ibid.
35. Brahman is here called *visajātiyam*.
36. AV 1.1.1, *yadārtha pramāṇam.*

37. VTN 136.
38. VTN 428–9.
39. VTN 122–9; 432–5.
40. AV 2.3.58; 3.2.56.
41. VTN Chap. 1.
42. AV 3.2.40.
43. Cf. BSB(M) 3.2.14–16; AV 3.2.56.
44. In Karma-Nirṇaya also there are a number of passages in which Madhva claims that reason shows Brahman to be *Saguṇa*.
45. BSB(M) 1.2.26; 1.4.16; 1.4.28; VTN 268, 451–2.
46. BSB(M) 1.4.28.
47. Ibid., 1.1.5 and 1.1.11.
48. VTN 50–9.
49. VTN 133. Commenting on '*neti, neti*', however, Madhva interprets *mūrta* (referred to earlier in this Bṛhadāraṇyaka passage) as 'that which is associated with sin', and *amūrta* as Śrī and Vāyu. As the supreme Lord is superior to both categories, he is 'not thus, not thus'.
50. BSB(M) 3.2.23–7.
51. AV 3.4.145ff.
52. VTN 82–7; cf. 99, 227–9; BSB(M) 3.2.19–23.

CHAPTER 7

1. BS 2.1.33.
2. BG 3.20–5.
3. Cf. BSB 1.2.2, 9; 1.4.23.
4. BSB 1.1.2; 1.4.23–8.
5. TUB 2.6.1.
6. BSB 1.4.23.
7. AUB 1.1.2.
8. BSB 1.1.4.
9. BSB 1.4.1–28; 2.1.1–17.
10. BSB 2.1.9. Here, significantly, follows a quotation from Gauḍapāda.
11. BSB 2.1.14.
12. Ibid.
13. Ibid.
14. Ibid.
15. *Ekatva-ekāntyād-īśitṛ-īśitavya-abhāva.*
16. Ibid. Sankara claims that he is not contradicting what he has said in Sutra 1.1.4, that creation is caused by the Lord. But he clearly recognises the problem of reconciling this with his assertion of 'the absolute oneness of the Self'.
17. BSB 2.1.16 (echoing the Sutra's words).
18. M. Hiriyanna, *Outlines of Indian Philosophy* (London, 1932) p. 339.
19. SB 2.1.15.
20. SB 1.1.4 (The Lord's creative power is not a mere *upalakṣaṇa*).
21. E.g. SB 1.1.1 (Thib. p. 75); 1.4.23; 2.1.15; 3.2.3.
22. VS 59. To think that Brahman actually suffers in the form of the embodied soul, argues Ramanuja, is like saying that 'Devadatta has one hand anointed with sandal-paste

and adorned with bracelets, and the other hit by a hammer and hurting as though in hell-fire'.

23. US 9.4–5; but cf. BUB 3.7.3.
24. SB 1.1.5; cf. 2.1.1–4.
25. SB 1.1.3 (CU 6.1).
26. SB 1.1.12, *sarveśvareśvaro nirasta-nikhila-doṣa-gandho . . . puruṣa-uttamo nārāyaṇa eva nikhila-jagad-eka-kāraṇam.*
27. SB 2.1.8–14.
28. SB 2.1.14.
29. B. Kumarappa, *The Hindu Conception of the Deity, as Culminating in Rāmānuja* (London, 1934) p. 278.
30. SB 2.1.14.
31. BGB.
32. Op. cit., p. 17.
33. SB 2.1.14.
34. SB 2.1.8; put forward by Samkhya, but acceptable to Ramanuja as far as it goes.
35. *Yasya cetanasya yad-dravyam sarvātmanā svārthe niyantuṁ dhārāyituṁ ca śakyam, tac-cheṣata-eka-svarūpam ca, tat-tasya śarīraṁ.*
36. SB 1.4.23.
37. Ibid.
38. SB 2.3.40.
39. SB 2.3.41.
40. SB 1.1.1 (Thib. pp. 88–9), *paraṁ brahma saviśeṣaṁ, tad-vibhūti-bhūtaṁ jagad-api pāramārthakam-eva.*
41. Ibid.
42. BSB(M) 2.1.35–43.
43. Dvādaśa-Stotra 3.6.
44. Sharma, op. cit., pp. 30, 267; cf. Mahā-Bhārata-Tātparya-Nirṇaya 22.184–8.
45. BSB(M) 2.3.41.
46. BGB(M) 7.8.
47. Ibid., 7.10.
48. Ibid.; cf. BG-Tātparya 7.7–10.
49. BSB(M) 2.3.11 (quoting Vāmana-Purāṇa).
50. Ibid., 2.3.41.
51. Cf. AV 2.2.33–8.
52. BSB(M) 2.3.37–9; cf. 2.1.22.
53. Ibid., 2.1.24.
54. Ibid., 2.1.26–41; cf. BGB(M) 2.24; 13.28.
55. VTN 262 (quoting Parama-Upanishad); cf. BSB(M) 3.2.1ff.
56. AV 2.2.33–8.
57. VTN 257–9.
58. VTN 259.
59. VTN 328, 340.
60. VTN 343–8, 368–9.
61. VTN 323–9.
62. VTN 370.
63. BGB(M) 7.25–6.
64. AV 1.4.81–5.
65. VTN 331.

66. In BSB(M) 1.4.25, quoting Rig-Veda 4.10.
67. BSB(M) 1.2.20, commenting on BU 5.8.22.
68. BUB 1.2.1; AV 2.2.14–30 is another typical passage on the Lord's determining will.
69. BSB(M) 1.4.27.
70. Op. cit., pp. 155–60.
71. S. Siauve, *La Doctrine de Madhva: Dvaita Vedānta* (Pondicherry, 1968) pp. 326ff.
72. Ibid., p. 328.

CHAPTER 8

1. In T. M. P. Mahadevan, 'The Idea of God in Advaita', *Vedānta Keśari*, May 1966. Cf. BSB 1.1.11; 1.3.13; 3.2.21–2; 4.3.14. We may note especially Sankara's statement in 4.3.14: 'But are there really two Brahmans, one higher and one lower? Certainly there are, for scripture declares this.' He goes on to qualify this quite radically, but the distinction between the two is not based merely on two 'aspects' of the one Brahman.
2. BSB 1.1.2.
3. BSB 2.2.1.
4. BSB 2.2.2.
5. BSB 2.1.24, 33.
6. BSB 2.1.33; TUB 2.6.1.
7. BSB 2.1.25. Note that the word *cetana* derives from *cit.*
8. Stanzas 237–40.
9. 408–10; cf. 464–471, 512–16.
10. *Nitya-śuddha-buddha-mukta-svabhāvaḥ.*
11. E.g. BSB 1.1.2; BGB intro.
12. P. Deussen, *The System of the Vedānta, according to Bādarāyana's Brahma-Sūtras and Çankara's Commentary thereon* (New York, 1973) p. 135. Cf. CUB 8.1.1.
13. TUB 2.5–9. Brahman is also identified with the *Bhūman,* also called Bliss, in 1.3.8–9.
14. Quoting 2.7.1.
15. TUB 2.7.1.
16. Ibid.
17. Ibid.
18. Ibid.
19. TUB 2.8.1–4.
20. Ibid.
21. TUB 2.9.1.
22. E.g. S. R. Bhatt, *Studies in Rāmānuja Vedānta* (New Delhi, 1975) pp. 53–5.
23. Op. cit., Chap. 5.
24. *Vedārtha-Samgraha,* p. 10.
25. VS para. 10.
26. VS para. 14.
27. SB 3.3.12–3.
28. SB 3.3.12; *guṇi-pṛthak-sthitatva-mātreṇa*. . . . The attributes are *aiśvarya, gāmbhīrya, audārya, kāruṇya.*
29. Op. cit., p. 97.
30. VS para. 6.
31. Cf. SB 1.1.21; 3.2.15.
32. VS 20.

33. VS 14.
34. E.g. GB 18.73. *Vīrya* (sometimes *dhairya*) has been interpreted by some later commentators as 'immutable', which Carman also does.
35. SB 1.1.2.
36. SB 1.1.1; 2.3.29; VS 84, 142, etc. GB intro.
37. Vedānta-Sāra 1.1.1. Cf. SB 1.1.1 (Thib. p. 84); VS 142.
38. SB 1.1.13.
39. VS 18; cf. Vedānta-Sāra 1.1.1.
40. SB 1.1.13.
41. VS 82.
42. VS 6.
43. VS 110.
44. Ibid.
45. VS 134.
46. *Svābhāvika*, VS 135; cf. SB 1.1.21.
47. SB 1.2.2, *aprākṛtika*; cf. GB intro. Later Vaiṣṇava doctrine said the Lord's body was made of *śuddha-tattva*, 'pure substance'.
48. SB 1.1.1 (Thib. p. 87).
49. Viṣṇu-Purāṇa 5.72ff (cf. VS 42), a passage (used also by Madhva) which goes on to say that *bhagavan* can be used of 'persons worthy of reverence in general', but is used 'in its primary sense of Vāsudeva only'.
50. VS 103.
51. VS 127; cf. 133, 135; GB intro.; Śaraṇāgati-Gadya 1, 7, 11–12.
52. Śaraṇāgati-Gadya 11.
53. VTN 461; also BGB(M) 2.37, 61; 4.10; 6.6; 7.19; 13.4, etc.
54. Karma-Nirṇaya 10.
55. Aṇu-Bhāṣya, or Sarva-Śāstra-Artha-Saṃgraha (The Essential Meaning of the whole of Scripture).
56. BSB(M) 1.2.12.
57. CU 3.14.1.
58. *Pūrṇaḥ ananta guṇaḥ*; VTN 437–64.
59. VTN 267; BUB 1.2.1; 1.4.17.
60. BGB(M) 17.23, taking *sat* as *sāttvika*; VTN 195.
61. VTN 196–7, 230.
62. VTN 263. Madhva comments similarly on these texts in BUB and CUB(M).
63. VTN 217, 190.
64. *Ekaḥ avibhaktaḥ, sa avikāraḥ paroḥ hariḥ, avibhāgāt parānandaḥ, nitya-guṇa. . . .*
65. Tātparya-Nirṇaya 1.12.
66. VTN 264, *sva-ānandaḥ*.
67. VTN 275, 439, etc.
68. BSB(M) 3.2.32.
69. VTN 451; cf. BSB(M) 1.1.1; 1.2.26; 1.3.2, 8.
70. VTN 265 (quoting Nārāyaṇa-Śruti), *svātantrya, sarva-jña, sarva-īśvarya*.
71. BGB(M) and Tātparya 7.12; cf. 9.4.
72. VTN 464; also 59, 98, 265, 437–8, 454, 461.
73. AV 3.3.16.
74. BGB(M) 2.37; 2.17.
75. Ibid., 5.14–15.
76. MaU, *icchā-mātram prabhos-sṛṣṭiḥ*.

77. BG-Tātparya 2.17; cf. BSB(M) 1.2.26; 1.4.3; 2.3.9.
78. VTN 457; also BSB(M) 3.2.31.
79. *Svarūpe 'pi viśeṣo 'sti svarūpatvād-eva tu.*
80. Mahā-Bhārata-Tātparya-Nirṇaya 1.11; . . . *svagata-bheda vivarjita-ātmā.* Sharma asserts that 'Madhva's view of the attributes of God is the same as that of the great Christian thinker, St. Thomas Aquinas' (op. cit., p. 250).
81. BSB(M) 3.3.41–2; BGB(M) 12.1–7; 15.1.

CHAPTER 9

1. BU 3.2.13.
2. BG 4.11.
3. BGB 18.62.
4. BSB 2.3.41.
5. 1.2.20 (cf. SU 3.20). *Prasāda* can also mean tranquillity, esp. as *sam-prasāda.*
6. 3.2.3.
7. G. Parrinder, *Avatār and Incarnation* (London, 1970).
8. BSB 1.1.20.
9. BGB 4.7–8; 10.39.
10. BSB 1.1.20, *sva-mahimā-pratiṣṭhasya.*
11. *Samasta-vedārtha sāra-saṃgraha.*
12. BGB intro.; cf. 12.3.
13. BGB 4.6.
14. BGB 4.7; 7.24; 9.11; BSB 1.1.20.
15. BGB intro.
16. BGB 7.24.
17. *Sulabhaḥ*, GB 8.14.
18. SB 3.2.37.
19. Ibid.
20. GB 8.14, quoting MuU 3.2.3.
21. BG 18.66.
22. SB 1.1.21, *apāra-kāruṇya-sauśīlya-vātsalya-audārya-mahā-udhatiḥ.*
23. VS 92; cf. 113.
24. E.g. GB intro., *bhū-bhāra-avataraṇa.*
25. GB 4.8.
26. GB intro.
27. GB 6.47; cf. 4.11.
28. GB intro.
29. GB 6.47.
30. GB 4.5.
31. GB 4.6.
32. Ibid.
33. BSB(M) 3.2.25–7, quoting Nārāyaṇa-Ādhyātma.
34. BGB(M) 4.11.
35. BSB(M) 3.3.53–4.
36. BGB(M) 9.32.
37. VTN 113–16, quoting Sauparṇa-Śruti.
38. BSB(M) 1.1.1 (also AV).

39. Ibid., 3.2.22.
40. Sharma, op. cit., pp. 315–16.
41. BGB(M) 12.5.
42. BG 18.66.
43. BG-Tātparya 18.56.
44. Ibid., 18.66.
45. Sharma, op. cit., p. 237.
46. BGB(M) 4.6. He also interprets it to mean 'by my knowledge', as did Ramanuja.
47. Ibid., 4.8, *līlā-kaivalyam, krīḍato bālakasyeva.*
48. BSB(M) 2.3.46.
49. Madhva interprets the BU text, 'Fulness from fulness, etc' (5.1.1) to mean that all the Avatārs of Viṣṇu possess the same 'fulness', without any diminishment of the *mūla-rūpa*, or 'root-form'.
50. VTN 453.
51. BSB(M) 2.3.48, quoting Caturveda-Śikha.

CHAPTER 10

1. BUB 1.4.7; BSB 1.1.4.
2. BUB 2.4.1, *tasmān-na sādhana-antara-sahita brahma-vidyā puruṣārtha-sādhanam sarva-virodhāt. . . .*
3. BSB 1.1.1. Sankara likens the Guru who helps the Brahman-seeker to a boat on an endless ocean. Its waters are the painful struggle in the cycle of rebirth, decay and death. Only when they are tired of this world with its means and ends, acts of right and wrong, their means and results, will they look for the saving boat.
4. BS 3.4, esp. 3.4.26.
5. BGB 8.22; 13.10; 18.54–5.
6. BSB 1.3.7; 1.4.14.
7. BSB 2.1.31, *na tarka-avagāhyam.*
8. BUB 2.4.10.
9. BSB 2.1.2.
10. BSB 2.2.38.
11. KeUB 1.4.
12. Śatapatha-Brāhmaṇa 10.5.2, 20; quoted by Sankara in BSB 1.1.11; BUB 1.3.16; 2.1.2; 4.4.16; BGB 8.6.
13. BGB 6.2.
14. Ibid.
15. E.g. VS 95, 139.
16. But see further discussion in this chapter, and cf. Van Buitenen on Ramanuja's exegetical method, op. cit. pp. 48–69.
17. SB 1.1.4.
18. Ibid.
19. VS 84; cf. 95.
20. SU 1.6.
21. Mahā-Upanishad; VS 96.
22. VS 38; also SB 3.2.21. '*Neti, neti*', BU 2.3.6; 3.9.23, etc.
23. SB 1.1.1 (Thib. p. 156). Cf. also the Small-Siddhānta in SB 1.1.1.
24. Ibid.

25. GB 18.46.
26. SB 3.4.26.
27. SB 3.4.27.
28. SB 4.1.1, 7; cf. 1.1.1 (Thib. pp. 12–16).
29. SB 3.4.12.
30. SB 3.4.26.
31. SB 3.4.8.
32. VS 91.
33. MuU 3.2.3; VS 92.
34. SB 3.2.40.
35. SB 4.1.4.
36. SB 4.1.5.
37. *Veda-vinirṇaya*.
38. VTN 3, quoting Brahmāṇḍa-Purāṇa.
39. Cf. ch. 6 supra; and VTN 14, 18–21, 23, 65, 68.
40. VTN 7–12; also 14–17.
41. Cf. ch. 9.
42. AV 1.1.46; BSB(M) 3.1.1.
43. BSB(M) 1.1.1.
44. Ibid., 1.1.7; 3.2.37, etc.
45. BSB(M) 3.3.5–6; 4.1.1. On Guru-bhakti cf. 3.3.44–6.
46. BGB(M) 3.20.
47. Ibid., 2.47.
48. Ibid., 3.20, 32, which stresses that only by direct knowledge can release be certain. Cf. BUB(M) 1.4.15.
49. Cf. BSB(M) 3.2.37; 4.1.4ff.
50. BUB(M) 1.4.7; cf. VTN 214–17.
51. VTN 112–13; BSB(M) 3.3.51–60; BUB(M) 3.4, in which Madhva contends that *mukti* is attained only through *bhakti*, and is in fact the desired End itself.
52. BUB(M) 3.4; BSB(M) 3.2.19, interpreting the Sutra's 'like water' in this sense of a flow of love.
53. BGB(M) 9.32; BSB(M) 3.3.53–4; cf. also VTN 115 and 3.2.22–7.
54. BSB(M) 3.3.54; VTN 112–26.
55. BSB(M) 3.2.19.

Bibliography

A. VEDANTIC TEXTS AND TRANSLATIONS

Bhasyam, K., *Śrī-Bhagavad-Rāmānuja's Śaraṇāgati-Gadya, with text, translation and commentary of Śrutaprakāśika Āchārya* (Madras, 1970).

The Brahma-Sūtra-Bhāṣya (text with footnotes and variants), ed. Narayan Ram Acharya, 3rd ed. (Bombay, 1948).

Bṛhadāraṇyakopaniṣat, with Bhāṣya of Śaṅkara and Ṭīkā of Ānandagiri, ed. Kāśinātha Śāstri Agase, 3rd ed. (1914).

Chandra Vasu Vidyarnava, S. *The Bṛhadāraṇyaka-Upaniṣad with the Commentary of Śrī Madhvāchārya*, a trans. revised by Nandlal Sinha, Sacred Books of the Hindus, vol. 14, 2nd ed. (Allahabad, 1933).

Gambhirananda, Swami, *Eight Upanishads, with the Commentary of Śankarācārya*, trans, in 2 vols (Calcutta, 1972–3).

Jagadananda, Swami, *Upadeśa-Sāhasrī: A Thousand Teachings of Śrī Śaṅkarāchārya*, text, trans. and notes (Madras, 1973).

Madhavananda, Swami, *The Bṛhadāraṇyaka-Upaniṣad, with the Commentary of Śaṅkarācārya*, a trans. 4th ed. (Calcutta, 1965).

Madhavananda, Swami, *Viveka-Cūḍāmaṇi of Śri-Śaṅkarācārya*, text with trans., notes and index, 9th ed. (Calcutta, 1974).

Narasimha-Ayyangar, M. B., *Vedānta-Sāra of Bhagavad-Rāmānuja*, trans., with text ed. V. Krishnam-acharya (Madras, 1953).

Radhakrishnan, S., *The Principal Upaniṣads* (text, trans. and notes) (London, 1953).

Subba Rau, S., *The Bhagavad-Gītā with Śrī-Madhwāchārya's Bhāṣyas, a Translation* (Madras, 1906).

Subba Rau, S., *The Vedānta-Sūtras with the Commentary of Śrī-Madhwāchārya, a Translation* (Madras, 1904).

Raghavachar, S. S., *Śrī Madhva's Aṇu-Bhāṣya*, text and trans. (Madras, 1973).

Raghavachar, S. S., *Śrīmad-Viṣṇu-Tattva-Nirṇaya*, text and trans. (Mangalore, 1971).

Sampatkumaran, M. R., *The Gītā-Bhāṣya of Rāmānuja*, a trans. (Madras, 1969).

Sarva-Mūla-Grandāḥ (*Works of Śrī Madhvācārya*), vol. I, *Prasthāna-Trayi* (being text of commentaries on the Gītā, major Upanishads, and Brahma-Sūtras) ed. Govinda Bannenje (Mangalore, 1969).

Śrī-Bhagavad-Rāmānuja-Grandha-Māla (text of complete works of Rāmānuja) ed. P. B. Annangaracharya Swamy (Kanchipuram, 1956).

Śrimad-Bhagavad-Gītā Śrī-Śaṅkara-Bhāṣyena Samhitā, ed. D. V. Ghokale, 2nd ed. rev. (Poona, 1950).

Thibaut, G., *The Vedānta-Sūtras, with the Commentary of Rāmānuja* (Part III), trans., Sacred Books of the East, vol. XLVIII (Delhi, 1966).

Thibaut, G., *The Vedānta-Sūtras, with the Commentary of Śaṅkarācārya*, trans. Sacred Books of the East, vols. XXXIV and XXXVIII (Delhi, 1973).

Van Buitenen, J. A. B., *Rāmānuja's Vedārtha-Saṃgraha*, ed. with intro. and annotated trans. (Poona, 1965).

Zaehner, R. C., *The Bhagavad-Gītā* (with a commentary based on the original sources) (Oxford, 1969).

B. SECONDARY SOURCES

Bhatt, S. R., *Studies in Rāmānuja Vedānta* (New Delhi, 1975).

Bhattacharya, H. (ed.), *The Cultural Heritage of India*, vol. III, *The Philosophies*, 2nd ed. (Calcutta, 1969).

Carman, J. B., *The Theology of Rāmānuja: An Essay in Inter-religious Understanding* (New Havan, 1974).

Das, S. K., *A Study of the Vedānta*, 2nd ed. (Calcutta, 1937).

Dasgupta, S. N., *A History of Indian Philosophy*, 5 vols (Cambridge, 1922–40).

De Smet, R. V., 'The Theological Method of Śaṃkara' (unpublished thesis, Pontifica Universitas Gregoriana, Rome, 1953).

Deussen, P., *The System of the Vedānta, according to Bādarāyaṇa's Brahma-Sūtras and Çankara's Commentary thereon* (New York, 1973).

Ghate, V. S., *The Vedānta: A Study of the Brahma-Sūtras with the Bhāṣyas of Śaṁkara, Rāmānuja, Nimbārka, Madhva, and Vallabha* (Poona, 1926; 2nd ed. 1960).

Hiriyanna, M., *Outlines of Indian Philosophy* (London, 1932).

Kumarappa, B., *The Hindu Conception of the Deity, as Culminating in Rāmānuja* (London, 1934).

Lacombe, O., *L'Absolu Selon le Védânta* (Paris, 1966).

Lott, E. J., *God and the Universe in the Vedantic Theology of Rāmānuja: A study in his use of the Self-Body Analogy* (Madras, 1976) (ATC, Brigade Rd., Bangalore, 1978).
Muller, F. M., *The Vedānta Philosophy* (London, 1904).
Murty, K. S., *Revelation and Reason in Advaita Vedānta* (Delhi, 1974).
Parrinder, G., *Avatār and Incarnation* (London, 1970).
Radhakrishnan, S., *Indian Philosophy*, 2 vols., 2nd ed. (London, 1930).
Raghavachar, S. S., *Introduction to the Vedartha-Samgraha of Sree Ramanujacharya* (Mangalore, 1957).
Raghavachar, S. S., *Śrī Rāmānuja on the Upanishads* (Madras, 1972).
Sharma, B. N. K., *The Brahma-Sūtras and their Principal Commentaries*, 3 vols (Bombay, 1971–7).
Sharma, B. N. K., *The Philosophy of Śrī Madhvācārya* (Bombay, 1962).
Siauve, S., *La Doctrine de Madhva: Dvaita Vedānta* (Pondicherry, 1968).
Smart, N., *Doctrine and Argument in Indian Philosophy* (London, 1964).
Smart, N., *The Yogi and the Devotee* (London, 1968).
Srinivasachari, P. N., *The Philosophy of Bhedābheda* (Madras, 1934).
Srinivasachari, P. N., *The Philosophy of Viśiṣṭādvaita* (Madras, 1943).
Von Glasenapp, H., *Die Philosophie der Inder* (Stuttgart, 1948).

Index